THE
GENTRY
MAN

THE GENTRY MAN

A GUIDE FOR THE CIVILIZED MALE

Edited and with text by Hal Rubenstein

HARPER
DESIGN

An Imprint of HarperCollins Publishers

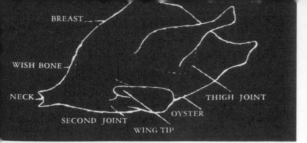

BREAST
WISH BONE
NECK
SECOND JOINT
WING TIP
OYSTER
THIGH JOINT

Saks Fifth Avenue

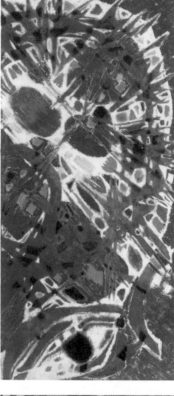

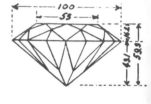

100
53

CONTENTS

Introduction

EVERY MAN
IS ONE
OF A KIND

GENTRY

NUMBER 1 WINTER 1951
PRICE   TWO DOLLARS

Do you know how to make a Buckingham cocktail, know what color "tea dust" is, or how to best an opponent at chess in just seven moves? Ever successfully diet while dining on baby lobster, experience the ease of a suit made from wool jersey, or play nine holes of golf on an eight-acre course? Have any idea what Confucius, Spinoza, and Dostoyevsky have in common with Aristotle, or why men admired Beau Brummell? Do you know what "two distortions" form the basis for modern art or which boldly unconventional chassis color made the 1955 De Soto Firelite Sportsman a classic car for the ages?

How many times did you silently say "Yes!" while reading the first paragraph? Well, don't feel so bad. It's doubtful there are enough men alive who can knowledgeably answer all eleven questions to complete a regulation softball team. How can one be so sure? Because it's a safe bet you never subscribed to *Gentry*.

Gentry is the men's magazine that defied the collective belief that the American Dream in the 1950s was fulfilled by a split-level home in suburbia, a four-door sedan, a wardrobe of blue blazers and gray flannel suits, and a happy to stay at homemaker tending to her breadwinner's every need while he coached Little League and mowed the lawn. What more was there to life than that?

Plenty, according to *Gentry*. Published quarterly from 1951 to 1957, the man portrayed in its pages could hardly wait to tackle a slalom course in winter, then fly cast in summer. He deftly decorated his office in what is now called midcentury modern (he called it contemporary), the perfect frame to show himself off in a three-piece Donegal tweed suit with matching vest. On the weekends, playing host at his spruced-up to the manor born country house, he'd sport tea dust–colored (that's green, by the way) Japanese linen Bermuda shorts, mix a shakerful of cocktails with his secret ingredient (applejack), whip up a beef goulash, and regale guests about driving the family up for a stay at the stately and still-popular Otesaga Hotel in Cooperstown, New York, in his sleek new 1953 Ford Sunliner convertible. He openly lusted for a painting by Paul Klee, had unapologetic fantasies about bull-fighting, confessed to yearning to learn more about Eastern philosophy—especially after reading an excerpt from Hesse's *Siddhartha*. He whispered of secretly planning a second honeymoon but couldn't decide which would be more fun—a weekend in Paris where there was a must-see Matisse exhibit at the Jeu de Paume or sunning in Barbados, where the beach attire was so wonderfully gay (and that word meant something else entirely).

The *Gentry* man's exuberance for the unexpected and sometimes the extraordinary had little in common with the domesticated bliss inhabited by two TV dads whom audiences deified as paragons of the American male during the 1950s: *Leave It to Beaver*'s even-tempered Ward Cleaver and Jim Anderson, the bemused sage who proved every week that *Father Knows Best*. But that's because William Segal, the man who created *Gentry*, was not only nothing like either of these characters, he wasn't like most men of his time.

A self-made millionaire by virtue of having created Reporter Publications, which included both *Men's Reporter*, the preeminent menswear trade publication during this same period, and the even more successful *American Fabrics*, the garment industry's handsome go-to quarterly handbook. For thirty-five years, *American Fabrics* was the textile industry's key source for technological innovation, such as nylon and polyester, as well as burgeoning trends in the industry. Segal also enthusiastically indulged in a limitless assortment of avocations including painting, Buddhism, exotic cuisines, you name the sport, Armenian mysticism, and travel by every means possible, especially to his beloved Far East. Segal did not ignore convention. Quite the contrary, it was always at the forefront of his passions—as the signpost to avoid. As famed documentarian Ken Burns, who created a short film about Segal, recalled, "He had a kind of vitality that—I had never met anyone like that—that kind of rearranged my molecules."

It's a shame the compliment is now carelessly applied to hail anyone who can speak more than one language or likes foreign films, because William Segal truly was a Renaissance man. He created *Gentry* magazine—fervently if foolhardily taking on the roles of both editor and publisher—because of an unshakable conviction that life was too exciting and diverse, bursting with mystery and the unexplored, for every affluent man not to want to stride constantly toward new horizons with elegance and a ready-for-anything spirit of adventure.

Though the foremost references in gloss-overs of the era include McCarthyism, liking Ike, Milton Berle, TV dinners, sock hops, and baseball, they overlook that America, during the early 1950s, was going through a time of rapidly increasing prosperity and hope, while retaining a sense of innocence. It was a postwar nation awkwardly coming to terms with two important social and economic developments. First, millions of young men returning from fighting overseas had discovered that the rest of the world wasn't exactly like their hometown. Europeans and Asians indulged in drastically different daily habits, manners of dress, favorite foods and sports, religions, and sources of leisure. These differences intrigued these young Americans so much that they wanted to incorporate them into life at home. Second, with the economy finally flourishing in peacetime, there was the first opportunity in many decades for masses of Americans to achieve the "good life."

There was no better expert on living, not just a good life—but a great one—than William Segal. That's why reading *The Gentry Man*, an anthology selected from the magazine's complete twenty-two issues, is going to surprise, charm, and perhaps even inspire you. First of all, the magazine instantly stands out due to its remarkably sophisticated design and production. The quality of its paper, use of engaging layouts, and inventive displays of color are ample justification for each of its issues costing a hefty two dollars apiece at a time when most periodicals stacked next to it on the newsstand sold for a quarter.

But then, *Gentry* wasn't designed for everyone. Segal admitted that if only one hundred thousand men took a liking to the publication and followed its aesthetic of intelligently executed affluence, not only would the magazine be a success, but nonsubscribers would pick up on the cues set by its select readership and follow suit. Such reasoning may appear elitist at first, but what Segal knew is that not every man had the time, the means, or the courage to stand out. But if those few

who did could flaunt their individuality with relish and generosity, he could instigate a quiet revolution in our culture: the rebirth of the civilized American male. To make this goal a reality, it was essential that *Gentry* look and feel special. But it was equally important to make readers aware that taking advantage of the information, opportunities, skills, destinations, and products presented in its pages would make their lives special.

Consequently, *Gentry* reveled in eclecticism. Amid the magazine's lavishly illustrated features on unspoiled ports of call and gleaming American roadsters were step-by-step how-to instructions on everything from packing properly for a trip around the world to building a Finnish sauna. (Segal said he didn't expect anyone to actually build the latter—though, of course, he had a sauna—but he admitted, "Wouldn't it be fun if someone did?") Dissertations varied widely, from "Ten Men Who Changed the World" to "The World's Biggest Gambling Game" to "In Praise of Booze." There were full-color inserts depicting the work of renowned artists, such as Michelangelo and Matisse, as well as soup-to-nuts seasonal recipe guides. Fashion pages even contained removable fabric swatches (to take to your tailor, naturally).

As for the clothes displayed on *Gentry*'s pages, they are startling in their joyous immersion of sartorial splendor. The ideal *Gentry* man's closet was an explosion of color, texture, and pattern, technological innovation, precision tailoring, and daring. Yet there was an insistence that however bold one's clothing choices were, a man should wear them with rakish nonchalance.

This attitude was not confined to the cultivation of an enviable wardrobe. Whether describing Whistler's brushstroke technique, comparing the whippet-slick lines of the 1955 Mercury Montclair to the Plymouth Belvedere, or revealing how to make eggplant caviar, *Gentry*'s lack of inhibition in accessing and presenting the original as something potentially life affirming is

> "They want always to know more, so that they may contribute more to people near them and to the world in which they live; they want to give more so that they can gain more from each breath, each hour, each day, each year of their lives."
>
> —William C. Segal, on the *Gentry* reader in a pre-launch advertisement for the magazine

striking. This almost-lost marvel of a magazine had an unbounded scope of curiosity, a lack of hesitation to reach back centuries for sources of knowledge and stimulation, and sought fearlessly to take on the most daunting obstacles without ever resorting to machismo. *Gentry* sent a clear declaration to its reader: "Stop wishing on a star. This is *your* life. Come and get it!"

That *Gentry* proved too expensive a project to succeed financially does not diminish either the potency of its mission or its lasting impact. Of course, you're likely to be amused by the clothing styles (the cabana outfits are a blast) and some cocktails of choice (can anyone swallow Chartreuse?), but much of the text and instruction, and more important, the magazine's rules of behavior are a valid barometer for identifying an educated, well-spoken, admirable, and perhaps even enviably civilized man.

William Segal died in 2000 at the age of ninety-five. He lived a consistently spectacular life, never anything less than the paragon of the ultimate *Gentry* man. What a treat it is to be able to reproduce the blueprint of his fortunate existence. Casually flip through this book and you will undoubtedly still find it entertaining, an ebullient exercise in time travel. But please don't do that: We live in such a cynical and stressful time; it's too easy to dismiss the world portrayed within these pages as being too happy, too wide-eyed, too full of possibility.

Your opinion is likely to change if you read the features that intrigue or perhaps initially baffle you with the same care you would a manual for installing a new home sound system. What you may discover is that this is an unexpected yet thoroughly winning handbook for a more exhilarating life. True, you may not be able to locate that coral-and-white De Soto with the fins that reach halfway to the Big Dipper, but there's no reason why you can't try on a patterned silk sport jacket when it's time to spruce up your wardrobe, or serve curry sauce on the side the next time you grill lobster. Armed with new insight on composition, try hitting a few galleries; you may realize that modern art isn't that impenetrable after all. Nor is it so difficult to select a hat that makes you look cool, turn to Eastern philosophy for guidance, or make a zingy gazpacho. And while it's highly unlikely that you will ever be able to cry "Checkmate!" in seven moves, now that you've read how it's done, you might be able to call it in twelve.

What's exciting, and hopefully lasting, is the possibility that this book will tempt you to be more open to shaking up your life, doing what you never used to, taking a risk—and loving it. When that happens, you will be well on your way to becoming a *Gentry* man.

— Hal Rubenstein

A Letter from *Gentry*'s Publishers

MOST READERS WILL SKIP THIS PAGE...

...and truth to tell, little will be lost by them if they do.

Somehow, when a new publication is put to press, the staff feels that something should be written in the first issue—a Credo, as it is generally called—explaining what sort of publication it will be, and why it has been brought forth.

Practically every Credo we have read has been a mishmash of claims, pomposity, and promises beyond the power of mortals to substantiate. So we killed the idea of a Credo; *Gentry* will either explain and justify itself, or it should expire quietly.

One of the prime considerations in launching a new magazine, aside from the human peculiarity of engaging in activity, is to make money, and we realize that to make money we must produce a publication which gives the reader something he does not get in other magazines. It is a law of business, as well as life, that one must give in order to get. We decided that the only way we could make *Gentry* a profitable property, would be by letting our editors do the kind of articles and presentations they like and we are able to execute. In the end, is this not the only way in which things of worth come into being? We do not think we will ever stick to—or stick our readers with—conventional handling of conventional subjects. We say that the readers of *Gentry* have a right to expect the unusual, both in thinking and in presentation, and that they have a right to look to every number for the choice and the unexpected.

Gentry will perhaps explain itself better than we can. Take the story on how to build a Finnish bath; we doubt whether many of our readers will ever actually get down to the job of building one, but isn't it a pleasant idea to toy with? Or the treatise on what it means to be a Man: in a world which places so much stock in money, medals, and muscles, isn't it worth pausing for a few minutes to wonder whether these are the things for which God granted us a higher intellect than the ape or the elephant? Then there's Thomas de Hartmann's quaint essay on the melodies and rhythms in nature; don't we know that Beethoven composed a full symphony around such motifs? And won't it be impressive, next time you walk through the countryside with a friend, to say, "Hear the bird chirping? That's in E-flat Major, 4/5 tempo!"

Much of what you gain from *Gentry* will result from the way in which you read it. Do so with an open mind about yourself and the world around you, and we believe *Gentry* may in some small measure satisfy and repay you for the time you spend with its pages.

— The Publishers

ABOUT YOU — THE

What are your interests? Your likes, dislikes?

TO GIVE YOU A PICTURE of the many interesting and unusual people who constitute Gentry's readership would be quite a job. Included, for example, are the President of the United States, the Prime Minister of Canada, Ambassadors, Congressmen, the heads of many of the nation's largest industrial empires, and important figures in the fields of the arts, the sciences, and the professions.

WHEN THE FIRST TABULATION of readers of Gentry began to take shape, the people who do the statistical work informed us (1) that 57% of Gentry's readers were presidents, vice-presidents, or proprietors of established companies, and (2) that over 80% enjoyed an income of more than $10,000 a year.

Frankly, we did not regard this information with the same warm glow as our statisticians. We wished, primarily, to ascertain those interests of our subscribers which were apart from their financial position and from their daily commercial lives. We know, as well as the next fellow, that money is one of the greatest motivating forces in life. But we have never set as our editorial goal the task of telling people, most of whom are obviously successful, how to go about the business of making money. What we did receive with the most lively interest were certain other facts, figures, and percentages . . . information which will help our editorial board to chart its course, and which we are passing on to you. In so doing we hope to be able to present a fairly accurate picture of the Gentry reader, giving you actual figures with as little embellishment as possible.

TO BEGIN, the Gentry reader is obviously an individual who is enterprising enough to know what he wants and energetic enough to be able to get it. We say this as we know that Gentry is not casually obtainable at newsstands nor is it offered broadcast through mass or bargain subscription channels. Aside from subscriptions secured through the preliminary public announcements, fully 70% of Gentry's present subscribers have come to us from subscription cards placed inside the issues and through the word-of-mouth recommendation of other Gentry readers. In most cases people have subscribed after seeing copies of Gentry in the homes of friends or in offices of business associates, and a great number of new subscribers was added during the recent holiday season when multiple gift subscriptions of 25 to 100 came in from executives of large corporations.

It may be that the tabulations, statistics, and percentages can help you to draw your own picture of the likes and dislikes, and even of the thinking, of the typical (if there is any such animal) Gentry reader.

Thirty-six thousand questionnaires were distributed, of which close to four thousand (11%) were returned.

ON GENTRY FEATURES MOST LIKED . . .

1.	Travel	69.4%
2.	Art	69.0
3.	Fashions	66.3
4.	Wines, Liquors	56.9
5.	Literature	54.4
6.	Food	53.9
7.	Science	51.6
8.	Sports	50.8
9.	Living	50.4
10.	Philosophy	46.4

ON THE FEATURES LEAST LIKED . . .

1.	Philosophy	25.8%
2.	Sports	17.7
3.	Science	17.5
4.	Art	15.9
5.	Fashions	14.7
6.	Wines, Liquors	13.1
7.	Food	9.9
8.	Travel	6.7
9.	Literature	6.7
10.	Living	3.6

MORE EMPHASIS WANTED ON FOLLOWING . . .

1.	Music	45%
2.	Theatre	38
3.	Sport Cars	12

PEOPLE WHO READ GENTRY

What are your preferences in sports... in hobbies?

ON CHIEF HOBBIES ...

1.	Music	61.5%
2.	Books	54.8
3.	Travel	
4.	Sports	46.4
5.	Art	42.5
6.	Fashions	37.7
7.	Photography	33.7
8.	Autos	32.1
9.	Antiques	24.2
10.	Boats	15.9

ON FAVORITE SPORTS ...

1.	Swimming	50.0%
2.	Golf	36.3
3.	Fishing	36.9
4.	Hunting	28.9
5.	Football	25.0
6.	Sailing	19.8
7.	Tennis	18.7
8.	Skiing	18.7

ON TRIPS TO FOREIGN COUNTRIES ...

74.5% have been abroad
25.5 have not been abroad

Advertising Men and Gentry's Readership

A well-defined audience of approximately 200,-000* ... plus Gentry's library-piece, long-life permanency** ... provides an audience that is possibly in a better position to buy what it wants than any other reading group of similar size in the nation. What this means in terms of automobiles, for example, is interesting. Consider the fact that while some sixty million autos are in use in the country, it is expected that about five million new cars will be purchased throughout the nation. Many may never buy a new car throughout a lifetime, while others will purchase a new car every other year. Gentry's readers, owning an overall average of two cars per family, are obviously a concentrated, highly potential, open-and-able-to-buy group of people for new automobiles ... as they are for quality products in every field, such as high fidelity equipment, new fashions, boats, and the finer things of living.

*Based on average of five readers per copy.
**We still receive inquiries on merchandise shown editorially in Issue No. 1.

ON MAKES OF AUTOS OWNED ...

1.	Cadillac	14.2%
2.	Buick	12.4
3.	Foreign Cars	11.5
4.	Ford	10.4
5.	Oldsmobile	8.5
6.	Chevrolet	7.7
7.	Chrysler	6.3
8.	Plymouth	5.2
9.	Pontiac	4.4
10.	Studebaker	3.6
11.	Lincoln	3.3
12.	Nash	2.5
13.	Mercury	1.9
14.	Packard	1.9
15.	DeSoto	1.9
16.	Willys	1.1
17.	Hudson	.2

OWNERSHIP OF AUTOS ...

50.6% own 1 car
29.5 own 2 cars
7.8 own 3 cars
.7 own 4 cars

ON NATURE OF BUSINESS OR PROFESSION ...

36.4% Manufacturing
32.0 Sales and Distribution
14.9 Professional (Doctors, Lawyers, etc.)
10.0 Miscellaneous
7.1 Arts

POSITIONS HELD BY MEN IN BUSINESS ...

35.6% are presidents or owners of companies
21.7 are vice-presidents of companies

ON THE SUBJECT OF PETS ...

52.8% own dogs
19.0 own cats
12.3 own horses
7.9 own other pets

CITY AND COUNTRY ...

54.6% live in cities
21.7 live in country
23.7 live in both

OWNERSHIP OF HOMES ...

63.8% own their own home
36.2 do not

P.S. To Gentry readers everywhere: Our thanks for your generosity and courtesy in making this survey possible.—THE EDITORS

WHAT

EVERY

MAN

SHOULD

KNOW

1

Some men will never stuff a turkey or slave over a hot convection oven to take on Thanksgiving dinner. No matter the regularity with which *Gentry*'s editors reveled in the power of cooking to stimulate immediate gratification as well as the ease with which such a sensually pleasing skill impressed others, and in spite of today's A-Team of do-no-wrong testosterone-infused chefs such as Bobby Flay, Mario Batali, and Tom Colicchio, it's simply the truth.

Nor will scores of others ever attempt a giant slalom, sail a ketch into the wind, button up a Norfolk jacket, or slide themselves behind the wheel of a Thunderbird. However reluctantly, *Gentry* founder, publisher, and editor William C. Segal accepted that reality. He admitted at *Gentry*'s inception that for some of its readers, virtually all the possibilities the magazine exposed them to would go no further than a vicarious thrill. After all, the magazine had a mission but claimed no mandate.

However.

Every now and then you came across an article that stated its instruction or information so matter-of-factly, so stripped of persuasion or humor that the implied message was obvious: If you didn't know how to do the task presented, you could not call yourself a man.

For example, a gent could refuse to cook a turkey, but there were few actions more damning to his manhood and his loved one's respect for the same than attempting to carve that gloriously roasted holiday bird with a finesse that recalls—depending on your generational point of reference—either the Boston Strangler, the cyborg in *Terminator 3*, or *True Blood*'s oversexed wayward vampires feasting on their prey. That's why the illustrated depiction of an on-the-spot carving is the paramount feature in this chapter. From Segal's point of view, there were no excuses or room for failure.

Mastering the throw of dice at a craps table was not to be downplayed either. Regardless of a casino's location—Monte Carlo, Macau, Las Vegas, or the local Veterans of Foreign Wars hall—the greatest concentration of high spirits and available women were always within an arm's toss of whoever is on a hot streak at the craps table. "The World's Biggest Gambling Game" promises that that man can be you. (Though for a right-handed guy, carving a turkey with one's left hand would probably be easier.)

Regardless of which hand you use to make your move, though, chess's "abstract beauty" and its stratagems made it "the most absorbing game in the world." If that wasn't inducement enough, a highly seductive "How You Can Checkmate in Seven Moves" was Segal's way of reminding a man that the only thing more satisfying than winning a game was doing so by flattening your opponent.

But it wasn't just actions that mattered. The *Gentry* man—every man—needed to know one universal truth. By daring to publish "The Golden Rule," this most basic of tenets, and declaring it as the universal standard for existence, the magazine put its rebellious status at risk. Backing up the Golden Rule's inarguable message with extensive quotes from disparate thinkers such as Shakespeare, Confucius, Aristotle, Spinoza, Mohammed, Henry James, and the Maharishi added to the validity of *Gentry*'s choice, but it also showed, however briefly, the magazine's heart.

Happily, that heart was only too glad to go back to being in the wrong place, especially when the time came to be "In Praise of Booze." Though well aware of the dangers of excess, Robert Paul Smith, the features author, dismissed them as easily as he might a game of canasta with the girls by admitting, "I don't drink to sharpen my appetite. I don't take to it for my arteries. I do not accept it as a social gesture…[or] because it is good for me. I drink because when I drink enough of it, I am a better, wiser, and a happier man." And who knows, maybe a few potent cocktails are all you need to go back and carve that turkey like Bobby Flay.

Gentry
Number Twelve
Fall 1954

**CLOCKWISE,
FROM TOP LEFT:**

Gentry, Number Twenty,
Fall 1956; Number Two,
Spring 1952; Number
Twelve, Fall 1954.

A Virginia gentleman, George Washington, aged 15, was living in the elegant home of his elegant half-brother Lawrence. Brother Lawrence ran the house at Mt. Vernon like a gay French court, filling it with guests who were "merry and handsome," the very cream of Colonial Society. But tall, narrow, awkward 15-year-old George, whose big hands fumbled with the teacups, whose big feet dragged on the dance floor, saw them through a glass darkly. Their clothes, he thought, were foppish; their conversation lewd; their table manners abominable. In a copybook, in the precise penmanship of his prudish adolescence, he set down 110 rules of "decent behaviour." Here follows a selection from those rules—which the proper young man was to follow the rest of his long life.

G Washington

Rules of Civility and Decent Behaviour

MOCK not nor jest at anything of importance; break no jests that are sharp or biting; and if you deliver anything witty or pleasant, abstain from laughing thereat yourself.

TURN not your back to others, especially in speaking; jog not the table or desk on which another reads or writes; lean not on any one.

WHEN your superiors talk to anybody, hear them; neither speak nor laugh.

IN the presence of others sing not to yourself with a humming voice, nor drum with your fingers or feet.

SPEAK not when others speak, sit not when others stand, and walk not when others stop.

THEY that are in dignity or office have in all places precedency, but whilst they are young they ought to respect those that are their equals in birth or other qualities, though they have no public charge.

LET your discourse with men of business be short and comprehensive.

IN visiting the sick do not presently play the physician if you be not knowing therein.

IN writing or speaking give to every person his due title according to his degree and the custom of the place.

UNDERTAKE not to teach your equal in the art he himself professes; it savours of arrogancy.

BEING to advise or reprehend any one, consider whether it ought to be in public or in private, presently or at some other time, also in what terms to do it; and in reproving show no signs of choler but do it with sweetness and mildness.

BE no flatterer, neither play with any one that delights not to be played with.

READ no letters, books, or papers in company; but when there is a necessity for doing it, you must not leave. Come not near the books or writings of any one so as to read them unasked; also look not nigh when another is writing a letter.

LET your countenance be pleasant, but in serious matters somewhat grave.

SHOW not yourself glad at the misfortune of another, though he were your enemy.

IT is good manners to prefer them to whom we speak before ourselves, especially if they be above us, with whom in no sort we ought to begin.

IN your apparel be modest, and endeavour to accommodate nature rather than procure admiration. Keep to the fashion of your equals, such as are civil and orderly with respect to time and place.

PLAY not the peacock, looking everywhere about you to see if you be well decked, if your shoes fit well, if your stockings set neatly and clothes handsomely.

BE not immodest in urging your friend to discover a secret.

SPEAK not of doleful things in time of mirth nor at the table; speak not of melancholy things, as death and wounds; and if others mention them, change, if you can, the discourse. Tell not your dreams but to your intimate friends.

BREAK not a jest when none take pleasure in mirth. Laugh not aloud, nor at all without occasion. Deride no man's misfortunes, though there seem to be some cause.

SPEAK not injurious words, neither in jest nor earnest. Scoff at none, although they give occasion.

BE not forward, but friendly and courteous, the first to salute, hear, and answer, and be not pensive when it is time to converse.

GO not thither where you know not whether you shall be welcome or not. Give not advice without being asked; and when desired, do it briefly.

REPREHEND not the imperfection of others, for that belongs to parents, masters, and superiors.

ASSOCIATE yourself with men of good quality if you esteem your own reputation, for it is better to be alone than in bad company.

WHEN another speaks, be attentive yourself, and disturb not the audience. If any hesitate in his words, help him not, nor prompt him without being desired; interrupt him not, nor answer him till his speech be ended.

GAZE not on the marks or blemishes of others, and ask not how they came. What you may speak in secret to your friend deliver not before others.

BE not angry at table, whatever happens; and if you have reason to be so show it not; put on a cheerful countenance, especially if there be strangers, for good humour makes one dish a feast.

LABOR to keep alive in your breast that little spark of celestial fire called conscience.

IN PRAISE OF

BOOZE

by ROBERT PAUL SMITH

The light imbiber, the steady drinker, the confirmed lush will find little interest in the following words, being already aware of the facts. This pagan hymn to earthly spirits is really dedicated to teetotalers everywhere

An honest man was over to my house the other night: I had some very good gin, so good that I had not yet been able to bring myself to do anything with it except pour it out of the bottle into a little glass and drink it. I had not put ice in the little glass, or vermouth, or bitters; I had just put the gin in it, and drunk it, and found it a total delight.

I said to the man—it was the first time he had been to my house and I did not yet know him to be honest, trustworthy, thrifty, loyal, brave, clean in mind and spirit, admirable, and my friend—"This is good gin. I will make it into a Martini, or you can have bitters in it, or there's some Scotch that—"

The man interrupted me in a loud clear voice. "I have not to date drunk anything alcoholic which I did not like."

This man is not, in my lexicon, a drunk; he is not, in somebody else's lexicon, an alcoholic. He is not any more neurotic than thee or me, except for his scrupulous honesty.

He is me, with courage. We drank some gin.

Because I am getting good and goddam tired of all the gumshoe moralizing about the evils of drink, I should like now to arise and say a few hundred words in praise of booze.

Alcohol is a substance which comes in a variety of more or less delightful forms. Its taste is not truly important; its effect is. I do not drink it to sharpen my appetite, I do not take it for my arteries, I do not accept it as a social gesture or a celebratory toy like a birthday snapper or a paper hat. There are a few kinds of alcohol whose taste I do not particularly like (cognac, because as a child I got it in tea when I had bronchitis; and rye, because as an adolescent during prohibition I drank it consistently and got sick ditto) and I must say that in general there are more foods that taste better than there are distillations. I do, then, not drink it because it is good for me.

I drink it because when I drink enough of it, I am a better and wiser and happier man.

I drink it because there are times when nothing—not the company of my friends, not the possession of money, not the kindnesses of my wife nor the pleasant doings of my children nor the postures of my cat, not the prospect of a new book by an author I admire nor a new recording of piano music by André Previn or an old recording by Bessie Smith, not the arrival of a friend with a Japanese print he promised to and did bring from Tokyo, not the first crocus in Spring or the last rose of summer nor the rising of the sun or the setting thereof—when not any of these things will make me as pleased as the introduction into my belly of a few ounces of gin, the wonderful internal benison of that magical liquid touching places in my interior which can be caressed in no other way. And then, the appealing, warm, witty and beloved person I become when that warmth rises to my rocky head.

There are times when I will surely cast myself from a high place and make myself dead, when I will assassinate my employer and antagonize the best of my friends and cause my wife to cry and my children to whimper and the cat to run away and hide, and nothing except a small glass container winking at the brim with beaded bubbles of Irish whiskey can cure this.

There was a summer when all was lost, and a man discovered to me Pernod, and my seat grew to the bar stool, and my elbows sent down roots into the mahogany of the bar, and I watched with delight the little swinging door that rocked so marvelously on its spring hinges.

There was a winter when my little boy had tularemia, or psitaccosis, or brucellosis, or undulant fever (and it was none of these and to this day it is not known what it was, but he was sick and I was scared) and there were days in that winter when the highest accomplishment of science was not what they were not doing for him with their miracle drugs, but what the ancient miracle drug that comes in bottles was doing for me.

There were all the times I was scared—and there have been plenty of them—and perhaps what booze gave me was Dutch courage, but I know of no other that you can get if you don't have it.

I have drunk too much booze on too many occasions, but I don't feel that the pain over the years has been even as great as the pleasure.

It has made me friends, it has made me brave, it has made me gentle and comic and kind and loose-lipped and maudlin. It is a product of civilization, and it civilizes me.

It is, I suppose, a great evil: but I am constrained to report that the pleasure which reformed alcoholics get from giving up booze seems to me to be exactly the same pleasure they got from drinking it. And that is not my pleasure.

My pleasure is the time-out that this fancy poison gives me, a kind of nap I can take sitting up and talking and walking around and making friends and being a charmer, as if the world were full of sun and small puppies and pink babies and pretty girls.

When a painter does it, it's art. When a writer does it, it's poetry. When a bottle of booze does it, it's getting a load on.

And I don't mean in moderation. I mean more than you can handle. A moderate poem? A symphony in the key of Moderation? A sober painting?

Nonsense. In matters of art, all things in immoderation.

Booze, too.

Booze is great.

My friend and I like it very much. ◆

JOHN SCARNE

TELLS YOU

HOW TO PLAY

THE
WORLD'S
BIGGEST GAMBLING GAME

Its name is "Bank Craps"
and it is played by more men and women
in more gambling casinos
than any other game
Here, from the No. 1 authority, is advice
on how—and how not—to play it

JOHN SCARNE once rolled the dice every day for 15 years, keeping score on every throw. He rolled 6,000,000 times. He wanted to see how many times the 7 would come up.*

Scarne's know-how is based on homework like that, not on any second-hand say-so from the percentage theorists. To call him an outstanding expert on gambling is to praise with a faint damn. He is, by all odds, the world's greatest.

Gentry's editors read Scarne's recent best-selling autobiography, *The Amazing World of John Scarne* and were forthwith prompted to ask him a question:

"What is the most popular game in the gambling casinos of the nation?"

"Reading from left to right," said Scarne, "Bank Craps."

"Would Mr. Scarne care to tell us something about Bank Craps?"

"Delighted," said the master.

It came up 1,000,001 times

THE RULES

THERE ARE VARIATIONS on the layout used for Bank Craps, but the one illustrated below is standard in most casinos.

The procedure of play is as follows:

A player throws the dice to form his "combination"—that is, the sum of the two numbers which show on the uppermost side of the dice. Before he throws, he must place a bet on either the "Pass (win) line," or on the "Don't Pass (lose) line." All other bets must be placed *before* the dice are thrown.

The Bets:

1. PASS

This means you win with a 7 or 11, you lose with 2, 3 or 12 thrown on the *first* roll. Any other number becomes your "point." Throw the dice until you have established your point, then continue throwing to try to make your point. If your point comes up again before a 7 is rolled, you win. You can then start rolling all over again. If a 7 comes up before you make your point, you lose. The dice are passed to the next player.

2. DON'T PASS

These are the opposite of "Pass" bets. You lose with 7 or 11, win with 3 and 12. Rolling a 2 is a "stand-off"—you neither win nor lose. You also lose if your point comes up before you roll a 7.

3. COME

You bet at "Come" after the point has been rolled. With 7 or 11 you win. You lose with "craps" (2, 3, 12). If any number comes out as 4, 5, 6, 8, 9, 10, this number becomes your point. If your "Come" number comes before 7, you win.

4. DON'T COME

The opposite of "Come" bets. You bet "Don't Come" after the point is out. If 7 or 11 is rolled, you lose. You win with craps 3 or 12. (There is no action with craps 2). If any number comes out as 4, 5, 6, 8, 9, 10, your bet goes to this number. If 7 comes before "Don't Come" number, you win.

5. HARDWAYS

The numbers 4, 6, 8, 10 win if a combination of doubles comes up before a 7 or an "Easy" combination of the same total. If you bet on the "Hardway 8," you win if a combination of two fours is thrown before an "Easy 8" (5 and 3, or 6 and 2) or a 7. "Hardway 10" wins with two fives, loses with a 6 and 4, or a 7. "Hardway 6" and "Hardway 8" pay 9 to 1. Hardways 4 and 10 pay 7 to 1.

The following "One Roll Action Bets" are placed before any throw, and they win or lose on that single throw:

Field—wins with any combination totalling 2, 3, 5, 9, 10, 11, or 12. Pays even money.

Any Craps or All Craps—wins with either 2, 3, or 12. Pays 7 to 1.

Eleven—wins with 11 only. Pays 15 to 1.

Craps (3)—wins with 3 only. Pays 15 to 1.

Craps (2)—wins with 2 only. Pays 30 to 1.

Craps (12)—wins with 12 only. Pays 30 to 1.

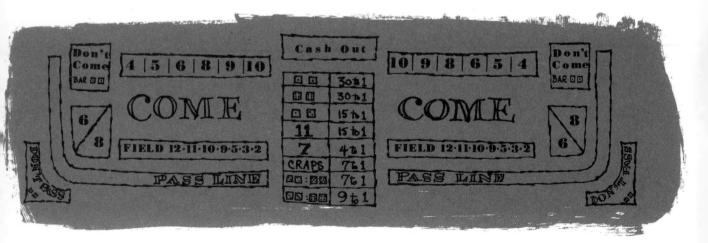

THE PLAY

We asked Mr. Scarne if there is any reliable system for playing Bank Craps. His reply is something for all devotees of the gambling dens to ponder:

"Systems are ridiculous. The only way to gamble properly is to know the percentages—to know when to bet, and how much. Anybody who gambles strictly on hunch is throwing his money away. But if a man makes a careful study of the percentages, goes into a casino with his eyes, ears and mind wide open, he might—I said *might*—do pretty good for himself."

The wise gambler always bears in mind the one great cardinal fact—viz: that he is playing against the house, and that *the percentage is always in favor of the house*. In the interests, then, of that Gentry reader, somewhere, who may occasionally take a flutter at the gaming tables, we herewith append Scarne's own list of percentages for the game of Bank Craps, worked out by the master himself after years of test, observation, and experiment.

They appear here, in full detail, for the first time anywhere.

The Casino's percentage on Bank Craps bets:

BET	% IN CASINO'S FAVOR
Win or pass line	1.414%
Come	1.414%
Lose or don't pass, Bar 6-6 or 1-1	1.402%
Don't Come, Bar 6-6 or 1-1	1.402%
Lose or don't pass, Bar 1-2	4.385%
Don't Come, Bar 1-2	4.385%

POINT BETS	CORRECT ODDS	% IN CASINO'S FAVOR
Bank lays 9 to 5 on 4 or 10	10 to 5	6.666%
Bank lays 7 to 5 on 5 or 9	7½ to 5	4.000%
Bank lays 7 to 6 on 6 or 8	6 to 5	1.515%
Player lays 11 to 5 on 4 or 10	10 to 5	3.030%
Player lays 8 to 5 on 5 or 9	7½ to 5	2.500%
Player lays 5 to 4 on 6 or 8	6 to 5	1.818%

FIELD BETS	
Field Nos. 2, 3, 4, 9, 10, 11, 12	11.111%
Field Nos. 2, 3, 4, 9, 10, 11, 12 with double payoff on 2 and 12	5.263%
Field Nos. 2, 3, 5, 9, 10, 11, 12	5.555%
Big Six	9.090%
Big Eight	9.090%

WIN OR LOSE BET PLUS BEHIND THE LINE BET

When a player has a bet on the "Pass" or "Don't Pass" line and the shooter throws a 4, 5, 6, 8, 9, or 10 on his first roll for his point number, the player is permitted to wager an equal number of chips behind the line. This is paid off at the correct odds. This in turn cuts down the percentage against the player on the Pass or Don't Pass line to less than 1% in favor of the Casino.

This is the best bet at the dice table.

The exact percentages in favor of the Bank on this bet are:

On a Win or Pass Line Bet plus a Back of the Line Bet, Casino percentage is .848%.

On a Lose or Don't Pass Bet plus a Back of the Line Bet, Casino percentage is .832%.

CASINO'S PERCENTAGES ON ONE ROLL OR COME-OUT BETS

THE BET	CASINO PAYS	CORRECT ODDS	% IN CASINO'S FAVOR
Two sixes (6-6) Two Aces (1-1)	30 to 1	35 to 1	13 8/9%
Eleven (6-5) Three (1-2)	15 to 1	17 to 1	11 1/9%
All Sevens (7)	4 to 1	5 to 1	16 2/3%
Any Crap (2, 3 or 12)	7 to 1	8 to 1	11 1/9%
7 with 3-4 7 with 2-5 7 with 6-1	15 to 1	17 to 1	11 1/9%

That says it. If you take your gambling seriously, live with these numbers until you've memorized them. Then—gentlemen—place your bets. ◆

How to Carve a Turkey

These step-by-step pictures show the correct procedure. To them we add: always use a very sharp knife and work standing up.

The first step in carving a turkey is cutting the leg (drumstick) down to the thigh joint. This involves starting well above the joint (1). When the knife reaches the bones, take the leg in the fingers and pull away from the bird revealing the joint, which the knife then severs (2). Next, separate drumstick from second joint (3), and slice dark meat from latter.

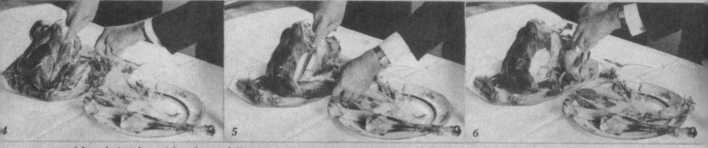

After placing drumstick and second joint meat on the serving platter, carve the wing. Cut from the breast toward the drumstick (4) as the wing joint is parallel to the thigh joint. As with leg, when knife reaches the joint, relinquish fork and use fingers to pull wing away from breast (5). After severing the joint, separate the two parts of wing at second joint (6).

Next carve the side of the breast, cutting the white meat in thin slices, starting at top. Cut toward the wing joint (7). For each slice the fork is placed low (8) and when knife is half way down, the fork is replaced above it to allow a continuous slice (9). Here is a trick: allow the bird to stand 30 minutes after cooking; this will firm meat, make it easier to slice,

Most delectable part of the bird is the "oyster", which is now removed (10). There are two, one on either side at the very bottom of the bird, between wing and drumstick. When the side breast has been carved to the bone (11) the bird is ready for the carving of the front breast, which is done in the same manner as the side. The other half of the bird is carved last.

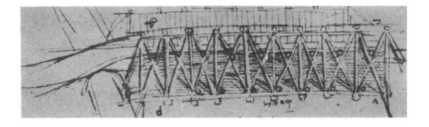

Leonardo applies for a position

PART OF A LETTER FROM LEONARDO TO THE DUKE OF SFORZA, OFFERING HIS SERVICES AND ENUMERATING HIS QUALIFICATIONS

. . . I shall endeavor, without prejudice to any one else, to explain myself to your Excellency, showing your Lordship my secrets, and then offering them to your best pleasure and approbation to work with . . .

1. I have a sort of extremely light and strong bridges, adapted to be most easily carried, and with them you may pursue and at any time flee from the enemy; and others, secure and indestructible by fire and battle, easy and convenient to life and place. Also methods of burning and destroying those of the enemy.

2. I know how, when a place is besieged, to take the water out of the trenches, and make endless variety of bridges, and covered ways and ladders, and other machines pertaining to such expeditions.

3. If, by reason of the height of the banks, or the strength of the place, to avail oneself of the plan of bombardment, I have methods for destroying every rock or other fortress, even if it were founded on a rock, etc.

4. Again, I have kinds of mortars; most convenient and easy to carry; and with these I can fling small stones almost resembling a storm; and with the smoke of these cause great terror to the enemy, to his great detriment and confusion.

5. I have means by secret and tortuous mines and ways, made without noise, to reach a designated spot, even if it were needed to pass under a trench or a river.

6. I will make covered chariots, safe and unassailable which, entering among the enemy with their artillery, there is no body of man so great but they would break them. And behind these, infantry could follow quite unhurt and without any hindrance.

7. In case of need I will make big guns, mortars, and light ordnance of fine and useful forms, out of the common type.

8. Where the operation of bombardment might fail, I would contrive catapults, mangonesi, trabocchi, and other machines of marvellous efficacy and not in common use. And in short, according to the variety of cases, I can contrive various and endless means of offense and defense.

9. And if the fight should be at sea I have many kinds of machines most efficient for offense and defense; and vessels which will resist the attack of the largest guns and powder and fumes.

10. In time of peace I believe I can give perfect satisfaction and to the equal of any other in architecture and the composition of buildings public and private; and in guiding water from one place to another.

on keeping healthy—

If you would keep healthy, follow this regimen: do not eat unless you feel inclined, and sup lightly; chew well, and let what you take be well cooked and simple. He who takes medicine does himself harm; do not give way to anger and avoid close air; hold yourself upright when you rise from table and do not let yourself sleep at midday. Be temperate with wine; take a little frequently, but not at other than the proper meal times, nor on an empty stomach; neither protract nor delay the (visit to) the privy. When you take exercise let it be moderate. Do not remain with the belly recumbent and the head lowered, and see that you are well covered at night. Rest you head and keep your mind cheerful; shun wantonness, and pay attention to diet.

THE

GOLDEN RULE

**WHATSOEVER YE WOULD THAT MEN SHOULD DO
TO YOU, DO YE EVEN SO TO THEM**

May I be no man's enemy, and may I be the friend of that which is eternal and abides. May I never quarrel with those nearest to me; and if I do, may I be reconciled quickly. May I never devise evil against any man; if any devise evil against me, may I escape uninjured and without the need of hurting him. May I love, seek, and attain only that which is good. May I wish for all men's happiness and envy none. May I never rejoice in the ill-fortune of one who has wronged me . . . When I have done or said what is wrong, may I never wait for the rebuke of others, but always rebuke myself until I make amends . . . May I win no victory that harms either me or my opponent. May I reconcile friends who are wroth with one another. May I, to the extent of my power, give all needful help to my friends and to all who are in want. May I never fail a friend in danger. When visiting those in grief may I be able by gentle and healing words to soften their pain . . . May I respect myself. May I always keep tame that which rages within me. May I accustom myself to be gentle, and never be angry with people because of circumstances. May I never discuss who is wicked and what wicked things he has done, but know good men and follow in their footsteps. ❧ FROM AN OLD PAGAN PRAYER ❧

In the pages following
Gentry presents a selection of passages from all religions and from all nations and races on the one definition of morality which has so commended itself to the heart of Man that it is universally known as the Golden Rule, or the Rule which transcends all others . . .

THE LI KI

What you do not like when done to yourself, do not do to others. In the way of the superior man there are four things, to not one of which have I, Khiu (Confucius), as yet attained.

To serve my father as I would require my son to serve me, I am not yet able; to serve my ruler as I would require my minister to serve me, I am not yet able; to serve my elder brother as I would require a younger brother to serve me, I am not yet able; to set the example in behaving to a friend as I would require him to behave to me, I am not yet able. In the practice of the ordinary virtues, and attention to his ordinary words, if (the practice) be in anything defective, (the superior man) dares not but exert himself; if (his words) be in any way excessive, he dares not allow himself such license. His words have respect to his practice, and his practice has respect to his words. Is not the superior man characterized by a perfect sincerity?

The superior man does what is proper to the position in which he is; he does not wish to go beyond it. In a position of wealth and honour, he does what is proper to a position of wealth and honour. In a position of poverty and meanness, he does what is proper to a position of poverty and meanness. Situated among barbarous tribes, he does what is proper in such a situation. In a position of sorrow and difficulty, he does what is proper in such a position. The superior man can find himself in no position in which he is not himself. In a high situation, he does not insult or oppress those who are below him; in a low situation, he does not cling to or depend on those who are above him.

THE ANALECTS OF CONFUCIUS

Some one said, "What do you say concerning the principle that injury should be recompensed with kindness?"

The Master said, "With what then will you recompense kindness?

"Recompense injury with justice, and recompense kind-

ness with kindness."

Tsze-kung asked, saying, "Is there one word which may serve as a rule of practice for all one's life?"

The Master said, "Is not RECIPROCITY such a word? What you do not want done to yourself, do not do to others.

"There is the love of being benevolent without the love of learning; the beclouding here leads to a foolish simplicity. There is the love of knowing without the love of learning; the beclouding here leads to dissipation of mind. There is the love of being sincere without the love of learning; the beclouding here leads to an injurious disregard of consequences. There is the love of straightforwardness without the love of learning; the beclouding here leads to rudeness. There is the love of boldness without the love of learning; the beclouding here leads to insubordination. There is the love of firmness without the love of learning; the beclouding here leads to extravagant conduct."

When a superior man knows the causes which make instruction successful, and those which make it of no effect, he can become a teacher of others. Thus in his teaching, he leads and does not drag; he strengthens and does not discourage; he opens the way but does not conduct to the end (without the learner's own efforts). Leading and not dragging produces harmony. Strengthening and not discouraging makes attainment easy. Opening the way and not conducting to the end makes (the learner) thoughtful. He who produces such harmony, easy attainment, and thoughtfulness may be pronounced a skillful teacher.

There is nothing more visible than what is secret, and nothing more manifest than what is minute. Therefore, the superior man is watchful over himself when he is alone.

The Master said: "They who return kindness for injury are such as have a regard for their own persons. They who return injury for kindness are men to be punished and put to death."

THE   G O L D E N

MENCIUS

Mencius said: All men have a mind which cannot bear to see the sufferings of others.

The ancient kings had this commiserating mind, and they, as a matter of course, had likewise a commiserating government. When with a commiserating mind was practised a commiserating government, the government of the empire was as easy a matter as making anything go round in the palm.

When I say that all men have a mind which cannot bear to see the sufferings of others, my meaning may be illustrated thus: Even nowadays, if men suddenly see a child about to fall into a well, they will without exception experience a feeling of alarm and distress. They will feel so, not as a ground on which they may gain the favour of the child's parents, nor as a ground on which they may seek the praise of their neighbours and friends, nor from a dislike to the reputation of having been unmoved by such a thing.

From this case we may perceive that the feeling of commiseration is essential to man, that the feeling of shame and dislike is essential to man, that the feeling of modesty and complaisance is essential to man, that the feeling of approving and disapproving is essential to man.

The feeling of commiseration is the principle of benevolence. The feeling of shame and dislike is the principle of righteousness. The feeling of modesty and complaisance is the principle of propriety. The feeling of approving and disapproving is the principle of knowledge.

Men have these four principles just as they have their four limbs. When men, having these four principles yet say of themselves that they cannot develop them, they play the thief with themselves, and he who says of his prince that he cannot develop them, plays the thief with his prince.

The benevolent man loves others. The man of propriety shows respect to others.

He who loves others is constantly loved by them. He who respects others is constantly respected by them.

THE HSIAO KING

(The superior man) speaks, having thought whether the words should be spoken; he acts, having thought whether his actions are sure to give pleasure. His virtue and righteousness are such as will be honoured; what he initiates and does is fit to be imitated; his deportment is worthy of contemplation; his movements in advancing or retiring are all according to proper rule. In this way does he present himself to the people, who both revere and love him, imitate and become like him. Thus he is able to make his teaching of virtue successful, and his government and orders to be carried into effect.

CHUANG TZU

The people of this world all rejoice in others being like themselves, and object to others being different from themselves. Those who make friends with their likes and do not make friends with their unlikes, are influenced by a desire to be above the others. But how can those who desire to be above the others ever be above the others? Rather than base one's judgment on the opinions of the many, let each look after his own affairs.

SAYINGS OF TSIANG SAMDUP

In this sense we are our brothers' keepers: that if we injure them we are responsible. Therefore, our duty is so vigilantly to control ourselves that we may injure none; and for this there is no substitute; all other duties take a lower place and are dependent on it.

LAO-TZE

To those who are good (to me), I am good; and to those who are not good (to me), I am also good; and thus (all) get to be good. To those who are sincere (with me), I am sincere; and to those who are not sincere I am also sincere; and thus (all) get to be sincere.

R U L E

THE BABYLONIAN TALMUD

Hillel was one of the greatest of the rabbis whose teachings and commentaries on Biblical law are included in the Talmud. Although born in Babylon, he lived in Jerusalem in the time of King Herod. Many of his sayings, which are recorded in the section of the Talmud called "Aboth," are almost identical with maxims which later appeared in the New Testament.

A Roman soldier once asked Hillel if he could teach him the all of Judaism while he stood before the rabbi on one foot. Hillel answered: "What is unpleasant to thyself, that do not to thy neighbor; that is the whole Law — all else is but its exposition."

BOOK OF TOBIT

Take heed to thyself, my child, in all thy works, and be discreet in all thy behaviour; and what thou thyself hatest, do to no man.

Another version reads:

Tobias is admonished by his father Tobit to love his brethren, saying "and what is displeasing to thyself, that do not unto any other."

THE NEW TESTAMENT

Therefore all things whatsoever ye would that men should do to you, do ye even so to them: for this is the law and the prophets.

Ye have heard that it hath been said, Thou shalt love thy neighbor, and hate thine enemy.

But I say unto you, Love your enemies, bless them that curse you, do good to them that hate you, and pray for those which despitefully use you, and persecute you.

— ST. MATTHEW

Owe no man anything, but to love one another: for he that loveth another hath fulfilled the law.

For this, Thou shalt not commit adultery, Thou shalt not kill, Thou shalt not steal, Thou shalt not bear false witness, Thou shalt not covet; and if there be any other commandment, it is briefly comprehended in this saying, namely, Thou shalt love they neighbor as thyself.

Love worketh no ill to his neighbour: therefore love is the fulfilling of the law.   — PAUL TO THE ROMANS, CH. 13.

THOMAS A KEMPIS

No man is sufficient of himself; no man is wise enough of himself; but we ought to bear with one another, comfort, help, instruct, and admonish one another.

AN ENGLISH ECCLESIASTIC, SAID TO BE JOHN FISHER. PAINTED TERRACOTTA. PROBABLY BY TORRIGIANO (1472-1528).

DOOMS OF KING ALFRED

It seemed good to the Holy Ghost, and to us, that we should set no burden upon you above that which it was needful for you to bear, now, that is, that you forbear from worshipping idols, and from tasting blood, and from fornication; and that which you will that other men should not do unto you, do not that to other men.

On this last precept the king observes:
From this one doom a man may remember that he judge every man righteously; he need heed no other doom book. Let him remember that he adjudge no man that which he would not that he adjudge to him.

SHAKESPEARE

If to do were as easy as to know what were good to do, chapels had been churches and poor men's cottages princes' palaces. It is a good divine that follows his own instructions: I can easier teach twenty what were good to be done, than be one . . . to follow mine own teaching.

HENRY SIDGWICK

Reason shows me that if my happiness is desirable and a good, the equal happiness of any other person must be equally desirable.

MOHAMMED

Anas reported on the authority of the Prophet — peace and blessings of Allah be on him. — He said: "None of you has faith unless he loves for his brother what he loves for himself."　　　　　　　　　　— BUKHARI 2:6

Abu Hurairah reported that the Messenger of Allah said: Who will take from me these sayings and act accordingly? I said: I, O Messenger of Allah! Then he caught me by the hand and counted five (sayings). He said: Fear the forbidden things, you will then become the holiest of men; be pleased with what Allah apportioned to you, you will then be the most contented of men; be good to your neighbour, then you will be a (true) believer; love for men what you love for yourself, you will then become a (true) Moslem; and laugh not much, for verily excessive laughter makes the heart dead.

Ali-b-Hasan reported that the Messenger of Allah said: The main part of wisdom after religion is love for men and doing good to everyone, pious or sinner.　— DARQUINI

THE HOLY QUR-AN

In the name of God, Most Gracious, Most Merciful.

> Woe to those
> That deal in fraud,
>
> Those who, when they
> Have to receive by measure
> From men, exact full measure,
>
> But when they have
> To give by measure
> Or weight to men,
> Give less than due
>
> Do they not think
> That they will be called
> To account?
>
> On a Mighty Day,
>
> A Day when (all) mankind
> Will stand before
> The Lord of the Worlds?

(Note: The translator, Abdullah Yusuf Ali, compares this with the Golden Rule and adds: "You must give in full what is due from you, whether you expect or wish to receive full consideration from the other side.")

APOLOGY OF ARISTIDES

They (i.e., the Christians) do not commit adultery, do not commit fornication, do not bear false witness, do not covet their neighbour's goods, honour their father and their mother, love their neighbours, judge justly; whatever they do not wish to be done to them they do not do to another; they exhort those who injure them and make them friendly to themselves.

ARISTIDES WAS AN ATHENIAN; HE WROTE THE APOLOGY DURING THE TIME OF HADRIAN, 117-138 A.D.

EPICTETUS

What you avoid suffering yourself, seek not to impose on others. You avoid slavery, for instance; take care not to enslave. For if you can bear to exact slavery from others, you appear to have been yourself a slave. For vice has nothing in common with virtue, nor freedom with slavery. As a person in health would not wish to be attended by the sick, nor to have those who live with him in a state of sickness, so neither would a person who is free bear to be served by slaves, nor to have those who live with him in a state of slavery.

ARISTOTLE

The question was once put to him (Aristotle) how we ought to behave to our friends; the answer was, "As we should wish our friends to behave to us."

SPINOZA

The good which each one who follows virtue desires for himself, he also desires for other men, and the more so, the more knowledge he has of God.

COLERIDGE

. . . Farewell, farewell!
but this I tell
To thee, thou Wedding-guest,
He prayeth well who loveth well
Both man and bird and beast.

He prayeth best who loveth best
All things both great and small;
For the dear God who loveth us,
He made and loveth all. . . .

DOSTOIEVSKY

. . Love will teach us all things; but we must learn how to win love; it is got with difficulty; it is a possession dearly bought with much labor and in long time; for one must love not sometimes only, for a passing moment, but always. There is no man who doth not sometimes love; even the wicked can do that.

And let not man's sin dishearten thee; love a man even in his sin, for that love is a likeness of the divine love, and is the summit of love on earth. Love all God's creation, both the whole and every grain of sand. Love every leaf, every ray of light. Love the animals, love the plants, love each separate thing. If thou love each thing thou wilt perceive the mystery of God in all; and when once thou perceive this, thou wilt thenceforward grow every day to a fuller understanding of it: until thou come at last to love the whole world with a love that will then be all-embracing and universal.

IMMANUEL KANT

So act as to treat humanity, whether in thine own person or in that of any other, in every case as an end withal, never as a means only.

CHESTERFIELD

Do as you would be done by, is the surest method of pleasing. To do as you would be done by is the plain, sure, and undisputed rule of morality and justice.

EMERSON

Love, and you shall be loved. All love is mathematically just, as much as the two sides of an algebraic equation. The good man has absolute good, which like fire turns every thing to its own nature, so you cannot do him harm.

The good are befriended even by weakness and defect. As no man had ever a point of price that was not injurious to him, so no man had ever a defect that was not somewhere made useful to him. Like the wounded oyster, (the good man) mends his shell with pearl.

Our strength grows out of our weakness. The indignation which arms itself with secret forces does not awaken until we are pricked and stung and sorely assailed. A great man is always willing to be little. Whilst he sits on the cushion of advantages, he goes to sleep. When he is pushed, tormented, defeated, he has a chance to learn something; he has been put on his wits, on his manhood; he has gained facts, learned his ignorance; is cured of the insanity of conceit; has got moderation and real skill. The wise man throws himself on the side of his assailants. It is more his interest than it is theirs to find his weak point. The wound cicatrizes and falls off from him like a dead skin, and when they would triumph, lo! he has passed on invulnerable.

THOMAS PAINE

The duty of man is not a wilderness of turnpike gates, through which he is to pass by tickets from one to the other. It is plain and simple, and consists but of two points. His duty to God, which every man must feel; and with respect to his neighbor, to do as he would be done by.

SWEDENBORG

That love to the Lord and love toward the neighbor comprehend in themselves all divine truths, may be manifest from what the Lord Himself spoke concerning these two loves, saying: "Thou shalt love the Lord thy God with all thy heart and with all thy soul. This is the first and greatest commandment. The second, which is like unto it, is, Thou shalt love thy neighbor as thyself. On these two hang the law and the Prophets."

THOMAS TRAHERNE

When you love men, the world quickly becomes yours; and you yourself become a greater treasure than the world is. For all their persons are your treasures, and all the things in Heaven and earth that serve them are yours. For those are the riches of Love.

HENRY JAMES

Where shall we find a definition of morality ratified by the universal mind of man? I know of none so commanding as that given by Jesus Christ, when he declared that it consisted in our doing as we would be done by. "All things whatsoever ye would that men should do to you, do ye even so to them: FOR THIS IS THE LAW AND THE PROPHETS."

LIN YUTANG

Whenever you do a thing, act so that it will give your friends no occasion for regret, your foes no cause for joy.

THE PERENNIAL PHILOSOPHER

I give an inch and the other guy gives an inch. He's human, just like me. — A NEW YORK TAXI DRIVER

SRI AUROBINDO

Our nature, our consciousness is that of beings ignorant of each other, separated from each other, rooted in a divided ego, who must strive to establish some kind of relation betwen their embodied ignorances; for the urge to union and forces making for union are there in Nature

TALKS WITH MAHARSHI

DISCIPLE: *What is my duty to Society? What should be my relation to it?*

MAHARSHI: You are a limb of Society. Society is the body, individuals are its members, its limbs. Just as the various limbs help and co-operate with one another and thus are happy, so each must unite with others in being helpful to all in thought, speech and action . . . One may see to the good of one's own group, i.e., the group that is immediate to him, and then proceed to others.

DISCIPLE: *What is the goal towards which mankind on earth is moving?*

MAHARSHI: Real equality and fraternity form the true goal; for then, supreme Peace may reign on earth, and the earth herself can be a single household.

THE GOLDEN RULE • END

HOW YOU CAN CHECKMATE IN SEVEN MOVES

*Chess, creatively played, involves a subtle expression of form,
design, and composition similar in many ways to those found in other arts.
The following pages illustrate a seven-move pitfall which combines
these elements in a swiftly formed pattern, classical
in its elegance and simplicity.*

The great charm of chess is its abstract beauty. It is an endless adventure in pure design, of inventions, compositions, stratagems, and forays. In its plays and counterplays symbolic devices are used to create arabesques of tension, each of which can convey the kind of emotion usually associated with the more familiar esthetic expressions.

All of which is to say that chess is perhaps the most absorbing game in the world. It can never become monotonous because the permutations of its designs are almost infinite and no two games are ever alike. Each new combination of pieces presents a fresh challenge to creative imagination. Every situation is the start of a personal communication, an exchange of ideas, a two-dimensional conversation in which symbols take the place of words.

Chess can be enjoyed on various levels. It is rewarding if played hit-or-miss, with only a rudimentary knowledge of basic moves. Pleasure here lies in finding original solutions to new problems; it is not necessary to know anything about strategic openings, gambits, defenses, or pitfalls. Many amateurs have acquired veteran status without concerning themselves with chess lore or logistics. On the other hand, like any other art, chess gains in charm and significance as its subtleties become apparent, and a little study is eminently rewarding.

An example of this is given on the following pages. Here we see a classical pitfall, famous in the literature of chess. In this stratagem White deliberately sacrifices his queen . . . a play which ordinarily has the quality of suicide. The sacrifice in this case makes possible a checkmate of Black within two moves.

This pitfall illustrates a creative design executed with chess men. In its simplicity, its imagination, and its forthright elegance, it embodies the basic materials of great art. Anyone familiar with the elementary moves can follow its structure without difficulty. For those approaching chess for the first time, however, an explanation of the essential moves is capsuled on the second page following.

FIRST MOVE. King's Pawn opening. White plays Pawn to King's fourth. Black replies with Pawn to King's fourth.

SECOND MOVE. White develops in an orthodox way, playing Knight to King's Bishop's third. Black counters with Pawn to Queen's third. This is a routine defensive move which supports Black's King's Pawn at King's fourth and at the same time opens the diagonal of Black Queen's Bishop, freeing it for offense.

THIRD MOVE. White brings out his King's Bishop to the Queen's Bishop's fourth. Black advances his King's Rook's Pawn to the Rook's third. This is a weak move, actually wasting precious time. Black is apparently afraid of the consequences of the advance of White's Knight and attempts to forestall the attacking move.

Basic Moves in This Pitfall

PAWN: Moves forward only, one square at a time. Two squares are permitted on the first move. The pawn effects a capture of an opposing piece by moving forward diagonally one square, and occupying square of the captured opponent's piece.

KNIGHT: Moves three squares in an L-shaped path. One square (or two) in one direction, then two squares (or one) to the right (or left).

BISHOP: Moves any number of squares backward or forward along a diagonal.

KING: Moves one square in any direction.

When a king is attacked by an opposing piece he is said to be *in check*. He is required to move out of check, or be protected from the check.

When a king is in check and can neither move away from the attack nor be protected — in short, when he is completely cornered — he is checkmated. The game is finished. The term *check* is derived from a Sanskrit root meaning Shah, or king; *mate* from death. Freely translated — *the king is dead!*

FOURTH MOVE. White's development is completely sound. He brings out his other Knight. Black brings out his Queen's Bishop and posts it at the King's Knight's fifth, pinning White's Knight. This looks like a clever move, immobilizing White's Knight. It isn't. Black's whole structure is weak. He should have developed at least one Knight before bringing out a Bishop. This usually establishes a sounder game.

FIFTH MOVE — WHITE. White takes advantage of Black's weaknesses and sets a trap. Despite the fact that his Knight is pinned against the Queen, he moves it into an attacking position, taking Black's King's Pawn. The White Queen is thus offered as a sacrifice.

FIFTH MOVE — BLACK. The temptation for Black is too great. He can see no reason why he should not take White's Queen. For the sake of such easy gain, Black walks head-on into the trap; he takes the Queen with his Bishop, overlooking the hidden threat to his King.

SIXTH MOVE — WHITE. The jaws now close. White sweeps across the board with his Bishop, captures Black's King's Bishop's Pawn, and declares Check.

SIXTH MOVE — BLACK. There is only one possible move for Black, blocked partially by his own men. Under duress he advances the King to King's second.

SEVENTH MOVE. The game is over. White brings up his Queen's Knight to the Queen's fifth. Checkmate!

STYLE

2

It's not exactly clear who's to blame for the major misconception about how men dressed during the 1950s because there are so many possible suspects. Among them are vintage shops filled with racks of plaid flannel shirts that never sell; late-night reruns of *The Adventures of Ozzie and Harriet* (Ozzie rarely took off his jacket or tie, even at home) and *I Love Lucy* (with Desi in either a Cuban guayabera shirt or a too-tight tux); the crisp, colorlessly buttoned-down cast of *Mad Men* (which actually takes place in the 1960s, but many fans are too young to make that distinction); and too many revivals of *Grease*.

Regardless of the source of the misinterpretation, we have cemented into our collective memory an image of men of this era dressed as if they were in costume. We've come to imagine them wearing attire that at one end of the spectrum represented stiff, humorless conservatism and on the other, leather jacket–clad *Rebel Without a Cause* kitsch.

This impression couldn't be more wrong, which is why *Gentry*'s fashion coverage is as unforeseeable as it is refreshing. The range of possibility packed into its pages is staggering, the avalanche of new ideas exhilarating, and the search for variation limitless. But what is most surprising is the constant encouragement to develop one's personal style.

Certainly, some of the features are now anachronistic, such as the imperative for a wardrobe of hats or the array of suffocatingly coy Tyrolean ski sweaters. But what's enlightening about *Gentry*'s approach to menswear is its joyful and fearless embrace of variety, and eagerness to find exactly the right outfit for every situation. Frankly, it's a very feminine approach to building a wardrobe. Yet, there is never any question or concern about whether being a clotheshorse is a "manly" goal. Ascots, foulards, striped patio slippers, formal shirts with lace placates secured by velvet ribbon, and evening coats with candy-apple red linings are presented without any hesitation as to what the guys in the office might think. Rather you sense *Gentry*'s editors' confidence in their point of view: If they do their job right, others will wish they were you.

Even geography comes into consideration. In a New York boardroom one would choose a close-fitting one-button silk and wool "town suit" with a pattern of broken stripes. In Barbados, well, though no one is implying anything untoward, the clothes are astonishingly gay, and not in the old-fashioned use of the word, either. Hats off to the grown man who can wear a sailor suit.

There are polished cotton shirts with a dizzying pattern of cooking utensils and wine bottles on them for manning the barbecue, "seaside red" velvet terry parkas for a weekend by the lake, dotted blue silk foulard blazers to get you noticed at the country club, the newest silhouette in three-piece suits with cropped waist-length vests, complete weekend wardrobes, and more variations on dressing for formal occasions than there are opening nights at the Metropolitan Opera.

The options are unnervingly endless. Thankfully, *Gentry* offers two guidelines. The first advised men to return to the standards detailed in the feature "Beau Brummell: A New Look at an Old Fallacy." This article is an enlightening assessment of the man not the myth, because unlike his depiction on film or his legacy as an adjective—both of which are the personification of dandyism—the real Brummell lived by three words: "Fastidiousness. Harmoniousness…cleanliness." Described by a contemporary as "the sworn enemy of foppery," he was admired for "the utter simplicity of his attire…Treatment was everything to him… His boots were said to be polished with champagne, but they were restrained in pattern. The beauty of the cloth lay in the cut." In simpler terms, no matter what you wear, your clothes should fit perfectly. That's why an article on "The Newest Version of the Double-Breasted Suit" details a nine-point checklist.

The second guideline was not as specific but was evident in every one of *Gentry*'s fashion spreads: Getting dressed should be a blast because here's how great you can look. Maybe Ozzie Nelson didn't think so. But after all, his entire world was black and white.

GENTRY

NUMBER TEN   SPRING 1954   TWO DOLLARS

CLOCKWISE, FROM TOP:

Gentry, Number Ten, Spring 1954; Number Sixteen, Fall 1956; Number 5, Holiday Issue, 1952.

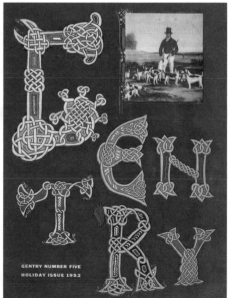

GENTRY NUMBER FIVE
HOLIDAY ISSUE 1952

GENTRY
FASHIONS

new approaches

1

informal evening clothes

In the male costume arts of today very little effort has been devoted to informal evening clothes. As a result, many men of taste and means have designed their own. For these men we offer our own new approach. Except for the velvet jacket by Alexander Shields and the velvet pumps by Capezio, the garments shown here and on the preceding two pages were designed by the editors of Gentry. The suit is made of W. Bill Ltd.'s black cashmere (Chipp, Inc.). The accents of jet on lapels, cuffs, pocket flaps and trouser stripes are of black silk velvet from Martin Fabrics. The jacket is back-vented; the trousers, self-supporting. The velvet slacks, cut along the lines of the Scotch breek, are designed to accompany the jacket for formals-at-home, or to be worn casually alone with the silk shirt. It was designed with a nostalgic nod to Douglas Fairbanks, Sr. New York's Poster-Holden cut it full and flowing at sleeve and cuffs, with many-buttoned front. Jewelry: velvet set by Destino, black pearl set by Jaguar.

2 the jersey suit

The use of worsted jersey for a fully tailored man's suit puts a versatile fabric to new use. Credit for the present accomplishment goes to Alexander Shields, who is shown here wearing one of his own suits in his handsome Park Avenue shop. The jacket has flapped pockets, one button front and no breast pocket. The use of worsted jersey (Sag-no-mor by Wyner) makes the suit adaptable to year-round wear. It is extremely light yet warm, drapes beautifully and is completely comfortable since it stretches with the movement of the body. Like a sweater, it is naturally crease-resistant. Mr. Shields also uses the jersey for sportswear in boldly colored contrasting jackets and slacks.

new approach 3

3

town and sport

The three jackets shown here reflect current trends in both fabric and design for town and country wear. *Upper left*, a new, slim double-breasted jacket by Lebow with short side vents. Note the narrow, horizontally notched lapels, the four-button front. *Upper right*, Jackman's country jacket uses a rare Scotch blend of cashmere (for softness), silk (for brightness) and worsted (for strength). *Lower left*, Baker Clothes contributes a new four-button single-breasted with horizontal peak lapels.

Designed by the editors of Gentry, here is a
new raglan sport jacket executed in Shetland tweed
by Barling Ltd., N. Y. Note details of shoulder,
one-button front, one-piece back, long side vents.

1

2

new approach

4

at home leisure clothes

*Photographed in the rooms of French & Co., N. Y.,
through the courtesy of the N. Y. Antique & Art Dealers Association*

3

4

The category of leisure clothes for indoor use is still a relatively new one. With the hope of stimulating further interest in this type of clothing, we present the four ensembles shown here. 1. Alpaca shirt-sweater by Dazza and Tremelloni. Velvet cord slacks with frontier pockets and glove-leather trim, by Vita. Italian slip-on shoes by Polli. All from George Grant. 2. Velvet shirt-jacket and worsted jersey slacks by Shields. Burlap shoes by Capezio. 3. One-piece house suit in washable Lanella by Poster-Holden. Polli buckle shoes in suede with crepe soles. 4. John Hatton of New York's Hatton-Case shop wears his design for a house suit. Shirt and slacks in black and tan, of featherweight wool serge. Pumps by Frank Bros.

new approach

5

from
the
barbados

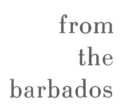

Resort fashions have been inspired by many
far and colorful places. Here is a new
contender—Barbados in the British West Indies.
Photographed aboard the Moore-McCormack
"good neighbor" ship S. S. Argentina, the garments
shown are part of a new resort collection
by Alfred of New York. They were inspired by
the native costume of harbor policemen
on the island. The ingenious adaptation to
American tastes is illustrated by the
accompanying photograph (above) of one of the
policemen in full regalia. From *left to right*
the ensembles include: "The Barbados"—a
beach shirt-jacket with sailor collar;
"The Islander"—a trimmed shirt with
detachable dickey front; "Calypso Pants"—with
sailor top-closing; "The Mormac"—a square-cut
boat-neck jumper with three-quarter
sleeves. Shoes are all by Capezio for Alfred.

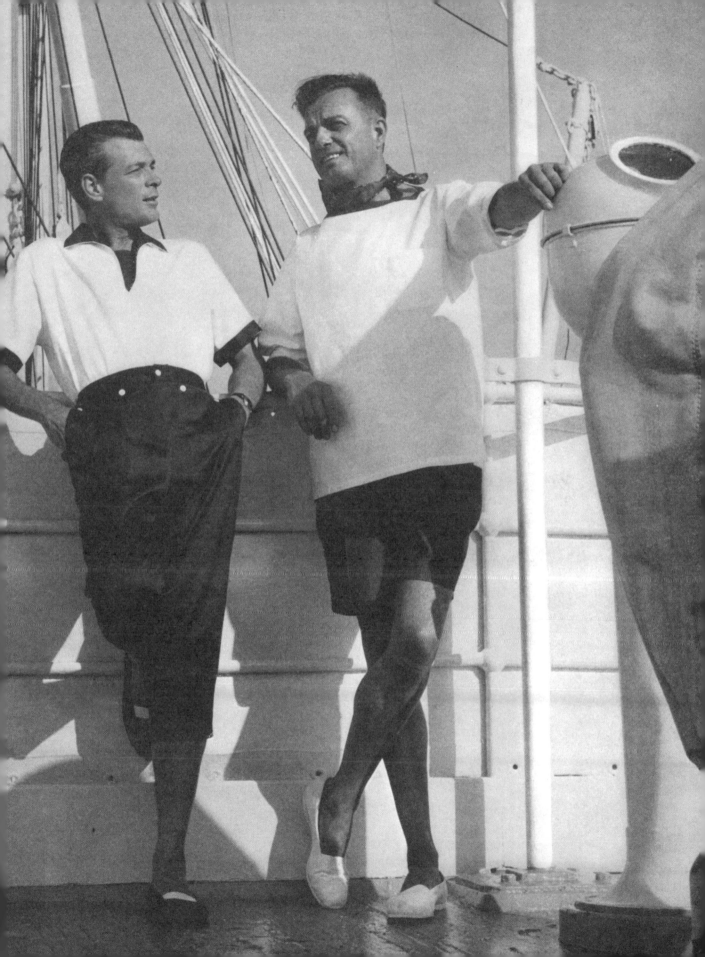

Gentry heralds the return of the double-breasted blazer and white flannel slacks. Here's an approach to fashion which served a more elegant era with great distinction; we believe these very fashions are destined for early revival. Shown here are two variations on a dominant theme. *Right*, Schumacher's Belgian linen (Gentry design), beige silk slacks (Battaglia) and chukka shoes (Peal). *Below*, navy flannel (Brooks), white doeskin slacks (Chipp) and a new white buckskin laceless slip-on designed by Gentry (Peal).

The trend toward brighter contrasts in men's clothing started with daytime apparel; it's been working its way only gradually into evening wear. This season, finally, it seems to be bursting into full flower. The evening shirt opposite is about the most daring venture thus far into neon hues for night life. Imported from Italy, it represents a combination of the frilled and pleated evening shirt with the colorful bull-ring shirt of the matador. The lace front can be worn all-white, or with a colored ribbon easily inserted into the lace. Comes with four ribbons of different colors.

Above, Lord Monson trims his white dinner jacket with black buttons. Below, Jeremy Monson wears his bright regimental blazer of the British Grenadier Guards with black evening trousers. Right, seen at Palm Beach, the black tuxedo is piped (lapel, collar, pockets) with black satin, the inevitable step before jackets of one color, piping of another

FOR THE *evening*

additions to
The Formal Kit

You're dressing tonight . . . it's raining . . . it's warm or moderately cool . . . and what do you wear? If you're like most men, even the most meticulous ones, chances are you'll slip on that tan raincoat you wear every rainy day in the week. You realize it's far from good looking and not in keeping with the rest of your apparel, but you have no other choice. To fill this void in the formal wardrobe, the raincoat illustrated, styled specifically for wear with formal clothes, was introduced by Schur of Southampton. Lawrence of London tailors it from a lightweight, pure silk fabric in black, lines it with the same fabric in red. When its military-type collar is worn closed at the neck, you see nothing but black . . . when the collar is open, it shows a small red lapel. You'll wear it almost anytime during the year, but it's especially practical for the hot and humid evenings of the summer months right ahead.

We saw them worn in Nassau . . . patent leather evening pumps with bright red bows. This method of adding smart, subtle and welcome color to formal wear prompted Mr. Capezio to style the pumps shown with removable bows. Use the white ones with a white dinner jacket; change to red when midnight-blue or black tuxedo is worn.

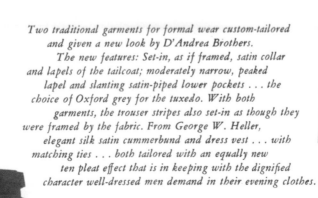

FORMAL
ELEGANCE

Two traditional garments for formal wear custom-tailored and given a new look by D'Andrea Brothers.
The new features: Set-in, as if framed, satin collar and lapels of the tailcoat; moderately narrow, peaked lapel and slanting satin-piped lower pockets . . . the choice of Oxford grey for the tuxedo. With both garments, the trouser stripes also set-in as though they were framed by the fabric. From George W. Heller, elegant silk satin cummerbund and dress vest . . . with matching ties . . . both tailored with an equally new ten pleat effect that is in keeping with the dignified character well-dressed men demand in their evening clothes.

ACCENT
on the
CUFF

The molded plinth of a corinthian column beautifully reproduced in 14-karat gold. Petit Musée, 16 West 58th St., New York. $125. pr.

This harness bit reproduced in 14-karat gold is effective, and popular for college men. Brooks Bros., 346 Madison Ave., New York. $48. pr.

Two 24-karat gold nuggets linked together produce a chunky and luxurious effect. Cartier Inc., 5th Ave. at 52nd St., New York. $140. pr.

Two small 14-karat gold nuggets are joined by a gold link. Day or evening wear. Black Starr & Gorham, 5th Ave. at 48th St., New York. $55. pr.

In the wake of the returning popularity of the French cuff, an increasing interest has developed in well-designed jewelry accessories. Collar pins, tie bars, cuff links, and matching sets are now available in new varieties of design, composition, color, size.

While the gold or sterling classic link retains its basic appeal, a growing trend is for more decorative cuff links which express masculine individuality. In this direction, sporting, traditional, and even seemingly surrealistic motifs are in demand.

The best of these styles are characterized by fine design, detail, and craftsmanship and they range in treatment from orthodox to whimsical.

Prices indicated are inclusive of Federal Tax.

18-karat white gold rim encircles a woven design of 18-karat yellow gold. Cartier Inc., 5th Ave. at 52nd St., New York. $90. pr.

Linked cuff link in an effective rope design of 14-karat gold. For day or evening wear. Cartier Inc., 5th Ave. at 52nd St., New York. $85. pr.

A surrealistic cuff link of hand blown imported crystal set in heavy lid of 18-karat gold and linked to an oxidized silver bar. Bronzini, 5 East 52nd St., New York. $165. pr.

Full Cry. Executed in 3-D effect by hand-cutting and painting, a piece of solid crystal set in 14-karat gold. Reverse design of a fox's mask. Tiffany & ·Co., 5th Ave. at 57th St. $320. pr.

The small circle knot has been a popular fastening design since early Regency days. In 14-karat gold with winged back. Black Starr & Gorham, 5th Ave. at 48th St., New York. $70. pr.

Genuine fishing fly encased in crystal and mounted in 14-karat gold is a delight for fishermen. Dunhill, 660 Fifth Ave., New York. $63. pr.

True Nordic tradition typified by this Viking ship. In sterling with winged back at Georg Jensen Inc., 667 Fifth Ave., New York. $13.50 pr.

Hand engraved college crests on mother-of-pearl create a smart black and white contrast. Finchley, Inc., Fifth Ave. at 46th St. $25. pr.

Chinese proverbs in 14-karat gold with winged back. Custom orders also executed. Benkin, 575 Madison Ave., New York. $60. pr.

A design in relief of Saint Christopher, 14-karat gold connected by curved shaft to small shield which can be custom-engraved. Alexander Shields, 15 East 60th St., New York. $60. pr.

Authentic 18th century Pennsylvania Dutch butter mold designs are reproduced on a winged back sterling cuff link. Black Starr & Gorham, 5th Ave. at 48 St., N. Y. $18. pr.

Wear a constant reminder— It's later than you think— executed in 14-karat gold with winged back. Black Starr & Gorham, 5th Ave. at 48th St., New York. $60. pr.

This intaglio, based on an archaic Greek gem design, is attributed to the Phidian School. In 14-karat gold with winged back. Petit Musée, 16 W. 48 St., N. Y. $165. pr.

Concave oval sterling cuff links with engraved initials are ideal for younger men. Winged back. Lord & Taylor, 5th Ave. at 38th St., N. Y. $10.85 pr. Initials, 30¢ each.

Traditional knot design with the larger, flat new look in 14-karat gold with winged back, Black Starr & Gorham, 5th Ave. at 48th St., New York. $120. pr.

A pleasing effect is achieved with this carnelian stone threaded with gold wire and set in a 14-karat gold case with winged back. Olga Tritt, 18 E. 57th St., N. Y. $55. pr.

Coiled rope and anchor design in 14-karat gold, with winged back. For the younger man with nautical interests. Brooks Bros., 346 Madison Ave., New York. $26.40 pr.

Engraved motif of St. Christopher, the patron Saint of travelers, on 14-karat gold cuff link with wing back. Mark Cross, 5th Ave. at 55th St., New York. $54. pr.

Finely detailed horsehead, modeled in relief, is connected by a shaft to a shield which can be personalized. 14-karat gold, from the new Alexander Shields collection, 15 East 60th St., New York. $60. pr.

Custom painted initials under crystal in 14-karat gold case are interpreted in flags of the international code. Winged back. Abercrombie & Fitch, Madison Ave. at 45th St., New York. $102. pr.

Neptune, God of the Sea, depicted rising out of the turbulent waters with a trident. In sterling silver, at Petit Musée, 16 West 58th St., New York. $18. pr.

Prince Philip, Duke of Edinburgh, with the Royal Princess Anne, wearing a jacket, wth Norfolk characteristics, which was tailored especially for him.

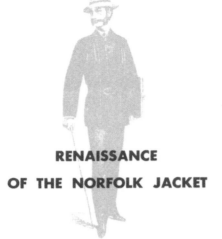

RENAISSANCE
OF THE NORFOLK JACKET

There has been some talk concerning the possible revival of certain Edwardian fashions (some of the fancy waistcoats described elsewhere in this section are examples). In the renewed acceptance of the Norfolk jacket, which takes its name from the 15th Duke of Norfolk, we have the revival of a style which is even older, having first come into being during the Victorian era. In the mid-1800's in England, with travel into the country made easy for the first time by railroads, there came into existence a group of clothes which could truly be given the name Country Clothes. As part of this trend, well-dressed men of that era adopted the style of the hunting coat worn by the Duke of Norfolk, combined it with what were then called knickerbockers (as at present, a revival of a previously popular fashion . . . knee breeches), and had them tailored from heavy tweeds to form a "country suit." The popularity rapidly accorded this style in England and on the continent soon spread across the ocean to our own shores. From this beginning until the present day the style has taken many forms (one in the vintage of the 1900's is shown above) . . . has been in and out of favor according to the dictates of the times . . . has added pockets . . . has

picked up front pleats . . . has inspired a whole family of sport coat fashions. Early in the 20th Century it was as popular with young men in America as is today's conventional single-breasted suit coat. In 1910 it was so well accepted that few small lads of that era were content unless they had a Norfolk coat just like their fathers'. Absent from men's wardrobes in recent years, it now appears that its revival is once again in the offing.

Overseas this revival has been given impetus because of the inclusion of the coat pictured on the opposite page in the wardrobe of Prince Philip. It should be pointed out that this jacket, made by Todhouse and Reynard (Norwich) Ltd., which is sometimes referred to in England as a "Norfolk House" and which has received orders from the Royal Family for several generations, incorporates only characteristics of the true Norfolk jacket. In place of the usual pleats, it is tailored with a forward fold on each forepart which is not sewed down but is left to expand. Retained, however, from true Norfolk design are the usual

A Norfolk jacket incorporating three-button front, pleats on each side and center of back, loose button-fastened belt, flapped patch pockets, free swing action pleats at back, and very deep center vent . . . tailored by H. Freeman of Philadelphia from a medium weight Shetland type fabric by Stroock. Silk print neckerchief from Italy by Handcraft.

vertical pockets and all-around belt. The sleeves, too, incorporate a change in that they are finished with a button band at the wrist in place of the conventional open cuff. In this country, too, there is a definite indication that acceptance of this jacket is on its way back. Our fashion scouts have seen it worn in the country and at sporting events in recent months, as evidenced by the candid pictures shown on this page. Several custom tailors report that they are tailoring garments of this type at the request of individual clients. This spring it will be seen in a limited number of fine stores throughout the country in ready-made versions, one of which is shown above.

Colors and motifs
of the great artists of Japan

GINGER ROOT PINK

Other shades:
swallow's breast
festival fire
fire-fly

FUJI BLUE

Other shades:
dragon-fly
brocade
temple twilight

BEAN SPROUT

Other shades:
castle moss
willow shoot
turtle

CEREMONIAL BLUE

Other shades:
coolie blue
kite-sky
wisteria

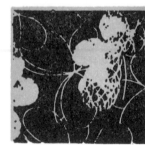

A few pages further on in this issue there is a portfolio devoted to Hokusai, one of Japan's great artists. In the year 1955 Hokusai, who died about a hundred years ago, will play a definite part in the American fashion scene. The link between art and fashion is a phenomenon which has been clearly marked in the last few decades. One of the fashion trends now in the making is the wider use of Japanese colors and motifs in both men's and women's apparel. As yet this trend is in the textile mill stage, but by Spring, 1955 you will see sportswear, neckwear, kerchiefs, robes, shirts and other items of apparel bearing the stamp of its influence. Gentry presents this advance chart of authentic colors and motifs for your personal guidance.

introduce a new fashion trend

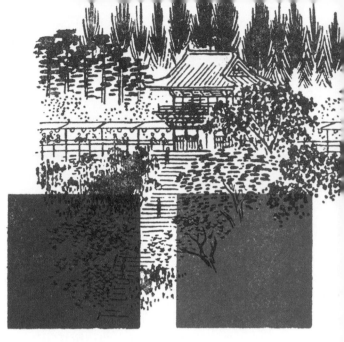

PLUM SKIN	**TEA DUST**	**EGG PLANT**	**INK STICK**
Other shades:	*Other shades:*	*Other shades:*	*Other shades:*
harvest drum	seaweed	bean-paste	charcoal
bronze bell	mulberry green	peony	incense stick
persimmon	moat stone	oriental spice	tiger's breath

Beau Brummell

A New Look at an Old Fallacy

His name is a synonym for sartorial splendor

Splendor he had, but not in loud adornment, not in gaudy tones

The real Beau was a clothes-horse of another color

ACT ONE: Youth, High Life, Success.

Here's a young buck named George Bryan Brummell, comes up to London after Eton and Oxford with the notion of breaking into high society. By the time he's twenty, against odds no gambler would take, he's the roaring lion of London. Duchesses grovel for his favors, for a kind word. The Prince Regent hurries to his rooms to watch him dress. He can make a man's social reputation by walking arm in arm with him down St. James. Lord Byron says the three most important men of the century are (in this order) Brummell, Napoleon, Lord Byron.

ACT TWO: Degeneration.

The incredible fellow gambles away an inheritance of £30,000, which would be half a million dollars by modern reckoning. He borrows. He gambles. He borrows. When he is 38, at the peak of his fame, he leaves England because he can't pay his debts. He flies to France. For 24 years he drifts, from small town to smaller town, from small hotel to smaller.

ACT THREE:

His mind sinks with him. He sits alone in dark little rooms, giving imaginary dinner parties for royalty. At 62 he dies, insolvent, insane, in a French convent.

It is not so much a life as a too-well-made melodrama.

Now in the first act his friends gave him the name "Beau." They meant it as a tribute—as a literal translation from the French, wherein *Beau* means fine, means handsome. But "Beau" is a word whose

This print, by Grego, is called A Ball at Almack's. Its subtitle:
"Beau Brummell in Deep Conversation with the Duchess of Rutland."
There are very few contemporary portraits of the Beau. He
simply refused to sit for artists, a fact which seems to belie
the theory that he was peacock-proud. This is the only view of him
that gives any sense of the personality, the pose, the poise that
dazzled London for so long. The arched back, the elegant hands,
the feet in a dancer's pose — all these we easily accept as
being typical of the man. But the dark clothing, the absence
of frills and jewels, the singular somberness of this costume —
these too were typical of the greatest of all dandies

Brummell

connotation changed overnight. The Regency moved out, the Victorians moved in. A Beau was suddenly a fop, and a fop is a fool. That is the way the Victorians regarded Byron's demi-God. A fop, a fool. It is the portrait the Victorians handed on to us.

Brummell would not have minded being called a fool. He was too intelligent to take umbrage at *that*. He always enjoyed being the cynosure of all lies. What the Beau would have minded, and that terribly, was the word *fop*. A fop he was not. He was the sworn enemy of foppery. It is time to realize, after a hundred years of character assassination, that Brummell was probably the quietest, the simplest, the solemnest clothes-horse of his day and age.

The testimony of the eye-witnesses first.

Here's the word of the Reverend G. Crabbe, who knew him well:

". . . (Brummell) certainly did not, either in manners or appearance, exhibit that compound of coxcombry in dress, and vulgar assiduity of address, which marks the 'Beau' (that is the dandy); I remember being struck with the misapplication of this title when I saw him one day at the Belvoir Hunt. He was dressed as plain as any man in the field, and the manly, even dignified, expression of his countenance ill accorded with the implication the sobriquet conveyed."

Or turn for the moment to the fount of most of our wisdom about Brummell, that Captain Jesse who wrote the first definitive life of Brummell:

"His chief aim was to avoid anything marked; one of his aphorisms being that the severest mortification a gentleman could incur, was to attract observation in the street by his outward appearance. He exercised the most correct taste in the selection of each article of apparel, of a form and color harmonious with all the rest, for the purpose of producing a

John Barrymore was the first to portray Brummell in the movies. He was the perfect choice, for his was also that blend of arrogance and wit, churlishness and charm so characteristic of Brummell. Beau would have approved of these skin-tight britches, the nice fall of the cape, the angle of the hat. But he would have sniffed at Barrymore's cravat. Sloppy, the Beau would have said. Very sloppy

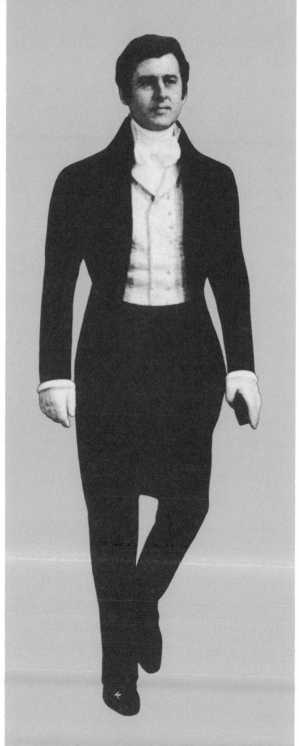

Stewart Granger in MGM's Beau Brummell probably
came closest to the true Beau in terms of dress.
The impeccable neckwear, the black jacket and
trousers, the white gloves — these were Brummell
to the life, as you can prove by comparing
Granger here to the Brummell in the Grego drawing. The perfect posture, too, was one of Brummell's
requisites for absolutely correct attire

Far off the mark was the most celebrated of all
make-believe Brummells, Richard Mansfield. He created the role in Clyde Fitch's play Beau Brummell.
The famous play and the great actor added woe-
fully to the Brummell myth. They made him "an
over-dressed and finical puppy," as the old photograph shows. This was the Victorian attitude
towards the Beau, and it was wrong, all wrong

Brummell

perfectly elegant general effect; and he spent much time and pains in the attainment of this object."

The word to mark here is "harmonious." For Brummell the key color in a gentleman's dress was black, and the best harmonies for black were, he always insisted, the quiet colors. It is significant to note that in a day when a gentleman's facade was gorgeously embellished, his vest a garden of embroideries, fobs and laces, Brummell never wore anything more *outré* than a plain vest of buff color.

Now let's move on to more recent critics of Brummell. Here is Max Beerbohm on the subject of Brummell's appearance:

". . . as in all known images of the Beau, we are struck by the utter simplicity of his attire . . . in certain congruities of dark cloth, in the rigid perfection of his linen, in the symmetry of his glove with his hand, lay the secret of Mr. Brummell's miracles. He was ever most economical, most scrupulous of means. Treatment was everything with him."

T. H. White, the English novelist and essayist, agrees, to the hilt: "He aimed," says White, "at the most difficult effect . . . simplicity. His boots were said to be polished with champagne, but they were restrained in pattern. The beauty of the cloth lay in the cut."

He dressed simply, without ornamentation, without ostentation. What was it then that set him apart so ostentatiously from the crowd? What made him the best dressed man of the century? The answer lies not, as history has decided, in his clothes. It lay entirely in the way he wore them.

He was of medium height, but proportioned like one of those quasi-Greeks his contemporaries so dearly loved to draw on their cups and saucers. Imagine him, at his tailor's, insisting on fittings worthy of that figure! "The beauty of the cloth lay in the cut," but until he attained the cut he must have sent battalions of tailors screaming into Bedlam. Merely putting on his hat was a ceremony; once it was on it stayed on. He, whose manners were as fastidious as his fashions, would not tip the hat to the ladies for fear of ruining its angle. "He spent much time and pains," says Jesse. That is an overwhelming understatement. Brummell never took less than three hours at his dressing, and he often dressed three times a day.

Fastidiousness. Harmoniousness. "Much time and pains."

And cleanliness. To Brummell that element came somewhere above Godliness in the scale. "No perfumes," was his advice to a disciple, "but very fine linen, plenty of it, and country washing." His concept of country washing was to spend two hours every morning in his tub scrubbing himself with a hair glove. To him the skin was the first layer of clothing. Over the impeccably scrubbed neck came his cravat. He would stretch out flat, pushing his chin back as far as possible. His valet would wind the freshly starched collar around the neck. Brummell would bring his chin down, slowly, agonizingly, coaxing the cravat into perfect folds. It did not always work on the first try. His valet stood on the stair one day holding an armful of limp cravats. "These," he moaned to Brummell's guests, "are our failures."

If all this sounds foolish, sounds (perish the word!) foppish, it is only because we fail to understand one vital fact about the man. Beerbohm recognized it, and cried it good and loud in "Dandies and Dandyism," which is the great defense of Brummell.

He was, said the cautious, incomparable Max, "an artist . . . in the utmost sense of the word . . . no poet nor cook nor sculptor ever bore that title more worthily than he."

SHADES OF PURPLE

Color highlight from the resorts . . .
a new family of colors
for Summer sportswear wardrobes

The newest family of sportswear color tones . . . deep plum to definite, but masculine, lighter casts of purple and lavender. Any shade too vibrant or extremely light should be considered taboo. In sport coats, deep, rich plum shades are most often observed. Slack preferences run from somber, deep shades to definite purples like those worn by golf match spectator at the Everglades Club in Palm Beach, pictured at right. Shirts most frequently combine medium shades with white, like the cotton woven plaid above, tailored by Peerless Sportswear.

The newest version of the
Double-Breasted Suit

From the Custom Shop of Dunhill Tailors, the changed double-breasted suit. Here is one good reason why this style has returned to deserved prominence in the well-dressed man's wardrobe.

Features:

• Natural but not squared-off shoulders.

• Coat cut with a short back so it does not rest on the hips, thus allowing it to achieve a straight look and avoiding bagginess.

• Front tailored waist-suppression gives the illusion of body tracing lines with no sacrifice of comfort.

• Straight-line narrowness of sleeves from top to bottom, not just at cuff, is achieved by high armholes, a feature that allows freedom of movement.

• Raised button spacing using small-sized buttons adds to the slenderizing illusion of the silhouette; positioning allows narrowed lapels to roll to lower button without giving the out-of-balance look of older garments.

• Blades at back are tailored so the fullness falls vertically rather than in the usual, mussy-looking horizontal manner.

• Side vents allow easy access to trouser pockets without unbuttoning coat.

• Buttoned cuffs are an extra custom detail.

• Trousers are self-supporting, cut on slim, straight lines with a seat patterned after riding breeches.

Result: A new slenderizing silhouette, becoming to men of all builds, in keeping with the times . . . and with the maximum of comfort.

Town Suit

Subtle interpretations of the patterned suit are again in favor for business wear. One of the newer patterned fabrics, shown in simulated swatch on facing page, is used by Baker Clothes to tailor the smart town suit photographed. The fabric, imported from Scotland, blends silk with wool to create a soft, subtle hand. The pattern feature: closely spaced, broken stripes which give an overall tie-weave effect when viewed at a distance. The model feature: natural-looking silhouette.

*Bright as the tropical climates
we recommend it be worn in.
A specific and smart interpretation . . .
the Heller slacks tailored
from tropical weight Thomas cotton.*

RED . . . in the sun

a

b

Striped Pants

In the event our title should confuse you, may we say we are not advocating that striped trousers, so long identified with weddings and foreign dignitaries, should now be worn on the golf course. They are perhaps the ancestors of these new slacks. Rather we think of the group of slacks shown on this and the facing page as a welcome, new and smart looking trend keyed to a specific use . . . wear on the most casual occasions.

a. Gordon's new Tropican Dacron and wool slacks in deep-tone stripings in a style that features adjustable back strap. b. Baker clothes uses a Swiss flannel loomed from Egyptian cotton with three stripes . . . one bright . . . one white . . . one a deep tone. c. Corbin Ltd. tailors a polished cotton featuring red, blue or black spaced hairline stripes on white ground into slacks with back strap, slim-proportioned leg styling. d. Country Life Sportswear's imported Irish linen slacks in a new light weight with 3/8" stripes. Blue, canary or olive green combine with natural tan.

c

d

black-green MICA
with lighter toned OLIVE

Left: A new method of handling gives these 6 x 3 rib cotton hose their smart, rough, wool-like appearance. From F. A. MacCluer, their softness makes them especially kind to the feet. Currick & Letken uses this imported Shetland fabric to tailor the natural-shouldered, three-button sport coat pictured at right. The subtle black stripe adds a distinctive masculine touch to the basic black-green Mica shade of the Shetland material.

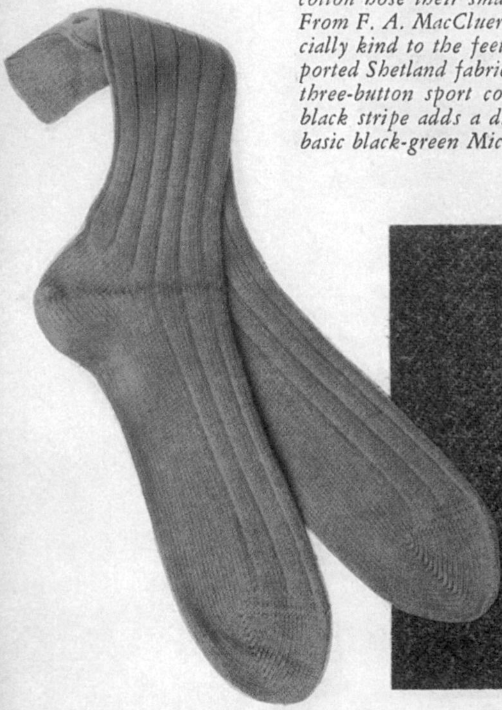

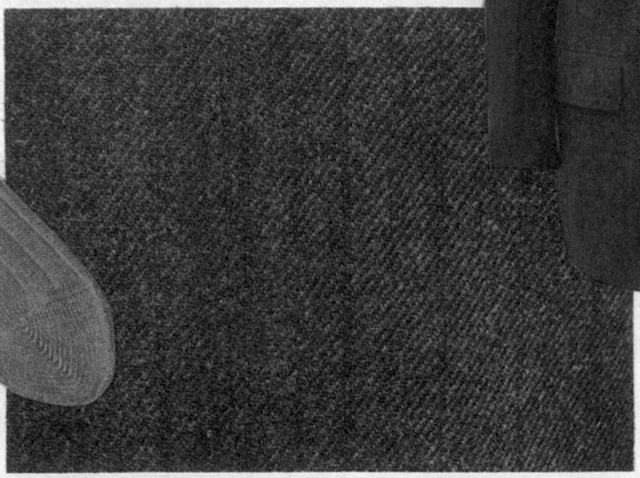

Two away-from-town shades of green . . . a family of colors very much on the ascendency in men's wear. Greens . . . ranging from the deep black-green of Mica, illustrated, through the yellow-tinted heathers like Lovat, to a soft, lighter shade like olive, depicted here . . . have that at-home-in-the-country look desired by well-groomed men. The two shades shown ensembled also lend themselves to combinations with contrasting but compatible notes . . . specifically: with dark browns, with greys from medium to dark, with black.

Left: Neckwear by Sambrooks in wool challis, woven silk rep or printed foulard utilizes olive green as the ground color smartly set off by muted shades of red and black in their patterns.   Right: A heavy-weight wool melton fabric is used by Corbin, Ltd. to tailor these slacks in the new, pleatless, narrowed leg style. The slacks also feature a rear back strap and buckle on the waistband.

Right: Lebow Clothes tailors this light-weight British worsted fabric, with its subtle red and dusty white stripes, into a model which carries three button holes but only two buttons. Thus, a two-button coat that gives the effect of a three-button one.

Black . . . unequivocal definition of the just as definite trend toward more formality in clothes worn in town for business or for informal evenings. A natural reaction to the increasingly popular, more colorful apparel now worn away from the city for leisure activities. By the same token, dark clothes, a necessary interpretation of this more dressed-up trend, call for accessory colors which give a lift . . . which strongly contrast in tone . . . which are vibrant yet masculine in hue. Chosen in this case . . . brilliant red . . . because it so perfectly adds this masculine touch of necessary color . . . because it is a color which makes such a handsome contrast with black.

in town...The Black Suit

...with it

Bright Red touches

Right: From England a hand-blocked silk foulard square to be used as a pocket handkerchief. A reversible muffler, the red side a soft wool . . . the black and white polka dot side, silk foulard. Both by Handcraft. Left: Adrian subtly places a single white dot to fall in stickpin position below the knot . . . surrounds it with black dots of the same size in this smart tie of woven fabric with rich, satiny luster. Left: In keeping with the formalized trend, a shirt with pleated front by Golden Arrow, tailored with an appropriate rounded-point collar to be worn pinned. The fabric . . . self-jacquarded white on white Madras . . . adds a further formal note.

Headlines and Footnotes

the hats and shoes that make up a complete autumn and winter wardrobe for the man of elegance

From left to right in both wardrobes: Headwear and footwear for formal, semi-formal and business occasions, for spectator sports or motoring and golf . . . and in the shoe wardrobe, the host shoe for wear at home (lower right-hand corner). The complete hat wardrobe from Saks Fifth Avenue. All footwear from Lefcourt, New York, except hiking boots and golf shoes (bottom right-hand shelf) by Foot-Joy.

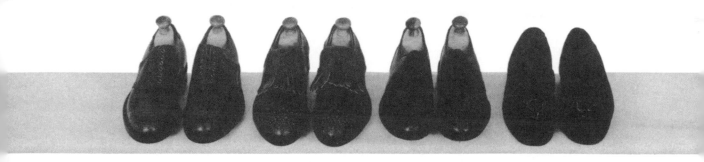

gentry's week-end wardrobe

BY ROBERT L. GREEN

FASHION EDITOR

The choice of new and interesting fashion items this spring is an exceptionally full one. Fabrics, textures and details are driving the dull and ordinary out of the well-balanced wardrobe. Here is Gentry's spring '57 collection. Start with a sport shirt of cotton and silk blend, inlaid Jacquard design and full-pleated front, by Alfred of New York. Hanging close by is the Vienease, by Baker Clothes—a belted and pleated back and front treatment reminiscent of the Norfolk hunting coat. Five brass buttons and a mandarin collar in Tussah raw silk are the main components of "Rangoon" by John Alexander. Pure off-white natural silk slacks and olive green moccasins by Battaglia. Knox's self band heather mixture "at ease" hat. The bistro plaid shirt in pure silk with covered buttons is by Val Desco.

Chippendale table on tripod
stand, courtesy French and Co., NY

A full and loosely fitting porous knit wool sweater by Baxer
of Milan tops a black and white polka dot silk sport shirt by Battaglia.
Classic lightweight cuffless flannels are by Majer, the pure design
of black grained leather walking shoe by Frank Bros. Slipover sport
shirt of chalis in paisley design by Knight and Petch of Ireland.
Natural color hand-knit tie in silk and linen by Threadcrafts.
Gourielli's narrow-stripe lounging robe of Rodier lightweight wool
is in beige and brown. Caswell-Massey's cologne has an amber
base with a fine, dry masculine scent.

Windsor writing chair,
circa 1760 (a favorite of Thomas Jefferson's),
leather fire bucket and iron candle stand
(1740) from Israel Sack, NY

"Have Black Tie . . . Will Travel"—a wine basket painted black bearing an assortment of furnishings for evening wear: Black silk cummerbund and tie by James Daniels, red moire suspenders and garters by Schoenfeld, narrow pleated shirt by S. A. Avery. Elizabeth Arden's multi-colored silk "Joseph's Coat" is a robe cut in "Teahouse" style. Four button, cuffed-sleeve jacket and frontier pants slacks in polished jet cotton make a versatile spring suit by Village Squire. Patent leather pumps, red-satin-lined for evening, and laced front burlap shoe for afternoons by Capezio. Cap in bold Scotch Tweed by Cap and Cloth Hat Institute. Copper Cologne in Venetian Glass by Countess Mara.

A wool cardigan hand-knitted by Alpine women. No two sweaters are made the same. Illustrated here from the collection available in the U. S. A . . . *Davoser*, designed by Georges Wolf for Titol Imports. Six colors are used in the intricate design. Buttons are replicas of old Bavarian coins.

Scene on opposite page was taken from the chairlift (100 chairs) to the "Octagon," 2,030 feet up Mt. Mansfield. Located at Stowe, Vermont, this skiers' paradise rises from the valley where "The Lodge" is located (the Den is shown in inset). The Lodge is the meeting place of the elite visitors to this area — the taking-off point for their daytime skiing activities and the rendezvous for night-time conviviality, as it is also the setting for many of the pictures shown on these pages.

Two-ply black nylon taffeta that is water-, wind-, and cold-repellent is used by White Stag in this parka which has the new *color touch* added. Styled with raglan sleeves, its hood is hidden. The bright red chest stripe conceals the zipper-fastened opening of a pouch-type pocket (see inset).

MODES AND MANNERS . . . SKIING

The use of black . . . highly contrasting color set-offs . . . functional improvements in design and fabric . . . these are among the significant developments in ski wear this season. Illustrated and described on these pages are some of the newer fashions from top designers both abroad and in America.

Five different colors are used in this sweater hand-knitted by fisherfolk in the Danish Isles. This pattern is of Old Viking design, styled with semi-turtleneck. It takes fifty to sixty hours to complete one sweater; no two are alike.

A new version of a Scandinavian design sweater in multicolor, made especially for Anouk Sportswear. Hand-knitted of fine wool yarns, the design features the bulk of the pattern in a yoke top. The body and sleeve design is composed of small, snowflake motifs, regularly spaced.

Bold raised cables . . . a new design theme in ski sweaters. Above is a hand-knitted creation by Anouk, featuring cables at front and sides of sleeves. Comes in black with red cables, grey with yellow, navy with white. The candid picture at left is another example of the cable treatment.

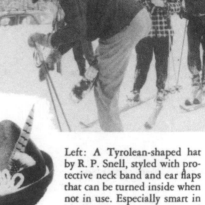

Left: A Tyrolean-shaped hat by R. P. Snell, styled with protective neck band and ear flaps that can be turned inside when not in use. Especially smart in black with white rope trim and colorful feather, it has elastic under-chin cord.

The Hat

Many Americans are adopting the Alpine custom of wearing Tyrolean hats for active skiing. Above: Devotee of this type of dress at Mt. Mansfield.

The Parka

On Mt. Mansfield well-dressed men favor black parkas, black trousers, black accessories as worn here. Lightweight but extremely warm nylon fabrics are often chosen for parkas and jackets.

The Ski Pants

A new feature is added by White Stag to worsted gabardine ski pants. As shown below, zipper closes an inverted pleat just above top of boot. When opened, an additional two inches in front leg are gained to afford greater ease when not skiing. In black, they are styled with tapered leg, four diagonal zipper-fastened pockets, elastic waistband liner, and tunnel belt loops.

The Tow Coat

Modern skiing involves frequent waits at tows and lifts which require "tow coats" for protection against cold and wind. Mt. Mansfield skiers shown here prefer double-breasted, fur collared sheepskin- or alpaca-pile-lined great coats. Professional type ear-flapped white cap, left, or sawed-off Austrian type stocking cap keeps head and ears warm.

The Sweater

Pictured in the Smugglers' Den at right, an Austrian batwing sleeve after-ski sweater. Above is an exact copy made in this country by White Stag. Smartest in black; other features are the horizontal rib and high crew neck.

The Gloves

Bottom left: The all-important rough weather over-parka in white with fur-ruffed hood. Below left: A new leather ski glove designed by James Couttet, coach of the French Olympic team, imported by Mont-Blanc. Made of horsehide, it features accordion-ribbed leather insets over knuckles. Comes in black, tan and navy, and in black and red.

The Footwear

Shown at bottom right are two styles of after-ski footwear — slipper socks for women, fur boots for men. Below right: A close-up of boot like that worn by Laplanders for skiing, hand-made and imported by J. G. Seaberg. The foot part is made from the tough leg skin of the reindeer, the upper part from the longer haired skin of the back and under portions.

Resort Wear Highlights

Jock McLean wears basic navy blazer, deep yellow slacks, tassel moccasin shoes.

Peter Jenkins ensembles a striped sport shirt with muted plaid shorts, preferred length.

At Everglades Club, Palm Beach: Ribbed knit slipover shirt, white linen cap, worn with two-tone golf shoes.

John Gafaell wearing a new double-breasted blazer, shawl collared.

Serge Obolensky supports his deep rust linen slacks with colorful necktie belt.

From the Riviera: Multi-color-striped patterned sport shirt with a new cuff detail.

D. E. Kaufman wears shirt which utilizes attached Ascot in lieu of conventional collar.

—and a new sportswear color trend...

Casual clothes for the resort season . . . and next summer as well . . . will be combined in a more orderly manner than in the past. This follows a trend already set in motion by recognized leaders of fashion today. This new mode of dress makes itself evident in many ways, one of the most prominent being the use of darker but still lively colors, set off prominently by the use of subtle black or white in the ensemble. So that GENTRY readers may better visualize the type of colors we speak of, we show on this page nine interpretations combined in three different ensembles. These swatches also make it possible for you to actually *see* and *feel* examples of the types of silk fabrics referred to on the preceding page . . . and the linen and linen-type fabrics which are elaborated on the next page.

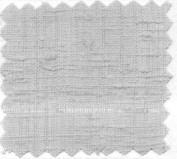

COAT or SLACKS of Honan fabric loomed from cultivated and tussah silk yarns by American Silk Mills.

COAT or SLACKS of crease-resistant Panama Cloth woven from finest combed yarns by M. & W. Thomas.

SPORT SHIRTING of Mallinson's washable, crease-resistant rayon Rusteena.

COAT or SLACKS of smart nub-surfaced Sil-Shan. A blend of viscose and silk by St. George.

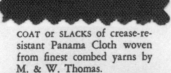

SLACKS of tropical weight Strea-Tone loomed from pure worsted yarns by Pacific Mills.

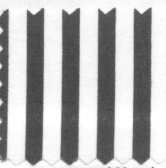

SPORT SHIRTING of Montauk cloth. A fine combed yarn cotton Madras by Clarence S. Brown.

COAT or SLACKS of light weight, crease-resistant imported Moygashel Irish linen.

COAT or SLACKS of washable Java Weave, a linen-like fabric by Palm Beach.

SPORT SHIRTING of linen-appearing rayon Boxa cloth from Ameritex.

Linen

On the links at the Everglades Country Club in Palm Beach: Linen in well tailored slacks. Black golf shoes with Kiltie tongue a fashion highlight.

Alfred of New York tailors this sport shirt of woven imported Moygashel linen. Interesting is the newly styled short point collar; adding additional interest is the loop-fastened gold color metal buttons.

. . . Right for Resorts . . . Right for Summer

Window shopping on Palm Beach's Worth Avenue: White linen blazer with deeper vivid shade of blue linen slacks. Side vents are popular.

Following a golf match at Palm Beach's Everglades Country Club: Knee length short slacks tailored of linen; a native inspired shirt and sun-protecting hat from the Virgin Islands.

Leaving the Southampton Beach Club: A linen odd coat and slacks. Interesting as well as cool, the tie is of native cotton India Madras in colorful plaid.

Linen . . . another of the once popular fabrics again returns to favor. There is no item, from headwear to shoes, in the casual wear wardrobe in which this fabric is not seen. The new heights of popularity being accorded these wearables is due primarily to the fact that 1952 vintages, differing from their predecessors, are cooler because they are lighter in weight and muss less easily because they are made crease-resistant.

THE BLAZER GOES

Here's a new chapter in our book on blazers. Its subject is foulard,
the pliable small-patterned silk which is usually reserved for
neckwear. Now we discover that the foulard's nice interplay of color,
its airily light weight, its resistance to creasing, make it a natural for
blazers too. The foulard pictured here is perfect for both daytime
wearing and informal country-club evenings. We saw it at the Montague
Beach Hotel in Nassau, in handsome red. Tailored by Currick and
Leiken, sold at most fine shops, it's also available in navy

COMBINATIONS IN COLONIAL tan

In light civilian disguise, uniforms worn by British Colonial officers
are turning up as leisure-time wear. For good reasons: the color—
darker than sun tan, not as green as khaki—belongs out in
the sun, and the ensembles have a distinctively masculine look.
We saw these at Palm Beach and at Montego Bay. Above: shirt and
Bermuda shorts form a matching ensemble with the new cotton fabric shoes.
Below: a short-sleeved, full-belted bush jacket replaces the shirt

straw hats COME

*Four years ago some nameless hero showed up at
one of the resorts, sporting the first off-beat summer straw.
He was a man of courage, a direct descendant of
the gent who first ate an oyster—and he had just as much
foresight. He started a trend. Headgear without
inhibitions is the big motif now, as these pictures prove.
We took them at beach, race track, country club and
hotel, but we couldn't quite cover the gamut of heights, weights,
shapes and sizes; the variety's too infinite for that. They're
designed to keep you cool, to keep the sun off your face or—most
important of all—just for fun. Most of the ones we saw were
coconut, raffia and unsized panama. The bodies are neutral tones,
the bands carry colors ranging from loud to explosive*

HANDSOME, WIDE AND HIGH

A bright new color, an exciting new imported fabric, and here's a parka that's perfect for drying off after a swim, for protection from sun and wind when you're on the beach, for warmth when you're out sailing. Its color: "Seaside red." Its fabric: "Velvet terry." It's been so named because on the inside it's pure, absorbent terrycloth, on the outside it has velvet's soft, luxurious look. Tailored in Denmark, photographed here at Round Hill, Montego Bay, the parka has a full zipper front and a zip storage pocket for change, cigarettes and matches

NEW CLOTH FOR parkas

These three gentlemen, photographed
at southern resorts, have discovered the secret
of "leisure-time formality"—the Ascot.
Wear it with a sport shirt and you're perfectly dressed
for lunch and cocktails. Matter of fact,
it can be ideal resort wear for almost any occasion.
There have been many attempts to create
a neckpiece especially for sport shirts, but Gentry
knows of nothing to compare with the Ascot,
in all its variations. Some of the new designs clip
on in the same manner as a ready-tied bow

ascot MAKES A COMEBACK

stripes ARE BLACK AND WHITE

Some liked them bold, some liked them subtle—but practically all the well-dressed men wintering at American resorts went for shirts with stripes, stripes combining black and white. In lines and details most of the shirts followed styles currently in favor. For example, Gary Cooper wears one of the more popular types. We also suggest for your consideration slip-over styles, knit fabrics and shirts with horizontal stripes. Handsome in combination with virtually any color, these shirts are especially striking when worn with slacks or knee-length shorts of pure white

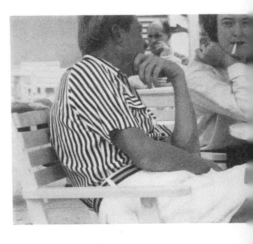

1

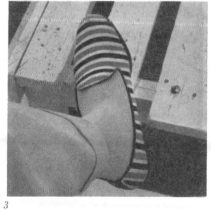

2

3

The fabric shoe is the perfect unconventional match for conventional shorts and slacks. Here are the three newest additions to the just-growing family of fabric shoes: 1. Cotton and rayon tweed; the upper has a rough look, the sole and the heel are leather. 2. Gondola style has upper of lightweight cotton Madras, flexible rubber sole and heel, and elastic instep strip. 3. Sailcloth upper is combined with molded rubber sole and heel; sawed-off tongue gives a special touch. All of them at least as comfortable as your best bedroom slippers, and all by Mr. Capezio

STRIPES ARE NEWS IN shoes

THE barbecue shirt

Gentry's conversation piece—a gourmet print on a shirt designed especially for the outdoor chef. The polished finish of the cotton fabric makes it look exactly like freshly wiped oilcloth—and back-yard gourmets are bound to love it. Designed and tailored by Damon Creations, the shirt has motifs in red, rust, green, brown and black. No guarantee that it will improve your cooking, but an odds-on favorite to make you the best-dressed man at your next barbecue

NEW TRENDS IN beachwear

*Big floral patterns and modernistic motifs on the way
out; restrained, simple patterns on the way in.
But beachwear will still be colorful, as exemplified
here in Alexander Shields' combination of a single bold
color with stark white. It's a wide (two-inch)
Roman stripe in a lightweight cotton Sahib robe,
cut like a Japanese kimono, and it comes with
matching swim trunks. The ensemble is worn by Sinclair
Robinson at La Coquille Club in Palm Beach. Two things you
can't tell from these pictures: the pockets are inside, and
the fabric is wonderfully easy to fold for packing*

HOME, CARS, AND TRAVEL

3

It's hard to believe that there was a time when the first questions one asked when buying a car weren't how many miles per gallon it got and what the results were of the latest crash test. Similarly, can anyone still recall when plane travel didn't inspire dread at the thought of glacially paced security checks, baggage restrictions, truncated leg room, and airports designed with the antiseptic panache of bus terminals? If you've come to think of all travel as an inevitable means to a measurable end, then we apologize in advance, because what you are about to encounter is likely to unnerve and upset you—or just make you flat-out jealous.

The 1950s was a decade in which the celebration of the American roadster was so fervent as to rival the devout. The current passion for technology is no match for the beaming adoration an entire nation exuded for those radiantly hued, thrillingly sleek, awesomely powerful, undeniably sensuous, and completely irresistible white-walled symbols of success and glory.

Great cars were such coveted possessions that new models were treated like Hollywood's hottest ingenues. Actual Broadway-scale productions were built around them. One of the most popular touring attractions at the time was General Motors' annual Motorama, a spare-no-expense "industrial" showcase. Featuring name-above-the-title performers (including Florence Henderson, prior to *The Brady Bunch*) and dozens of chorus boys and girls singing and dancing, extolling the wonders of GM's stable of Chevrolets, Oldsmobiles, Pontiacs, Buicks, and Cadillacs while the most recent models of each arrived onstage by either dramatically descending from atop the proscenium, entering suspended from the wings, or rising up on platforms from below the stage floor—all to furious standing-room-only ovations.

Gentry's passion for these gleaming chrome-edged chariots was no less rapturous and affectionate. Henderson, who was the Rocket 88 Girl, sang, "It's a thrill to take the wheel of your rocket Oldsmobile" at the Motorama—and staring at the two-tone sky-and-turquoise blue 1955 Super 88 Holiday Coupe ready to zoom off *Gentry*'s pages, the sentiment was clearly justified. On a nearby page is an endlessly long azure 1956 Cadillac Sedan de Ville that will instigate an invigorating rush of envy and lust. Chrysler Corporation's mammoth De Soto owned the color coral, not exactly one of today's go-to chassis colors,

but we think you'll agree that it's sorely missed. And then there's the 1955 Plymouth Belvedere Sport Coupe convertible, a midcentury design marvel that deserves a place alongside the best works of Le Corbusier.

No less fascinating are the ideas and wish lists expressed by six designers *Gentry* asks, "What Would You Like to See in an Automobile?" Some of the answers include privacy shades, automatic windows, back video panels, multiple-way seat adjustments, storage compartments, and heaters—even a type of radar that allows the driver to plot his position and trip. About the only prediction that hasn't come true yet is a floral-patterned ceiling. Darn.

Naturally, a car of distinction belongs in a driveway that does it justice, and the featured "Bachelor's Country House" does just that. Anything but a "pad," *Gentry*'s available "catch" lives in a hydrangea-flanked Tudor home with butler and footman. With a dressing room more lavish than any offered as a home channel sweepstakes prize and a dining table set with such attention to detail it should have been described by Thackeray, many a prospective bride might be scared off due to feelings of inadequacy.

But then, she wouldn't be the right girl, because whether at home, in the air, or on holiday, the *Gentry* man lived big and traveled well. That's why the "Round the World Guide" carefully selected the right fabrics and garments to pack (the story also resonates with great taste in luggage). Even if today's voyager no longer checks in with sixty-six pounds of baggage, the tips for balancing and maximizing the elements of a travel wardrobe are just as valid.

However, there's no reason why you can't pack as much as you'd like to if you were to motor up to the rustically handsome Smuggler's Notch Inn in Jeffersonville, Vermont, as recommended in "Summer Resorts…American Planned." Except if you were to get behind the wheel of the ravishing, streamlined-as-a-bullet burgundy 1956 Lincoln Continental Mark II—the same coupe *Gentry* touts in the same story—you may be tempted not to step on the brake until you reach the Canadian border. Luckily, you'd probably run out of gas first. These cars never did get great mileage, but then, they were so beautiful, who cared?

Gentry Number Eleven   Summer 1954

**CLOCKWISE,
FROM TOP LEFT:**

Gentry, Number Eighteen,
Spring 1956, Number
Eleven, Summer 1954;
Number Fourteen, Spring
1955.

IT'S A BIG

World

There are many places to visit and many things to do when you travel. Gentry's Editors suggest that your next trip, whether it be five or five thousand miles from home, can be a little more pleasurable, a little more rewarding. Before you plan, before you pack . . . please turn.

Chevrolet Bel Air Station Wagon

SUMMER RESORTS
...American Planned

Resorts have been harshly treated at the hands of history, both etymologically and socially. One dictionary gives the derivation of the word resort as *haunt,* another as *sporting house,* while Cleveland Amory's *Last Resorts* points out that this country's major social resorts just aren't what they used to be. However, there's still good news for the summer resorter of 1956, for if the old resorts aren't what they used to be, our new resorts, which were not in existence in the days of Mr. Amory's Four Hundred, are better than ever and enjoying great success.

The resort boom, the largest in the history of our country, can be attributed to the lessening of distances by air travel and super highways, the present prosperous state of the union, and the all-important fact that the resort operator of today has gone to the trouble of learning what you personally want to find when you arrive at his inn . . . whether you want to relax, pull a Garbo, be gregarious, or run the gamut of the sports

Stables at Smugglers' Notch, Stowe, Vt.

Continental Mark II

Left: Treadway Inn at Coonamessett in North Falmouth, Cape Cod. Right: Newagen Inn on the rockbound Maine Coast.

SUMMER RESORTS . . .

Cadillac Sedan de Ville

Left: Rolling bar at pool in Black Inn, Prout's Neck, Me. Right: At Basin Harbor Club, Vergennes, Vt.

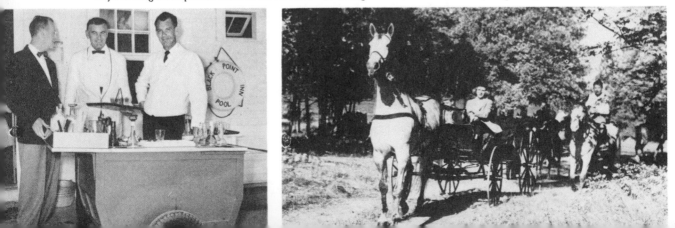

Imperial Sedan

SUMMER RESORTS . . .

parade...all is provided by American planned resorts. The distinguished resorts which we have assembled for you are designed to tickle the most discriminating palate with good food, fine accommodations.

Cape Cod has appealed to the traveler's imagination ever since Lief Erikson first discovered its wonder strands . . . but where to stay seems to have been just as much of a problem to the visitor of today as it was in 1003 until Richard Treadway took over The Coonamesset Inn at **North Falmouth** and made it **The Treadway Inn** three years ago. Imagine 2,300

acres of your own private reserve . . . real Cape Cod cottages . . . swimming and sunning on a white sand lake beach as you find only on the Cape . . . or ocean bathing privileges if you wish . . . golf at the door . . . and a few minutes walk to Richard Aldrich's Falmouth Playhouse . . . and last but of first importance, fabulous Treadway Inn meals and a well stocked wine cellar. Cottage Doubles $20 to $24 daily, European Plan. Inn and Lodge doubles $14 to $16 daily.

Newagen Inn on **Cape Newagen, Me.** owned by John D. Brooks, has a special charm in a rare setting

Packard Caribbean

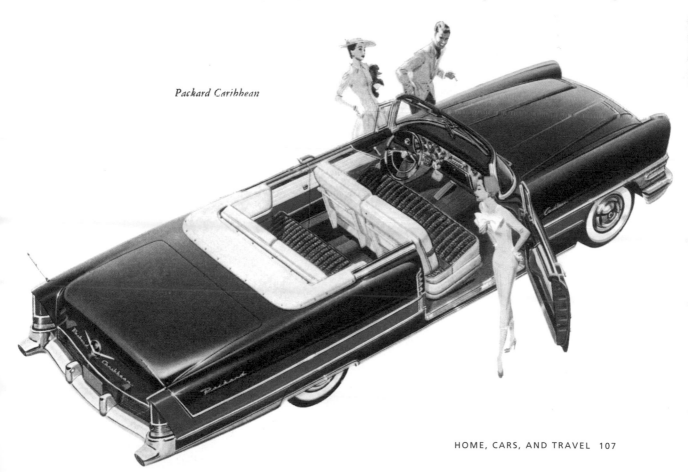

Oldsmobile Holiday Sedan

Church at Stowe, Vermont

SUMMER RESORTS . . .

of rugged nature: it is bordered on three sides by the Atlantic . . . appeals to congenial, conservative people with a kindred taste for simple, gracious living who are seeking respite from busy responsible lives. Tempered ocean swimming pool . . . weekly clambakes, outdoor cook-outs . . . secluded cottages along the shore. Double rooms with bath $27 to $31 daily, American Plan; single rooms with bath $15 to $17.50 daily, American Plan.

At **Stowe, Vermont,** Sepp Ruschp, famous Austrian ski champion, has built a summer resort that proudly takes its stand with its winter counterpart. **The Lodge at Smugglers' Notch** has its own heated swimming pool, the tastiest food west of Maxim's in Paris, and a pitch and putt golf course at the door. Sightseeing galore, with trips up Mt. Mansfield by car and chair lift, up Spruce Peak in the new double chair lift, or to

Ford Thunderbird

Ford Victoria

Mercury Montclair

De Soto Adventurer

Buick Estate Wagon

SUMMER RESORTS . . .

nearby Bingham Falls and Lake Elmore. Double rooms with bath $44 and $48 daily, on the American Plan.

A winning twosome, **The Otesaga at Cooperstown, New York.** A tranquil atmosphere under elm shaded lawns overlooking the tree lined shores of Lake Otsego, where James Fenimore Cooper conjured up his *Leatherstocking Tales* of Hawkeye. Superb 18 hole golf course along the lakeshore, swimming, canoeing . . . glamorous new cocktail lounge . . . all set against a backdrop of historic interest . . . the National

Octagonal Barn near Stowe, Vt.

Pontiac Station Wagon

Nash Rambler Cross Country Station Wagon

Baseball Museum and Hall of Fame, where the eyes of all male creatures whether eight or eighty take on a gleam as they cross the threshold . . . The Farmers' Museum filled with ingenious Yankee inventions such as a rocking bench, complete with built-in cradle and attached butter churn to produce butter while mother rocks . . . and Fenimore House, with its collection of early American folk art, second to none in the U.S. The Otesaga is a Treadway Inn managed by H. J. "Skip" Merrick, Jr. Double rooms with bath $22 to $30 daily; single rooms with bath $13 to $20 daily, both on the American Plan.

Dodge Custom Sierra Station Wagon

A corner of the master's library or study, paneled in pine. Predominant color, primrose yellow; furniture, walnut; fireplace, Georgian.

*L*ife in an English bachelor's country house has little that is formal. There is no fixed schedule of events or program for what one does during the day. An atmosphere of tranquillity and do-as-you-like always prevails, and the same applies to the clothes, which generally consist of tweed jackets and flannels or plus-fours for day wear, with an ordinary dinner suit, soft silk or cotton shirt with collar attached and black tie for the evening. Many men wear colored smoking suits made from cashmere, vicuna, or other soft-hand cloths, in navy, saxe blue, wine, or dark green; one sees also brown and tan.

Women's clothes are equally informal, with the evening clothes never very decolletté.

For week-ends, guests generally arrive on Friday for dinner, and leave on Sunday after dinner, as men like to get to their offices early on Monday.

The country house that is illustrated is owned by a bachelor; the staff consists of a butler, footman, housemaid, and cook. He is lucky inasmuch as he has old-fashioned servants who have been with him for many years, but there is a saying in England that bachelors run the best houses and have no trouble in getting servants. Probably it is because a man does not *chivvy* the servants in the same way that a woman does.

The house itself dates back to 1500, and is a beautiful example of Elizabethan architecture. There are five master and four servants' bedrooms with bathrooms, servants' hall, and of course the usual butler's pantry, kitchen and scullery. The great Lord Nelson lived there for a time. It was originally sold in the sixteenth century to the Draper's Company, one of the great City companies, who in turn sold it with a thousand acres, the proceeds being used to build the Queen Elizabeth Alms Houses at Greenwich.

ィ　ィ　ィ

The house is quite near several golf clubs and one or two hunts. Its very fine garden is open to the public on Saturday and Sunday during the spring.

Food, these days, is a great consideration; breakfast is generally served in the bedrooms or, if there is a large party, then all go down to the dining room where there are several dishes on a hotplate. A typical luncheon provided at a recent week-end included mushroom soup, roast chicken, broccoli, potatoes, and sweets or cheese. At dinner were served melon, sole mornay, roast pheasant, Japanese salad, Mont Blanc (a puree of chestnuts with whipped cream). Sherry was served with the melon, a vintage claret with the pheasant, and liqueurs with the coffee.

Servants' clothes are interesting. Butlers very rarely wear the evening tailcoat during the day. They prefer the black jacket and waistcoat and striped trousers, and very often this dress does also for the evening. Footmen still wear their owner's livery, generally black or a dark navy form of tailcoat with no facings, and carrying the owner's crest on silver or brass buttons; trousers match. The waistcoat in the correct colors match the owner's crest. Housemaids no longer wear caps in England,

Bachelor's Country House

BY CAPTAIN J. A. MURDOCKE

The main living room, paneled in old oak, is furnished with beautiful Queen Anne furniture.

A week-end guest arrives and is received by the butler and footman. Note the butler's black short jacket and waistcoat and striped trousers, and footman's livery.

A CORNER OF A BACHELOR'S BEDROOM, *showing the built-in cupboard. At the top, in boxes, are underclothing for summer and winter, silk shirts and pajamas; on the next row are kept day shirts for town and country wear, the latter of course carrying collars. Then come the lounge and country suits carried on hangers with the trousers on each hanger rail. The next shelf carries a selection of hats, and on the lower are shoes for every occasion. On the left-hand door are neckties — top row, black grounds; second row, navy grounds, and lower row, country or sports ties; browns are on the left-hand inside wall of the cupboard. To the left of the cupboard is a Queen Anne chest of drawers; the top left-hand drawer holds linen collars, and the right, handkerchiefs. The next drawer is given to country or colored handkerchiefs and such accessories; the third drawer holds navy ground socks, and the lower drawer, black ground socks.*

Built-in cupboard in the hall, for both country and town overcoats. The large checks on the left are in the Balmocan style; on the right are dark double and single breasted Chesterfield overcoats. A waterproof coat divides the groups. Soft, country hats at top.

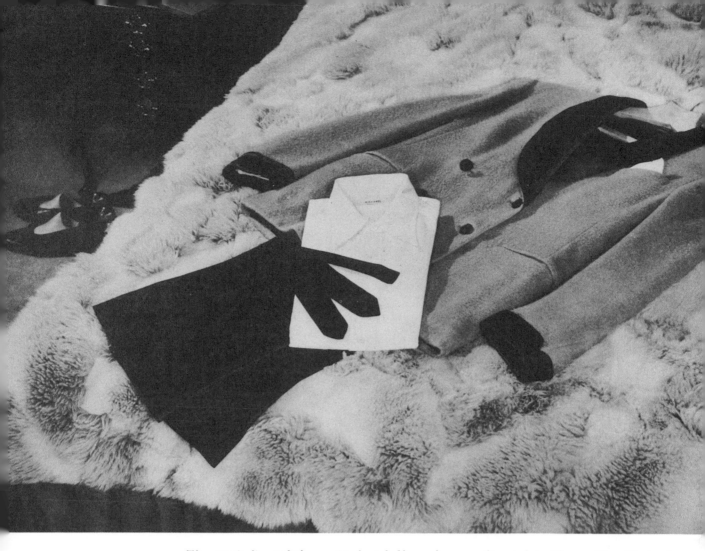

The owner's dinner clothes consist of a pale blue cashmere smoking jacket with navy blue silk shawl collar and turnback cuffs, navy blue cashmere trousers matching the jacket, white silk shirt with polo collar, and black dinner tie. On the left can be seen a pair of court shoes which are worn with navy blue socks.

Bachelor's Country House ... continued

or the old-fashioned aprons, but a brown, grey, wine, or dark green dress with a tiny fancy apron.

What happens in an English country house in the evening? Dinner is always about eight o'clock. Afterwards there is conversation, canasta, bridge, or music. The house described is not far from Tunbridge Wells and guests sometimes come in for cards; in the summer months many people arrive before lunch and dinner to see the gardens, and sherry is generally served. Cocktails are rare because of the difficulties in making and finding the necessary ingredients.

Of course, as most Americans who have visited England are aware, English entertaining has changed greatly from the years before the war; difficulties in getting servants and food, to say nothing of the high costs, have curtailed large house parties to a great degree.

The dining room is in Elizabethan style and appointments. Walnut top table requires little attention; cut-glass candlesticks are old English; silver is George II period.

Gentry's Portfolio

Lincoln *for 1955 has new sweeping lines, longer rear fender treatment, and a brand new grille design. Superlative upholstery is matched by outside paint combinations. Unseen but highly important to the consumer is the new, smooth turbo-drive with greater low-speed torque, built to work in harmony with new high-torque V-8 engine, which delivers 225 horsepower. New also is the rear deck design with dual exhausts.*

Mercury *has concentrated on even lower and sleeker lines in 1955, placing their emphasis on fabrics, patterns and color in the interior. On the Mercomatic there is improved low speed torque for faster and smoother getaway, better rear springing for improved riding at high speeds, and wider brake drums, all of which increase the safety margin at all speeds. A new engine brings power up to 188 and 198 horsepower.*

of 1955 Automobiles

Oldsmobile's *1955 Super 88 Holiday Coupe combines bright, colorful styling with luxurious upholstery and motoring refinements. The flying color motif as applied to body finishes utilizes the sweeping side moulding for color separation. Front end design has been completely restyled, with recessed headlights and new bumper contour. Power is supplied by a 202-hp. Rocket engine with 8.5 to 1 compression ratio.*

Plymouth's *1955 Belvedere Sport Coupe is longer, lower, more spacious than ever before. Chrome-framed headlights are deeply recessed. A new full-view windshield, with side-posts that slant upward and backward out of the way, gives maximum vision at eye level. Available with either a new Chrome-Sealed PowerFlow Six or Hy-Fire V-8 engine. Power steering, power seats, and power windows are optional features.*

De Soto *Firelite Sportsman of 1955 is the longest, widest and lowest De Soto ever built. It stands barely five feet high, measures 18½ feet long. The new wrap-around windshield is fully 20% bigger. Inside, the upholstery of nylon, vinyl and leather presents a harmonious color scheme. The car is powered by a 200 hp. V-8 engine, and comes with power features. Model above is Amberglow with surf white color sweep and top.*

Dodge *in 1955, has returned to the big, long car with sleek, streamlined body, projecting headlight hoods, swept-around windshield, cut back doors, flared wheel openings and streamlined rear deck — in short, the Forward Look. There is a lower roof line accented by two-tone, and in one model by three-way, paint combinations, the latter combination being an innovation this year. The V-8 engine develops 183 horsepower.*

ROUND the WORLD GUIDE

of

Helpful Do's . . . A Few Don'ts

for

Air-Minded Travelers . . .

The scene takes place in the Men's Bar of the Waldorf-Carlton, or any other center where the problems of the world can be settled without the tintinabulation and distraction of women.

DRAMATIS PERSONAE

MR. B.O.A.C. SPEEDBIRD. *He is lean, tall, tanned and in the best British tradition. He is at home anywhere for he is a professional traveler.*

MR. SAKS. *Obviously an American who, in the course of his wide travels, has become a collector of excellences.*

MR. GENTRY. *He has the relaxed and speculative eye of a connoisseur. The world is his garden.*

The time is any five o'clock.

Mr. Speedbird: (raising a glass) Cheers. Both you fellows keeping fit, I see. Good show.

Mr. Saks: Never better, thanks. Here's how!

Mr. Gentry: Good health, gentlemen! (after a reflective pause) If more people had wider interests, they would be better off. Half the poor health today is due to the fact that people worry about themselves. Ought to see more of the world. Do them a world of good. Traveling much these days, Speed?

Mr. Speedbird: All the time. All over the shop. Just leaving on another round-the-world flight. Fun, you know. Fast, too, in these days of jet airliners. My Comet flies eight miles a minute, eight miles high.

Mr. Saks: Must present a problem in deciding what to take in the way of clothes, doesn't it?

Mr. Speedbird: Eighty-eight pounds you're allowed on a round-the-world trip. It's ample. Packing, laundry and pressing are a bit of a problem though. Hate to turn up looking like an unmade bed.

Mr. Gentry: There's no reason why you should with all these new fabrics for suits, shirts and everything. No wrinkle, dry overnight after washing. Wonderful. Ever try them?

Mr. Speedbird: I've heard about them, that's all. Don't know whether they are all they're cracked up to be.

Mr. Saks: Sceptic. You fly jet planes and stick to old-fashioned fabrics. These new fabrics are the equal of anything on the market. I should

If the reader will consult the enclosed Wardrobe Guide, the results of this sensational drama will be unfolded on location in word, picture and chart.

In front of the Coliseum in Rome, wearing navy blue topcoat over grey nailhead Irish tweed suit.

Wearing Kabaya sports jacket and grey flannel trousers, with Chief Guide Rangi in front of her home in Rotorura, N. Z.

In garden at Aw Boon Haw Villa in Singapore, wearing white washable linen slacks, silk print shirt.

Wearing the Orlon and acetate warm-weather suit while visiting Aw Boon Haw Villa on the outskirts of Singapore.

Government reception following display of ancient musical instruments in New Delhi, India.

In white silk dinner jacket . . . enjoying late snack at food stall in famous Albert St., Singapore.

Air-minded Travelers . . .

	know. I sell them.
Mr. Gentry:	That gives me an idea. Saks, why don't you and I outfit him and let him prove to himself how good they are. After all, BOAC, you spend more time in these far-away places than anybody. I don't know anyone better qualified to check up on the right clothes for every country.
Mr. Speedbird:	You mean, sort of flight-test them for you both? I'm going to be in a lot of different climates, you know. A bit of a problem.
Mr. Saks:	I'll buy that. Where are you going?
Mr. Speedbird:	England. *Bit moist occasionally.* India. *Hot. Cold, too.* Far East. *Cold. Hot, too.* Australia. *Moderate.* N. Z. *Quite moderate.*
Mr. Gentry:	He sounds like the poor man's Noel Coward. He thinks he can scare us, but he can't. Can he, Saks?
Mr. Saks:	Certainly not. Drop in to see me in the morning, BOAC. I'll fix you up with clothes for every occasion. How about it?
Mr. Speedbird:	Good show, gentlemen. You're on.
Mr. Gentry:	That's my boy. Give the clothes the best workout they can get. You'll find a new lease on travel style and comfort. (Pause, very brief). Barman. Another round. Mr. Saks and I wish to drink to our friend here, Mr. BOAC Speedbird, well dressed world traveler. Man-about-the-World.

Three experts express satisfaction . . .

A. GUSTAFSON, clothing executive of Saks Fifth Avenue. *"We knew that the right clothes would enable our man to cope successfully with any vacation, social, or business occasion . . . and the actual test proved it."*

G. IRVING, well-known furnishings executive of Saks Fifth Avenue: *"Our man-about-the-world has proved that it is possible to combine style and comfort in any climate, any season."*

F. GRUMMT, luggage specialist of Saks Fifth Avenue: *"The luggage was chosen to stand up under all sorts of conditions in all parts of the world. It did the job."*

Amelia Earhart's *Flying Trunk* is made of canvas . . . has twelve-hanger capacity. Packed with average weight clothes, it weighs less than 66 pounds. 36"x22"x12" . . . approximately 27 pounds unpacked . . . costs $157.80.

Oshkosh luggage made of durable woven striped canvas. Suitcase is three-suiter size complete with hangers and attachments . . . made on aluminum frame . . . with leather trim, metal hardware . . . weighs 11 pounds. Cost, $95.40. Matching soft-sided bag with heavy duty zipper, 20"x20" . . . 4½ pounds. Cost, $45.00.

Combination clothes brush and collapsible hanger from England. Brush is of leather; hanger, hook, and arms, of brass. $10. Wallach's, New York.

Left: Softly constructed shoe case made from woven plaid canvas in green, blue, and gold combination. Has six cotton felt compartments which can be removed. Trimmed with leather straps and metal hardware, it weighs 1¾ pounds, measures 17½"x14"x7". Costs $24.00. Center: Bottomless folding carryall matches shoe case. 28"x16" jumbo size, it folds into matching envelope which can double for miscellaneous item-carrying case. Weighs 1½ pounds . . . leather handles and corners, zipper closure. $35.40 from T. Anthony, New York.

Cowhide brief case has special water-repellent compartment at bottom with its own zipper opening that holds collapsible umbrella. Case has conventional top zipper closure: Umbrella ten-ribbed man-size, is covered with acetate fabric. 16"x11". Costs $27. Mark Cross, New York.

The Norelco Battery Shaver operates on three self-contained flashlight batteries or plugs into an automobile lighter socket, thus avoiding possible difficulties with plug-in razors in foreign voltage. $29.95, Lewis & Conger, New York.

ROUND THE WORLD WITH 88 POUNDS

When traveling by air, staying within your 88-pound allowance for Round-the-World flights . . . 66-pound allowance for overseas flights . . . requires careful planning not only of what you pack but what you pack it in. Here are some helpful suggestions on the latter subject. In the large photo above, leaving Raffles Hotel, Singapore, Malaya, Laird Loftus carries complete flight-tested wardrobe in two Hartman suitcases . . . and had poundage to spare. This canvas-covered plywood-frame luggage when so packed actually weighed 72 pounds. The four-suiter size is $108.00 . . . the one-suiter size, $85.00. Both suitcases are from Saks Fifth Avenue, New York.

Extremely lightweight luggage made from brown cotton duck. Hanging wardrobe case holds five suits, with accessories in upper and lower zipper-attached voluminous pockets. Weighs 6 pounds and, when folded over double for carrying suitcase-style, measures 24"x18". Cost, $51.00. 29" suitcase with soft drum-type top and bottom holds three suits plus accessories. Weighs 8½ pounds. Cost, $54.00. Vendome carryall features big flapped pockets on each side with open center compartment for magazines, papers, etc. Ideal to take inside plane . . . holds shirt without folding, and personal items. 16"x12½"x4½" . . . 1¾ pounds. $23.40. Leather-trimmed; metal hardware. T. Anthony, 751 Madison Ave., New York

Where Federal Tax applies, the tax is included in the prices given.

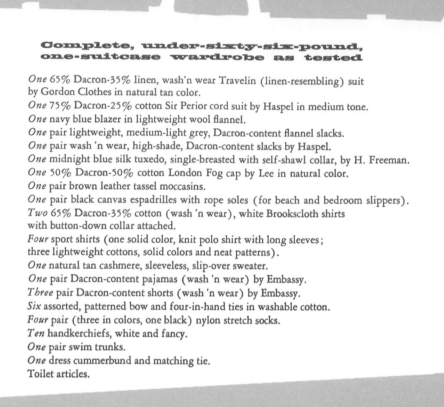

Complete, under-sixty-six-pound, one-suitcase wardrobe as tested

One 65% Dacron-35% linen, wash'n wear Travelin (linen-resembling) suit by Gordon Clothes in natural tan color.

One 75% Dacron-25% cotton Sir Perior cord suit by Haspel in medium tone.

One navy blue blazer in lightweight wool flannel.

One pair lightweight, medium-light grey, Dacron-content flannel slacks.

One pair wash 'n wear, high-shade, Dacron-content slacks by Haspel.

One midnight blue silk tuxedo, single-breasted with self-shawl collar, by H. Freeman.

One 50% Dacron-50% cotton London Fog cap by Lee in natural color.

One pair brown leather tassel moccasins.

One pair black canvas espadrilles with rope soles (for beach and bedroom slippers).

Two 65% Dacron-35% cotton (wash 'n wear), white Brookscloth shirts with button-down collar attached.

Four sport shirts (one solid color, knit polo shirt with long sleeves; three lightweight cottons, solid colors and neat patterns).

One natural tan cashmere, sleeveless, slip-over sweater.

One pair Dacron-content pajamas (wash 'n wear) by Embassy.

Three pair Dacron-content shorts (wash 'n wear) by Embassy.

Six assorted, patterned bow and four-in-hand ties in washable cotton.

Four pair (three in colors, one black) nylon stretch socks.

Ten handkerchiefs, white and fancy.

One pair swim trunks.

One dress cummerbund and matching tie.

Toilet articles.

Addenda: *Other items which might be included in more complete wardrobes*

Sport coats in white or high solid colors, tailored from linen, linen-like fabrics, Palm Beach, silk, tropical-weight woolens; tailored from year-round weights: solid or patterned Shetlands, tweeds, cashmeres, etc.

Slacks in varied colors (black, pink, red, blue, yellow, white) tailored from such lightweight fabrics as linen, linen-types, polished cotton, silk, tropical worsteds; tailored from black-grey, regulation year-round-weight wool flannel.

Knee-length shorts in similar colors and fabrics suggested for slacks above.

Single-breasted, white dinner jacket, self-shawl collar, tailored from silk, tropical worsted, Palm Beach fabrics. Long- and short-sleeved sport shirts: knits, solid or striped, crew, boat or collar-attached necklines; cut-and-sewn styles, solid colors, neat patterns.

Beach robe, jacket or shirt of terry cloth or other absorbent material in bright colors.

Swim trunks, plain or patterned, boxer style or with waistband; knitted or woven fabrics.

Colored dress shirts (blue, pink, tan, white), Oxford or broadcloth, varied style collar attached.

Four-in-hand or bow ties, various colors, patterns, in silks, cottons and man-made fibers.

Conventional lightweight shoes in brown or black.

Silk or cotton foulard lightweight dressing gown, plain or neat pattern.

Plain or fancy (argyle, box or neat panel plaids) socks; knee-length socks for wear with shorts.

Single or double-breasted business suit in medium-dark casts of blue, grey, brown, tailored from silk, mohair, tropical worsted fabrics.

A business suit in year-round weights and fabrics. Solid-color, slip-over or cardigan sweaters with sleeves or without, medium-weight wool, Dacron, Orlon (latter two wash 'n wear).●

What would you like to see in an automobile?

PHOTOGRAPH COURTESY CHEVROLET DIVISION, GENERAL MOTORS

We asked six famous designers,
three men and three women, to tell us
what they would like to see in an automobile.
Here is what they wrote and sketched
as their suggestions for the American automobile.

Car of the future by William Pahlmann

William Pahlmann, interior and industrial designer, first gained recognition, while at Lord and Taylor, by creating a series of exhibition rooms which impressed press and public. He went on to become Design and Decoration Editor at Harper's Bazaar. Since founding his own firm, Mr. Pahlmann has been responsible for interiors of Bonwit Teller stores in Boston, New York, Chicago and Cleveland. He has also designed furniture, fabrics, carpets and bedspreads.

There should be less color on the outside of a car and more inside. The rather flashy, two-toned jobs that have been rolling off the assembly line in the last few years, and some of the sharp putrid pastels, quite often make the people inside these circus boats look a little bit silly. A heavy, bearded laborer dashing to work in a pale blue or shrimp pink car doesn't make much sense to me and it certainly doesn't lend to the dignity of the road. I prefer gunmetal greys, charcoal grey-blacks, brown-blacks, and some deep blue colors, and black itself. In a sports car, I do think whites and greys and beige tones are all right; but any of the other pastel colors are a little bit on the *sharp* side.

The Car Interior

The inside of a car is a rather personal thing. I see no reason for having so much glass on the sides that you appear to be a wilted flower in a showcase. There should be some way of screening the windows on the sides of the cars, keeping, of course, the windshield and the rear window clear for safe driving. I don't understand why the inside tops of cars should be dull and uninteresting. Why not have flowered ceilings, or one of woven fabrics that have a design or texture to them? Why shouldn't the floor coverings have a tweedy look or a small over-all design?

We've already touched on fabrics slightly in reference to the ceiling and floor. As far as the seats are concerned, I rather like the effect of permanent slipcovers. I personally use this sort of thing and, at one time, I used a pandanus cloth or straw as a seat covering. I now have black Lurex in a semi-permanent slipcover.

Figured carpets or, if it's possible, vinyl tile could be used over the floor boards; if these floor boards could be stamped out of plastic or Fiberglas with a scarified

top, it would take the wear and tear and still be attractive. I think this could be done and eliminate the constantly moving carpet on car floors.

The interior lighting should be better. There should definitely be a map-reading light, and lights concealed in more spaces in the car to make it easy to read a theatre program or to make notes without disturbing the vision of the driver.

Styles of Interiors

There could be different styles of interiors on the insides of cars. Why shouldn't there be subtle indications through hardware, and decorative materials to give a car an Empire look, a French Provincial look, a Directoire look, or perhaps even a Spanish look? Why shouldn't there be loose cushions to fit into the small of the back? These can be of straw or of other sturdy materials, but they can be bright, cheerful and comfortable as well as practical. And why couldn't there be scented interiors in cars? This was done in the old-type car I know, but what is wrong with having a scent of pine or some other scent indicative of the owner.

The car of the future should release heat from all parts of the car, not just from the dashboard heater. There should be a heater for the back of the car and there might even be a heater in the trunk, where clothing and other items packed there become quite cold and uncomfortable in the wintertime. There is a similar need in summer — the trunk should be well ventilated and cooled, particularly in cars of high cost.

On Conveniences

The glove compartment should be given more design attention. It should be larger and fitted like a desk, with slots for maps, and perhaps a small drawer for pencils, etc. It is near this compartment that there should be an

"Why can't window shades come up from the door like windows do, by pressing a button . . ."

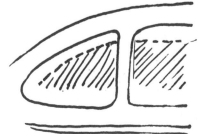

"The car of the future should have wheels that turn sideways when a lever is thrown, for parking . . ."

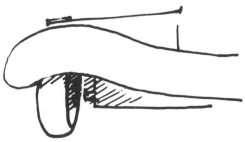

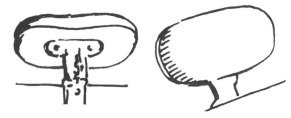

luminous paint here

"The entire inside of the trunk could be sprayed with a bright red, luminous paint which would glow when an approaching car's headlights hit it . . ."

adjustable, map-reading light. I know most cars have some sort of a map-reading light, but you have to bend your back and almost stand on your head to use it. This light should be shielded so that it does not interfere with the driver. There should be two ashtrays on the dashboard, one for the driver and one for the person next to the driver, and two in the rear.

There should be side-pockets, as in the old-fashioned cars, on the doors. These sidepockets could be on the door next to the passenger in the front seat, and not necessarily next to the driver, although even here a flat pocket would not be a bad idea. These could be used for maps, magazines, Kleenex and such, that might conceivably be left out of the glove compartment.

On Seat Comfort

The front seat of the car should be so designed that the driver's seat can be adjusted to any height or distance from the controls. Of course, this has been done to an extent, but the seat next to the driver should also be more adjustable. I, personally, prefer the front seat split so that the passenger riding in the front seat can not only adjust his seat up and down, front and back, but can do this without disturbing the driver's seating arrangement. There should also be plenty of leg room for a tall person such as I.

On this passenger seat, we could have an adjustable headrest, such as I have installed in my car, and which has been more than successful. These headrests are similar to the headrest on a barber's chair, but they should be wider and have small wings on each side so one's head has some support when it lolls over to one side. A headrest such as this could also be installed in the rear of the car; in fact, the backs of this rear seat should be higher and made quite similar to the seats in an airplane so there is a permanent headrest when it is needed. If this is too high to make for an attractive appearance to the car, then an adjustable headrest can be inserted into a slot in the back of the seat.

The car of the future should have wheels that turn sideways when a lever is thrown for parking, and I believe this improvement will come in time.

On Special Features

There should be a combination lock similar to that on safes on the driver's door, so when he forgets his key he will be able to unlock the door.

There should be an electrical plug in the trunk in the rear similar to the one that can be put into the cigarette lighter on the dashboard. This same plug will come in handy to plug in food warmers or coolers or any appliance which is needed for camping and picnics. This plug should be able to take a fairly long extension.

And here's an idea that I am trying to have copyrighted. The entire inside of the trunk could be sprayed with a bright red, luminous paint, which would glow when an approaching car's headlights hit it and be an instant danger signal. Too many serious and fatal accidents happen when a parked car is not seen by an oncoming driver. This inside paint job should be standard practice on all models with trunks. Also, bumpers and other portions of the exterior should be treated with such a warning device.

Why can't window shades for privacy come up from the door like windows do, by pressing a button. This might not be necessary if plate glass could be installed whereby you can look out but no one can see in.

The Car of the Future that I would like to see is a car suited to a man 6'2" tall, a car low in depth but not so low that you seem to be sitting on the road or one that would give you the feeling that you're sitting in a pocket on one side of the crankshaft. The seat should be extremely comfortable, but still give enough support to one's back on a long tour.

"The glove compartment . . . fitted like a desk."

"Two ashtrays on the dashboard, one for the driver."

". . . we could have an adjustable headrest, such as I have installed in my car . . ."

Sports car styled for tomorrow by **Howard Ketcham**

Howard Ketcham is probably the most color-conscious person in the world. In twenty years as head of his own organization, he has developed new colors and styles for more than 500 products. His touch is seen in fabrics, plastics, pre-fabricated housing, commercial and military aircraft, household appliances, railroad passenger equipment, ships, automobiles, offices, factories and display showrooms. He is color editor of American Fabrics Magazine.

Some day soon, you'll see dazzling new sports cars totally unlike today's concepts streaming down the colored highways! A flash of line and color. A deep throated roar of nuclear power. A bold fleetness of style and utility both inside and out. That's the car for your tomorrow!

Powered by nuclear energy, this unique vehicle has no moving parts in its engine! Instead, a self-contained atomic reactor transmits motive power to the rear driving wheel. And there's no need for servicing — for the entire atomic fuel unit in the rear is simply rented from the manufacturer, and exchanged periodically for a fresh unit!

Automatic Features

Atop the nuclear engine is a luggage rack, which actually opens at the *snap of a finger*. Noise made by your fingers actuates an electronic circuit which pops open the compartment automatically. The same *snap* opens and closes the front compartment housing radar, television and high frequency sound-generating units.

Radar circuits operate the nuclear engine, steering mechanism, and brakes from the passenger compartment. While television and supersonic-impulses tell of road conditions for a radius of 50 miles! All this, plus automatic, proximity-operated parking *brains*.

And just look at all the dramatic new features for increased riding comfort. The plastic, seat-enclosing, solar-dome reflects heat rays in the summer, and absorbs just enough energy from the sun to heat the car interior throughout the winter! No special heating unit is ever needed. Air-conditioning, of course, for year-round comfort. And the most striking features of all: Foam-rubber dashboard, crash panel, and seats — styled in the most advanced, eye-appealing synthetic fabrics. There's utility to spare in this brilliant sports car.

There is no limit to the colors that can be used to achieve striking decorative combinations for automobiles.

*Ketcham's concept of an atomic powered automobile with
heat reflecting solar dome. engine with no moving parts.*

The three different color styling plans for the car are described below:

Combination of Fuchsia and Peacock Blue

This striking concept in color coordination uses fuchsia for the car body and tires, while peacock blue serves as the trim and interior accent color. For example, the steering wheel color is the same as the trim color — peacock blue — so that the interior will effectively echo parts of the car exterior color scheme!

There already is an upholstery fabric which is a special blend of these two car colors. Maroon is used as the warp, and peacock blue as the filler. Result: An excitingly new color combination, unlike anything seen today in car interiors!

Combination of Blue and Green

In this scheme a gay, youthful effect is achieved. Here, blue is used as the body color, while green serves as the color for the trim and interior accents.

What makes this color combination so unusual! Simply the fact that it has never been successfully achieved before in cars. Designers said it couldn't be done . . . that blue and green can't be used together. But the simple fact is that it is possible when you know which varieties of these two hues to combine. Blue and green can work wonders together to attract and please the eye — if they are blended correctly. It's all in the skill of color-application.

Combination of the Unusual

The third category of color schemes stresses the unusual and unexpected. Lime yellow is combined with blue . . . chartreuse with coral pink . . . orange with pink. One color is used for the body, and the other for interior and trim. Although the combinations are unorthodox, they will present a pleasing impression because they are skillfully blended.

The creation of gay and brilliant effects is a logical conclusion from domestic and industrial experience.

Talking design ideas around by **James Amster**

James Amster's background includes heading the decorating department at Bergdorf Goodman and designing sets in Hollywood. He now owns a successful designer-decorator firm. He has worked on the Decoration Committee for the World's Fair, the Terrace Club, the National Advisory Committee Building, the Mount Washington Hotel at Bretton Woods, and recently designed the Peacock Alley Cafe at the Waldorf Astoria and the Swedish-American Liner "Kungsholm".

It seems to me that metal trim for cars has been chrome-colored for so long, it would be a fine idea to use some new, gilt-colored metal for all exterior and interior trim. As a matter of fact, the end has almost been reached in the tremendous quantity of metal trim used, and I think it is time to cut it down to a minimum. With less metal, there could certainly be finer detailing in all the trim.

When it comes to exterior colors I would prefer to see more of charcoals, seal browns and deep reds, instead of the prevailing pastels. To take the place of the eliminated metal trim, there could be contrasting stripes in lighter tones of the body color.

There is also the possibility of a revival of early wooden spoked wagon wheels, this time with the heavy spokes in metal, finished in the same color as the car body. This is a refreshing change from the solid masses of metal or the squirrel-cage wheels now popular.

On Interior Styling

The interior should be tied to the exterior of a car by means of a monochromatic color scheme. The light-est value of the color would start at the ceiling and be carried down to the level of the window and door divisions. The functional metal parts in this area should be lacquered to match the ceiling. The seats could be the darkest value of the color — and I favor deep tufting with, perhaps, gilt buttons sunk in the tufts; triangular flat tufting; box pleating; quilting. Let's not have any antimacassars or contrasts between back and seat or added head rests. For the floor I would want a carpet in a combination of the darkest and a medium value of the overall color. It could be a tweed, a salt and pepper weave or a very small pattern. It might be a fine idea to cover the floor of the rear section and carry the carpet up the back of the front seat about twelve inches. This would afford added protection against scuffing, and increase the apparent size of the floor area.

Fabrics for car interiors should be chosen much as if they were for your home. Plain fabrics, small patterns, and twills are all suitable. The fabrics can be treated to be moisture-, soil- and flame-resistant and yet not have the clammy plastic feeling.

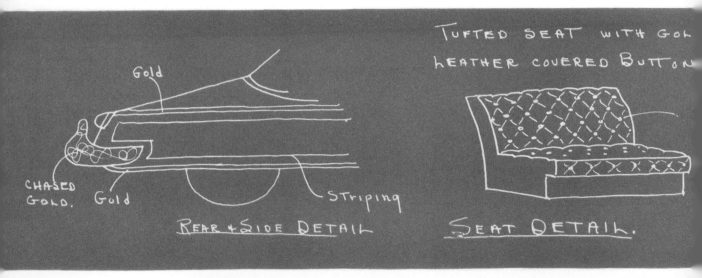

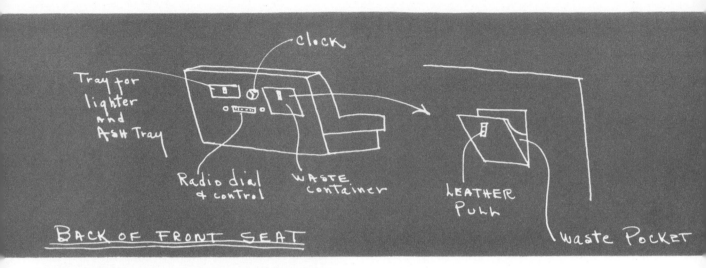

clock

Tray for lighter and Ash Tray

Radio dial & control

WASTE container

LEATHER PULL

waste POCKET

<u>BACK OF FRONT SEAT</u>

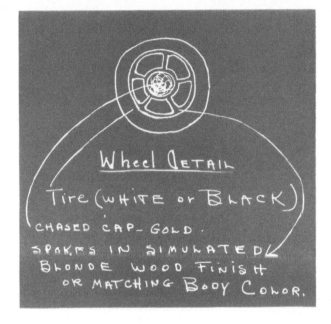

<u>Wheel detail</u>

Tire (WHITE or BLACK)

CHASED CAP- GOLD.

SPOKES IN SIMULATED BLONDE WOOD FINISH OR MATCHING BODY COLOR.

There should be no real contrast in fabrics or paint. I would limit the interior trim to occasional welting on upholstery and to metal. By the way, metal fixtures could well be more finely detailed. Ashtrays, for instance, should be larger, more attractive, easily washable — and placed so all passengers can use them.

On Important Accessories

Dashboard equipment could also be more simple in design. A secondary dashboard might be established in the rear with a small clock (the one in front is rarely visible), radio controls, and a concealed wastebasket. The latter would be placed in the back of the front seat, and equipped with a liner for easy emptying.

Automatic controls for windows are a must. Concealed lights should be added in the rear which light when the doors are opened. A telephone is an asset for emergencies, but not advisable for casual conversation. Air conditioning is a joy in most areas. Television is possible but I don't approve of it unless it is in the rear of a chauffeur-driven car where the driver cannot see it.

BODY

PLAIN BRUSHED GOLD COLOR METAL (NON-TARNISHING

CHASED LINES ON LARGE MASS OF GOLD

CHARCOAL PAINT BODY BRUSHED GOLD. STRIPS LIGHT GRAY STRIPING

Front detail

The car is the family's second home by **Dorothy Liebes**

Dorothy Liebes' textile designing has netted her awards from Lord and Taylor, Paris Exposition, American Institute of Architects, and Neiman-Marcus. She has contributed to several shows at the Museum of Modern Art and to the Chicago Home Furnishing Market, as well as participated in twenty-five museum and gallery shows. She holds the title of director or board member on about twenty organizations, and is retained as designer and stylist by many concerns.

It is almost a truism that proper relationships make for rhythm in life. Hence, the automobile — the family's second and often favorite home — should be largely related to the locale. A country car and a city car should have some distinguishing features that identify each for what it is. Indeed, this fact has already been partially recognized in the so-called *town car,* as contrasted with the station wagon.

For one color scheme, I would like an earthy palette, making use of the colors of the out-of-doors. Too many models today have the same color-schemes as a tea-room or a lady's boudoir.

The Country Car

The country model I would design with large dashes of warm autumn color. Instead of the too-familiar chrome, all metal trim would have a copper finish. This should cost no more than the conventional chrome.

The colors of body and hood are close in value. I don't like sharp contrasts here. A combination of tan deep and tan light, copper trim, and black tires — preferably with a lacquer red line — would produce a warm, eye-attracting whole.

The logical place for a color-scheme is the top inside. It is now uniformly dismissed with a mouse-colored, coffin-like pile or duveteen cloth. A screen print by Ivan Bartlett sets a gay and happy atmosphere. The cloth is linen or nylon and treated to repel dust.

The upholstery color also combines colors of close value, sage-green and tan. The linen is treated to be fire-, water- and dust-proof.

For the floor, laminated wood shavings is a handsome and practical product, closely related to the nature setting where the car will most often be seen.

The town car, naturally, will have a more sophisticated look. On the lining of the top, a Miro-like print, chamois upholstery, and everything treated to be proof against dirt, fire and water. As in the other model, I visualize substituting copper wire for the grill and copper wire for the wheels, instead of the tired chrome for the wheels, instead of the tired chrome accessories.

Functional Features

A costly survey conducted by a large advertising agency (among other things, they checked thousands of cars in parking lots) showed that the worst housekeeping in the world is in the rear seating space of the family car. Everybody complains about it, but no manufacturer has done anything about it.

It is perfectly feasible to have a car that can be hosed out on the inside without damage to upholstery, fabric or any of the fittings. Everything in the interior is waterproof. Apart from that, all that would be necessary is a drain in the floor, closed with a plug.

One reason for the untidiness of the average family car is that little or no provision has been made for the thousand-and-one articles that find their way into the car. For example, why not racks attached to the back of the front seat? There should be two racks that fall forward when not in use, to hold magazines, and a deeper one for parcels. No more papers and magazines blowing all over the rear window. We can take a leaf from, and improve on, the methods used in airplanes to handle the problem of reading matter and potential litter. In side pockets, there should be space for thermos containers, one side for the hot, the other for the cold.

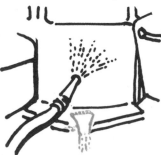

"All that would be necessary is a drain in the floor . . ."

"There should be two racks . . . to hold magazines and parcels."

"In the side pockets . . . a space for thermos containers."

TOWN CAR

"The logical place for a color scheme is the top inside, now uniformly dismissed."

DESIGN BY IVAN BARTLETT

"For one model, an earthy palette . . . too many models today have the same color schemes as a lady's boudoir . . ."

FABRIC BY DOROTHY LIEBES

"For body and hood combine tan deep and tan light . . ."

LAMINATED SHAVINGS BY U.S. PLYWOOD

STATION WAGON

"A screen print sets a gay and happy atmosphere. The cloth is linen or nylon and treated to repel dust . . ."

DESIGN BY IVAN BARTLETT

"The upholstery color combines colors of close value . . . sage green and tan. The linen is treated to be fire-, water- and dust-proof."

FABRIC BY DOROTHY LIEBES

interior seating for comfort
and elegance in appearance
made with a fabric that offers
the least abrasion
and allows for maximum breathing
and coolness of touch in summer

tufted upholstery

Family outing or long distance coach by **Doris Tillett**

Heavily influenced by the addition of Linnaea Tillett to the growing firm of Leslie, Doris and Dek Tillett, Doris Tillett has devised the practical car of tomorrow on this page. The Tilletts are primarily designers of fabrics and maintain their own plant where they test new techniques in fabric printing. Their shop serves as a proving ground for the experimental work and as a spring board for ideas for interior decorators and architects. Currently, they are consultants to the Owens-Corning Fiberglas Corp., and have contributed to the new Fiberglas fabrics.

translucent fabric with print

interior canopy for privacy
made of translucent fabric
printed with shadowy leaves
and white on white branches
which operates like baby carriage hood

bubble roof for light
and to give an airy joyful illusion
made of unbreakable glass

luggage space and refrigerator compartment

seating arrangement for relaxed conversation
and play area
is obtained with tufted couch
following oval contour of car
fitted picnic, luggage, toidy, refrigerator
compartments under seating

I remember, years ago, needing a car immediately and, being very busy at the time, I sent a friend to find one for me "—any kind, as long as it's yellowish-green, convertible, and leather lined." You see, I'm completely female and quite average in tilting with the engineering miracles of our lives. The men in my family despair of my *ever* knowing anything about the innards of a car—but, just watch my weight being thrown at point-of-sale if I don't like the looks of it. I repeat, I'm Mrs. Average Consumer in this respect, and never underestimate the power of fashion in the steel and oil industries! The hand that rocks the cradle can firmly rock the back seat of a car, too.

Much of my life has been spent in my native state, California. There, one practically lives in a car, and barnstorming (as I like to call it) around the country is my favorite sport. The call of the open road is irresistible, and much of my designing in fashion is influenced by this. One of my favorite and most successful early designs was a car robe to be worn poncho-like while driving, or used as a lap robe.

On Creature- and Vanity-Comfort

Comfort in a car, to a woman, is a prime requisite — and comfort can mean a lot of things besides the very able job the design engineer accomplishes. Of course, there's mental-comfort in knowing he's done a safe construction job. But there's creature-comfort — like upholstery that's kind to the touch and doesn't catch clothes. And there's vanity-comfort — like knowing that the color is a very flattering background. Believe me, I thoroughly respect the job the automotive industry has done but, as long as I'm asked, here are some strictly personal thoughts on "if I had my way!"

If I had my way there would be very little chrome trim, if any, and only for a good reason. No fake streamlining and modernistic (awful word!) embellishments for my dream car. I realize that simplicity is the most difficult thing to achieve in *anything* — but *please* less gadgets. I'm all for the sports car trend, especially the hard top variety, but the creature-comfort side of me rebels at having to stoop so low to enter some of them. What do people with long legs do? And statistics prove they're getting longer!

On Interesting Tones and Textures

I think a much more interesting job could be done with color and combinations of color. It's not the color itself so much, as *tone* and *texture.* I'd have someone like Dorothy Liebes do me a tough, beautiful fabric impervious to rain, dirt, and Junior's pet puppy. I'd then have a paint chemist mix some wonderful harmonizing tones — and maybe use them all on the one car, but you'd never know it for the blend would be a beautiful whole, like a painting. Or — I'd love a striped top, say green and white on a green car, like the gayest awning ever, and, though the top would be sturdy and fixed, it would be designed of some material which would give that soft translucent effect that a canvas awning gives. None of the bold overhead glare of a glass window for me. I'd consider the inside of the top — its color, and the kind of a light it would cast on my face. I'd be sure it was flattering and made me *feel* pretty. I'd banish carpeting on the floor forever and use smart resilient plastics — maybe a mosaic pattern to dress up an otherwise mono-colored car.

I'd love to do a series of car accessories. Why not loose, soft pillows matched to the upholstery? How often I've rolled up a coat under my head for a nap in the back seat! There are lots of ideas for that growing barnstorming population which could be worked into chic as well as practical items. Better conveniences for hanging clothes and packing them, for instance. Luggage that is designed as one with a car — to be nested like Japanese boxes. Whole exciting design area here — and one which a woman would appreciate, with all the odd-sized luggage around to confuse one. Whatever happened to the ancient robe-rack? It *was* useful. And so on, and on "if I had my way!" Maybe I'm not really thinking about my dream car — but a sturdy camel pack!

Maybe I'm not thinking about a dream car, but a sturdy camel pack says **Bonnie Cashin**

Bonnie Cashin is a women's fashion designer whose clothes have been described as being akin to contemporary architecture inasmuch as they interpret a sense of time, space and function. Her diversified background (she has designed for the Roxy Theater, 20th Century Fox in Hollywood) gives her clothes the kind of versatility and movement that designing everything from period costumes to musicals inspires. A winner of the Neiman-Marcus Award and Fashion Critics' "Winnie", Miss Cashin has designed rain and stormcoats, evening and daytime separates, "at home" clothes, packaged bed sheets with matching pillow slips, knitted dresses, coats and suits.

FOOD

AND

DRINK

4

Nowhere in *Gentry* is there any mention of the "little woman" being relegated to slicing and dicing while the "master of the house" sips a Drambuie and watches the game on his new black-and-white Philco TV.

That's what's so noteworthy about the prominence of food and dining in the magazine: the goal wasn't simply to educate the palate. On the contrary: *Gentry*'s editors believed that it wasn't enough for a man to provide food for his family. He was obliged to prepare it for them as well, and to do so with skill, confidence, and relish, literally and figuratively.

So get ready, weekend chefs and fearless gourmands. With more than sixty recipes to satisfy such varied occasions as New Year's Eve supper or an "around the world" dinner (each course comes from a different country), not to mention the formulas for making more than forty different cocktails, punches, grogs, and nogs, this chapter is a veritable *Gentry* cookbook.

Since *Gentry* had no test kitchen, recipes often came from fabled eateries of the era, such as Luchow's in New York City, the Beverly Hills Hotel in Los Angeles, and Tour d'Argent in Paris. Tastes change over time, so rarified delicacies such as Beef Tongue with Beet Sauce or Chicken Liver and Pea Soup may not prompt anyone to buy a new set of Calphalon, but the gazpacho has a feisty kick to it, and it's one of the rare recipes for this soup that doesn't cheat with a tomato juice base.

Of course, *Gentry* offers a grilling and broiling guide by no less than the esteemed James Beard. His guide's presentation reveals the essence of what made this magazine so unique. Who wouldn't be tempted by eight variations on the classic hamburger, including an herbed burger dense with parsley, chive, and rosemary, a corned beef burger, and a bunless burger served between two slices of grilled eggplant? But Beard insists that a smart cook must do more than follow a recipe's marching orders. For example, he cites that all cuts of meat are neither created nor to be treated equally, comparing the doubled thickness with which one should cut a porterhouse as opposed to a sirloin, and explaining why a pork steak requires different handling than pork ribs.

Happily, the enthusiastic gourmand is not always tied to apron strings. Just to ensure that going out to eat remains one of life's great pleasures, *Gentry* offers some pragmatic table manners to add some couth to youth. Should you suffer the stings and sorrows of Rabelaisian indulgence, the editors also provide ten really sound pieces of advice on dieting that still hold up today.

Since the magazine was published in the 1950s, long before nonalcoholic beer and twenty-four-hour news stations eagerly featured the latest Hollywood celebrity picked up on a DUI charge, one must forgive *Gentry* for its wholehearted, unabashed immersion in the wonderful world of alcohol. Here are drinks such as the Exterminator and an ancient cavalryman's Dragoon Punch (made with champagne and brandy), as well as an ode to the "character-building" qualities inherent in "The Unadorned Truth about the Great American Martini." Try as you might to fight it, the latter manifesto reads like poetry.

Finally, to drive home the point that cooking isn't meant to be solely women's work, the first step in the preparation of pressed duck is as follows: "Take a fine duckling, six weeks to two months old, hang it until strangled, pluck, dress, singe, and draw it." Luckily, these days, you can also call for takeout.

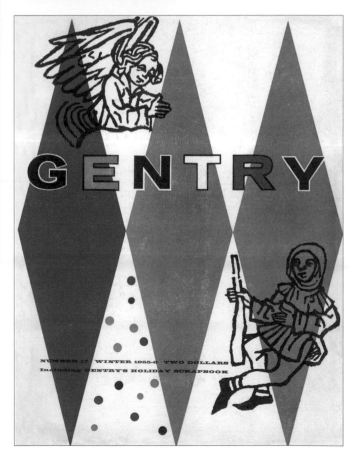

the
UNADORNED TRUTH
about the
GREAT AMERICAN MARTINI

*no two Martini-ists
are the same . . .*

BY ROBERT WINTERNITZ

To begin with, don't think of the martini primarily as a beverage. Oh no. It is first of all a great character builder.

Are we pulling your hollow leg? Not a bit of it. Anyone who can withstand the belt of a brace of martinis, and repeat a couple of times, must have a strong character on top of a strong constitution. Otherwise he would land

    . . . in the arms of Morpheus
    . . . in the ash can
    . . . in flagrante delicto
    . . . in jail

The martini not only separates the men from the boys, but ordinary human beings from characters with copper-lined interiors. It marks the dividing line between bartenders with reverence for their calling, and converted soda jerks.

The martini is by all odds the most famous American alcoholic beverage, justly celebrated in song and story. Its fame has spread abroad. More people drink martinis in more English novels than any other kind.

Have you ever heard a Somerset Maugham character mention a manhattan or a side car or a julep or scotch on the rocks? Never, it's always a martini. Unfortunately, though the English fictioneers have discovered the martini, they have not learned how it should be made. They still *shake* their cocktails, a revolting practice long since abandoned even in the most dismal bistros.

Never speak disrespectfully of a martini, for the devotees of this tipple constitute a fanatical cult who know all the answers. They look upon anyone who does not know the leading gins and vermouths as the personification of a social error.

Above all the martini is a cocktail no one should ever take a double of. The distillers will hate you if you do. They admire to stay in business, suh, and the last thing they want is problem drinkers.

The worst of doubletons, however, is not their lethal voltage; it is the law of diminishing returns for those precious, pampered taste buds of yours. By the time you have sipped your way through the tandem size, your drink is tepid if not torpid. And that, dear boy, is the unforgivable sin. The authentic martini is the coldest drink in the world, served in a crystal-clear, frosted, super-chilled glass. Once a drink rises above the lowest potable temperature, it ceases to be a martini. So raise your right hand high as you can and promise never again to specify the twin-screw model.

What makes a martini so strong, asks the little lady in the front row? It's the alcohol in it, sis; not the olive or the slice of lemon, just the plain little old last year's alcohol. The joker is that you get more alcohol in a martini than in any other concoction listed in the bartenders' guide. There's no dilution from ice as in an old fashioned, nor from citrus fruit as in a daiquiri or a sour. Sure, the vermouth isn't as strong as the gin, but how much vermouth do you get? The manhattan, the nearest alcoholic competitor, with its 2 parts of liquor against 1 part of wine can never claim the voltage and joltage of the martini's 3½ to 1, all the way up to 7 to 1 (brrrrrrr).

When it comes to the emotional department, the world's foremost cocktail does an extra special job. No matter who you are, it will fill you full of some kind of love; almost any kind, such as

    . . . love for your neighbors and friends
    . . . love for your neighbor's wife
    . . . love for rassling and/or fisticuffs
    . . . love for nothing but more martinis
    . . . love for a nice, long nap

Do other drinks give you the same emotional surcharge? Yes, but they're not a pale patch compared to a martini.

Since you have only one stomach to give to your country, why not join the Scotch-and-branch-water fraternity? No one will stop you, laddie, but you will be missing the most exalted taste sensation of all: the first sip of a properly mixed, properly served martini, man's closest approach to civilization. If you don't feel that way about it there is only one thing for you to do: resign from the human race at once. You don't deserve to have your character lifted.

Recipes suggested by Gentry
for
GRACIOUS DINING
and prepared in collaboration with the chefs of la Toque Blanche, le Pavillon, le Cafe Chambord, the Colony and Jack and Charlie's "21".

Once in a while an occasion arises which demands exacting attention to the dinner menu — whether the occasion is a business or a family one — and then all but a very few hosts become aware of the limitations of their repertory of dishes suitable to offer guests.

With this in mind, and for the many lesser occasions when good eating is in order, Gentry's editors offer you a complete dinner. Each dish is the special offering of a famous restaurant, and their chefs have given their own personal recipe for its preparation.

MENU

Quiche Lorraine
(La Toque Blanche)

Hot Madrilène
(Le Pavillon)

Lobster des Gourmets
(Le Café Chambord)

Soufflé Potatoes   *French Green Peas*
(Le Pavillon)   (The Colony Restaurant)

Caesar Salad
(The Colony Restaurant)

Crêpes Soufflés "21"
Sauce Grand Marnier
(Jack and Charlie's "21")

WINE

Chilled White Burgundy
(suggested by Le Café Chambord)

FOR THE CHEFS' RECIPES FOR THIS MENU, TURN THE PAGE

The Dishes Comprising Gentry's Gracious Dinner, and how to make them . . .

Ernest Luthringshauser of la Toque Blanche

MENU

Quiche Lorraine

Hot Madrilène

Lobster des Gourmets

Soufflé Potatoes   *French Green Peas*

Caesar Salad

Crêpes Soufflés "21"
Sauce Grand Marnier

WINE

Chilled White Burgundy

Marcel Grangé of le Café Chambord

FROM LA TOQUE BLANCHE

Quiche Lorraine
(Egg, ham, and cheese pie)

5 eggs	½ lb. Swiss cheese
1 pt. heavy sweet cream	salt, pepper
½ lb. smoked ham	nutmeg

Roll out a good quality pie crust dough, and mold lightly into an 8 inch pie pan.

Beat the eggs well and season with salt, pepper and nutmeg to taste. Add to this the sweet cream. Shred the Swiss cheese and ham in thin pieces and mix together with the eggs and cream. Fold this mixture into the pie dough. Bake in a preheated oven at 350° for 45 minutes. Cut into wedges and serve hot. Serves eight to ten.

———

FROM LE PAVILLON

Hot Madrilène

5 qts. beef stock	1 diced celery stalk
2 lbs. very lean beef, ground	4 diced tomatoes
	chopped parsley
4 diced carrots	2 red peppers—diced
2 diced leek	4 oz. tomato paste
	6 egg whites

Assemble in sauce pan the meat, vegetables, and tomato paste along with egg whites, mixing well. Add beef stock, bring to a slow boil, stirring occasionally, and allow to simmer gently for 1½ hours. Pass through cheese cloth, season to taste. Serves ten.

———

FROM LE CAFE CHAMBORD

Lobster des Gourmets

8 1½-lb. lobsters	1 qt. dry white wine
14 oz. sweet butter	heavy sweet cream
4 tbs. chopped shallots	chopped herbs (tarragon,
4 oz. Pernod	chives, chervil, parsley)

Clean the lobsters, remove the green roe and set aside. Cut lobster in pieces and season with salt and pepper to taste. Heat a saute pan with 12 oz. of sweet butter. Cook the lobsters in this pan for 4 minutes. When the shells turn red, add the chopped shallots, and allow to simmer for a few minutes. Flambé the lobster with Pernod. Pour the wine into the pan, and reduce. (Simmer over a low flame until the wine almost evaporates.) Cover with heavy sweet cream. Cook for 15 minutes. Mix 2 oz. sweet butter with the roe and add to sauce. When ready to serve, sprinkle chopped herbs over it. When serving, you may again flambé with ¼ glass of Pernod. Serves eight.

———

FROM LE PAVILLON

Soufflé Potatoes

Using large Idaho potatoes peel to form oval shapes. Cut uniformly even slices ⅛ inches thick, wash in very cold water, dry in towel and place in deep hot fat. Turn heat high to make up for heat lost when potatoes were added. Keep heat high until potatoes are done, (When they reach the surface). Drain without shaking for a few seconds then plunge into more hot fat (much hotter than previously). This will cause the potatoes to puff up. Drain off well, spread on dry towel, salt lightly and serve.

FROM THE COLONY RESTAURANT

French Green Peas

1 qt. fresh green peas	4 oz. butter
1 heart of lettuce	1/3 oz. salt
parsley, chervil	2/3 oz. sugar
12 small onions	3 tbs. water

Mix together peas lettuce, herbs, onions, butter, salt and sugar. Add water, cover and cook gently. Add butter before serving.

FROM THE COLONY RESTAURANT

Caesar Salad

(The Colony recommends that the following recipe be made according to individual taste. There are no specific ingredient amounts.)

Using Romaine lettuce, mix some croutons of bread, grated Parmesan cheese, chopped anchovies, and slightly warmed egg with French dressing. French dressing is made with oil, vinegar, salt, pepper and a little mustard according to taste. Garlic may be used.

FROM JACK AND CHARLIE'S "21"

Crêpes Soufflés "21"

Crêpe Suzette Batter

8 tbs. plain flour (rounded)	2 egg yolks
2 whole eggs	4 tbs. oil
	8 tbs. milk
	½ tsp. salt

Beat all ingredients except milk with a whisk until smooth. Add milk until creamy consistency is achieved. Put into refrigerator for 10 minutes. Pour batter into a very hot pan spreading a thin layer over entire pan.

Be sure the pan is very hot. Rub butter over pan bottom with wax paper or a rag to help prevent batter from sticking. Pour excess batter with a quick movement back into bowl. Take rounded knife and lift edges up to prevent sticking. With spatula, execute a quick movement to turn over the pancake. Make the crêpes slightly brown and not more than 5 or 6 inches in diameter. Set aside 2 crêpes for each person, which is considered an average portion. This makes 16 to 20 medium size pancakes.

Filling

6 generous tbs. butter	1 cup sugar
3 tbs. flour	2 tsp. vanilla extract
2 cups milk	8 egg yolks beaten
6 pinches salt	10 egg whites beaten stiff

Melt butter in a saucepan and mix with the flour. Gradually add the milk and salt. Stir constantly. Add the sugar and vanilla extract. When sauce is thick and smooth, remove from fire. Add egg yolks and beat all ingredients well, folding in the egg whites. The sauce should be thick and smooth. Let ingredients cool.

Place enough stuffing in each of the crêpes and place them neatly in a semi-deep casserole in a flat pan with hot water. Put into an oven which has been heated to 400° F. Let this cook for 15 minutes, then reduce to 375° F. for an additional 20 to 25 minutes.

Sauce Grand Marnier

2 tsp. vanilla extract	2 cups heavy cream
2 cups milk	3 or 4 pinches salt
8 egg yolks	2 delmonico glasses
1½ cups sugar	Grand Marnier

Add vanilla to the milk and scald. Beat the egg yolks until light and add the sugar while beating. Add the heavy cream and gradually the scalded milk. Add the salt. Beat vigorously until ingredients are well blended. Cook over a pan of hot water. Then remove from fire and add the Grand Marnier. Mix again until well blended.

When crêpes are cooked, remove from oven. Sprinkle a generous helping of almonds or "amandines" over top and dust with powdered sugar. Flambé with a good quality of brandy and serve with sauce on the side. Serve immediately since the crêpes have a tendency to deflate when cooled. Serves eight.

Yves L. Ploneis of Jack and Charlie's "21"

FOR GENTRY'S

FALL REFRESHERS

PLEASE TURN

THE PAGE

GENTRY FALL REFRESHERS

Any good barman will tell you that most men prefer to stay with their Scotch, Bourbon, or whatever else personal habit dictates. But there comes a time when the guests have gotten too accustomed to the usual routine and circumstances demand a change of pace. Here is what some top experts suggest:

COLONEL SERGE OBOLENSKY,
VICE CHAIRMAN OF
THE BOARD OF DIRECTORS,
AMBASSADOR HOTEL

The Exterminator

1/2 oz. dry Sherry
2 oz. Vodka 80 Proof

Pour over cracked ice, stir and strain. Pour into well chilled cocktail glass and serve with a twist of lemon peel.

Colonel Obolensky suggests fresh salted cucumbers to serve with this cocktail. Wash and cut into wedges cold small fresh cucumbers. Do not remove the cucumber skin. Salt and eat with the Exterminator.

VICTOR FERASIN, HEAD BARTENDER
THE SHERRY-NETHERLAND HOTEL

Orgeat Sour

1 oz. Orgeat Syrup
Juice of one lime or lemon
2 oz. Rye
2 drops Peychaud's Bitters

Pour over cracked ice. Shake well and strain into sour glass. Add 1 slice of orange, a maraschino cherry, and a squirt of seltzer on top.

Pompier Special

1/2 oz. Creme de Cassis
2 oz. French Vermouth
1 oz. Gin

Stir in stem glass with cube ice. Fill the rest of stem glass with seltzer.

SALVATORE BERTOCCI
HEAD BARMAN,
THE SAVOY PLAZA

Buckingham Cocktail

2 oz. Gin
1 dash of Scotch

Pour over cracked ice, stir and strain into well chilled cocktail glass.

Champagne Fraisette
Savoy Plaza

To be served in a thirty-ounce crystal stem glass.

Place in glass 7 or 8 ice cubes of even dimension. Pour on ice:

3/4 oz. Cointreau
3/4 oz. Cognac
8 medium size strawberries
1 split French Champagne

Insert spoon and serve immediately.

OSCAR HAIMO, MAITRE DE BAR,
THE HOTEL PIERRE

Fall Prize Winner

3/4 oz. Dry Vermouth
2 oz. Rye
3 Dashes Cordial Médoc

Pour over cracked ice, stir and strain. Decorate with twist of lemon peel, serve in chilled cocktail glass.

The Oscar Haimo

1-1/2 oz. Scotch
2 dashes Van Der Hum
Twist of lemon peel

Serve on the rocks.

EDWARD WARD, HEAD BARTENDER
THE PLAZA HOTEL

Paradise Cocktail

1/3 part Gin
1/3 part apricot Brandy
1/3 lemon juice

Shake well, strain and serve.

to aid and abate your hearty summer appetite

james beard
offers a man's primer on how to

grill *and* broil

the steer

the lamb

the chicken

the pig

the fish

and the dog

to which is added an important memorandum on
drinks
for summer days and summer nights

grilling and broiling beef

steak

Beefsteak is probably the most popular meat in America, and certainly there is nothing more hearty or satisfying than a good big steak, thick and juicy, and sizzling hot right from the grill.

Good beef is a cherry-red color when fresh, and of a purplish hue when well aged. The flesh of steaks should be well marbled with fat, and edged with firm, flaky fat that is creamy colored. The top grade is stamped U. S. Prime on the untrimmed cuts, and the next best grade is stamped U. S. Choice. Some packers have their own names for various grades, such as Swift's Premium and Armour's Star.

You won't generally find aged beef in a supermarket where the turnover is large and attention to individual customers is small. Particularly when it comes to steaks, you'll do well to patronize a butcher who takes pride in handling choice meat and will advise you honestly. Order your extra-special steaks well in advance and get properly aged steak, which is tenderer than strictly fresh meat and has a touch of gamey flavor.

porterhouse

This is the steak with the cross-shaped bone in the middle, the filet on one side of the bone and the contra-filet on the other. It is probably the choicest cut of steak. For outdoor cooking, order it cut extra-thick—1½ to 3 inches.

sirloin

This is a fine cut from lower down on the loin. It is excellent eating and economical for a large group. Have it cut not less than 1½ inches thick. In England and France this cut is preferred for roasting, being considered far better than the rib cut generally used in this country.

rib steaks

These are called *entrecots* by the French and considered a delicacy. They are best when cut from the first three ribs. Have them cut with or without the bone, as you choose.

mexican hamburgers

To 1 pound of hamburger add 1 small green pepper and 1 onion, both chopped, 1 tablespoon chili powder, 1 tablespoon of chili sauce, and salt and pepper to taste. Mix well, form into cakes, and cook as detailed above.

VARIATION: Serve plain hamburgers with chili con carne.

filet

This is really the tenderest part of the tenderloin. If you are serving several people, it is best to buy the whole tenderloin and either cut it yourself into individual steaks or cook it whole. Or you can put part of it into steaks and spit and roast the rest. You will find it cheaper per pound when you buy it in a whole piece.

other cuts

Some of the less expensive grades of steak, such as top round and rump, as well as short ribs, may be broiled if they are first marinated.

To cook chunks of beef on skewers, the best choice is sirloin, though the cheaper cuts may be used if marinated to make them tender. Buy beef for this purpose by the piece and cut it into cubes yourself; it is more economical.

barbecued steak

Make a paste of 2 to 3 teaspoons of dry mustard, salt to taste, and enough Bourbon or other whiskey to moisten. Spread this on the steak and let it stand for ½ hour. Broil as usual.

minute steak

Minute steaks are thin slices cut from the loin or sirloin. They should not be over ½-inch thick. They must be pan-broiled or sautéed. Be sure the pan is sizzling hot, grease it lightly with butter or fat, pop in the steaks and cook quickly—about a minute to a side. Season to taste and serve.

A

hamburger cheese sandwich

Arrange two thin patties of hamburger sandwich-fashion with blue cheese spread between. Wrap with strip of bacon around the rim, secure with toothpicks, and broil until the bacon is really crisp and the cheese starts to ooze.

corned beefburgers

Here's a tasty change from the usual hamburger fare. Use a good brand of canned corned beef hash or—much better—make your own mixture. To 4 cups of chopped corned beef add 2 cups of cubed, lightly boiled potatoes, freshly ground black pepper to taste, 1 or 2 onions chopped, and a pinch of nutmeg. Mix well and form into patties. Brush with melted butter and grill over hot coals or in a hot skillet. Cook slowly until the patties are crusty and brown on the outside. Serve with poached eggs and a tart sauce, such as a chili sauce.

VARIATION: To the corned beef mixture add 4 tablespoons of chili sauce and 1 green pepper chopped very fine. Mix well, form into patties, brush with butter and grill.

plain hamburger

Have your coals or fire glowing hot. Grill the patties, searing them quickly on both sides, and cook them until they are crusty on the outside and still juicy and pink in the center. Turn often, seasoning with salt and freshly ground black pepper on both sides.

If you prefer to pan-broil your hamburgers, grease the pan very lightly with butter, or cook them in a dry skillet that has been well sprinkled with salt. Have the pan sizzling hot, sear the meat quickly on both sides and then cook until just done to your taste.

herbed hamburgers

To 1 pound of hamburger add ¼ cup each of chopped chives and parsley, 2 teaspoons of dried rosemary, 1 egg, and salt and freshly ground black pepper. Mix well and form into cakes. Cook as above.

cheesed hamburgers

To 1 pound of hamburger add 1 small onion finely chopped, 1 tablespoon of Worcestershire sauce, ½ cup of grated sharp cheddar cheese, and pepper to taste. Mix well, form into cakes, and broil.

marinated steak

You can broil the less tender cuts, such as top round steak, with delicious results by first marinating the meat. Mix 1 cup of olive oil, and juice of 1 lemon, 1 crushed clove of garlic, a dash of salt, and 1 teaspoon of freshly ground black pepper. Pour this over the steak, turn several times to be sure it is evenly coated, and let stand in a warm place for several hours or overnight. Grill as usual, omitting any further seasoning.

shell steaks

The porterhouse that is left when the filet has been removed. They are the best choice if you want to serve individual steaks.

hamburgers

The secret of making excellent hamburgers is to be sure you have good meat, freshly ground. Select a whole piece of meat—top round, rump, and sirloin are good choices—allow about ¾ pound per person and have it ground to order. It should be coarsely ground, and put through the grinder only once. When you are ready to grill the hamburgers, shape the meat into good-sized patties about 1½ inches thick. Don't knead and mold the meat in your hands—simply pat it gently into shape. This will give you a juicier, more flavorful and plumper hamburger.

hamburger and eggplant

You will need 2 rather thin slices of eggplant for each serving. Dredge them in seasoned flour and grill them lightly, just until they are brown and tender. Keep them hot. To 1 pound of hamburger add 1 small onion grated and 1 smallish clove of garlic grated. Season to taste with salt and freshly ground black pepper. Form into patties about the size of the eggplant slices and fairly thin—½- to ¾-inch thick. Grill quickly. Serve each hamburger patty sandwiched between two eggplant slices, with your favorite barbecue or tomato sauce poured over each serving.

B

grilling and broiling **lamb**

steak

There is a great difference between real spring lamb and yearling lamb. The latter more nearly resembles good mutton. True spring lamb is hard to find in some parts of the country. Check with your butcher and see what he can do for you.

Lamb steak is cut from the leg. It should be about 1 inch thick. If good mutton is available in your neighborhood, it's even better for steak. Grill slowly, turning often, and season to taste just before serving. Be sure to serve it on piping-hot plates. If you like the flavor of tarragon, sprinkle a little on the steaks as they grill. Or press rosemary into both sides of the steak and grill.

For lamb steaks, you may have to buy a whole leg of lamb and ask your butcher to cut you some slices off the meaty end. (You can use the shank end to braise with lentils for another meal.) You should get 4 to 5 good sized steaks from the average leg. If this seems too extravagant, have a shoulder of lamb boned and rolled and then cut into slices for steaks.

Mutton may be treated in the same way, but be sure to cut away the excess fat that comes on it.

lamb and curry marinade

Crush a clove of garlic, add 1 tablespoon of curry powder, a bit of ginger and ¾ cup of soy sauce. Marinate the steaks in this for 1 hour before grilling.

chops

When buying lamb chops for the outdoor grill or other broiling unit, be sure to get good-sized, thick—2 to 3 inches—loin chops. Rib chops can be grilled if they are thick, but are not as tasty as the loin cut. Good thick chops are grilled over a hot fire in the same way you grill steak. They will be far juicier and better flavored if they're cooked just until they are crusty brown on the outside but still rare in the center. Season to taste and serve on hot plates. The hot plate is especially important with lamb, as its grease is distasteful if cold. Serve big thick chops.

mutton chops

If those big English-style mutton chops are available in your neighborhood, by all means serve them instead of the usual lamb. They are delicious and hearty—a natural for the outdoor grill. They should be a good 2 to 3 inches thick, and are extra delicious with the kidney skewered inside, and bacon wrapped around the outside. First trim off the excess fat—they generally come with quite a bit—and grill as you would lamb chops. As with lamb, you will have a better dish if you serve them on the rare side. Hot plates again and a big baked potato with plenty of butter.

breast of lamb

Breast of lamb makes a delicious dish if prepared in much the same way as pork spareribs (see following). Select as lean a piece as you can find, as this cut of lamb tends to be fatty. Marinate in your favorite barbecue sauce (use one with plenty of garlic, which does things for lamb) for 2 to 3 hours. Broil as you would spareribs, basting frequently to keep meat moist.

grilling and broiling **fowl**

chicken sauté with chile

Dredge the chicken pieces in flour. Sauté until brown in hot grease. Season to taste with salt and pepper, add a dash of cayenne, a crushed clove of garlic and 1 onion chopped. Cover and simmer for a few minutes. Add ¾ cup of tomato purée, 2 teaspoons of chili powder and a pinch of dried basil. Cover again and simmer until the chicken is tender. Remove the chicken pieces to a hot platter, thin the sauce down a little with dry red wine and pour it over the chicken pieces and serve.

C

broiled chicken

When serving broiled chicken, allow at least ½ broiler per person. Select small birds with plenty of meat on them. Have the butcher split and clean them, and remove the backbone and neck. The broiler halves will then lie flat and cook more evenly. For each half broiler, melt 2 tablespoons of butter, add a scant teaspoon of paprika and salt and pepper to taste. Brush this all over the chicken. Arrange the chicken halves on the grill, flesh side to the flame, and about 4 inches from the heat. Let them cook on this side for about 10 to 15 minutes. Brush with more melted butter and turn. Watch them carefully after turning to be sure the skin side does not become charred and black. Turn several times toward the end to get an even browning and brush liberally with melted butter. Be sure not to overcook or your broilers will be dry and tasteless. Test for doneness with a sharp fork at the thigh joint. If the juice still runs pink the chicken needs a little more cooking. If it is colorless, the bird is done.

marinated broilers

Make a marinade with 2 parts olive oil to 1 part dry white wine. Add 1 chopped onion, 1 crushed clove of garlic, tarragon and salt and pepper to taste. Soak the broilers in this mixture for 2 to 3 hours. Broil the chicken as above, basting with the sauce during cooking.

chicken sauté with wine

Do not sprinkle chicken pieces with flour. Merely brown them in hot grease. When all the pieces are browned, season to taste with salt and pepper, and sprinkle with dried tarragon and chopped chives. Pour ½ cup of dry white wine over the chicken, place a cover on the pan and let it simmer until the chicken is tender. Serve on hot platter.

barbecued broilers

Soak broilers in a good barbecue sauce for 2 to 3 hours, making sure to turn them often. Broil, basting frequently with the sauce during the cooking process.

old-fashioned fried chicken

Have the fryers cut into serving-size pieces. Dredge each piece with flour. Heat fat or oil in a large skillet. You will need plenty of fat, about 1 to 1½ inches in depth. (A good idea is to fry several rashers of bacon, set the bacon aside to keep warm and use the bacon fat to fry the chicken. Then garnish the platter with the bacon.) Have the fat hot but not boiling. Brown each piece of chicken thoroughly. Season to taste, cover and simmer until done. This should take 20 to 30 minutes. When the chicken is tender, remove it to a hot platter. Skim off all but about 4 tablespoons of fat. Add 3 or 4 tablespoons of flour, blending it in and stirring all around the bottom and sides of the pan to scrape up any pieces of meat or skin that are sticking there. Slowly add a pint of half milk and half cream, stirring constantly until smooth and thickened. Taste for seasoning and serve sauce separately in a gravy boat.

broiled turkey

In recent years, American turkey growers have developed a small but meaty bird which is very popular with families who hate to be faced with leftovers. These young, tender birds make excellent eating broiled. Select a plump 4- to 5-pound turkey and have it split and prepared for broiling as you would a chicken. Melt at least ¾ cup of butter, add a squeeze or two of lemon juice, some paprika and 2 or 3 teaspoons of dried tarragon. Brush the turkey thoroughly with this mixture. Place it on a hot grill, flesh side toward the flame and about 4 inches away from the heat. Cook it for 15 minutes and turn, seasoning and brushing again with melted butter. Cook it on the skin side for a good 10 minutes and then turn again. Continue turning and basting every four or five minutes until the meat is tender but not dry. Test for doneness by thrusting a sharp fork in at the thigh joint. If the juice runs pink, the turkey needs more cooking. If it is colorless and the joint pulls away easily, the turkey is done and ready to serve.

marinated grilled duckling

Carefully skin the duck and cut in quarters. Then cut the wings off, so that the four pieces will be equally thick. Place the pieces of duck in a bowl and sprinkle with the following: 2 teaspoons of lemon juice, 1 teaspoon of Kitchen Bouquet, ½ teaspoon of salt, ¼ teaspoon of onion salt and ½ teaspoon of ginger. Toss the duck gently to coat it evenly. Let it marinate for 30 minutes to soak up the seasonings. Then place the pieces on a broiling rack 15 to 18 inches above glowing coals, or beneath your electric or gas unit, at moderate heat. Cook for 15 minutes and turn. Continue cooking 15 minutes longer.

D

grilling and broiling pork

marinated pork steak

1. Chop a large onion very fine, add ½ to ¾ cup of soy sauce, a bit of chopped fresh ginger and a dash of whiskey. Let the steaks stand in this marinade for several hours before cooking. Turn them often. Pan-broil as above, or grill them over slow heat, turning often and basting with the marinade.

2. Crush a clove of garlic, add ½ to ¾ cup of soy sauce and a teaspoon of dry mustard. Proceed as detailed above.

3. To 3 tablespoons of sesame seeds add 2 tablespoons of olive oil, 1 tablespoon of chili powder and ¾ cup of tomato juice. Salt to taste. Proceed as above.

pork steak

Pork steaks are usually cut from the leg and should be about ½- to ¾-inch thick. If you wish to grill them, they should first be marinated, otherwise they will become stringy. Plain pork steak is best pan-broiled.

Grease the pan lightly with a little of the fat off the pork. Season the steaks with salt, freshly ground black pepper and any one of the following herbs—thyme, basil, oregano. Brown them slowly on one side and then turn to brown on the other. Continue cooking until the meat is thoroughly done. Slices of onion may be browned in the pork fat and served with the steaks. Or core tart apples, leaving the skin on, and cut them in slices right through. Brown in the pork fat.

barbecued spareribs

Buy a good pound of spareribs for each serving and a few extra for the pot. Have them cut in long thin strips if you intend to lace them on a spit, otherwise leave them in whole slabs. Put them in a pot with an onion stuck with 2 cloves, a bay leaf and a couple of cloves of garlic. Add 1 teaspoon of salt for each 2 pounds of ribs and barely cover them with water. Bring to a boil, lower the heat and simmer for a little less than an hour, or until ribs are nearly, but not quite, done. Remove the ribs to a flat pan and cool.

Prepare a sauce with 2 cloves of garlic grated, ½ cup of soy sauce, ½ cup of white wine or sherry, 4 tablespoons of grated fresh ginger and ½ cup of honey. Brush the ribs well with this mixture and let them stand for an hour or two. Broil them over charcoal and brush them once or twice during the cooking with more sauce. They should take about 15 minutes to finish cooking and get a good glaze. SAUCE VARIATION: To ½ cup of tomato sauce or catsup, add ½ cup of soy sauce, 2 cloves of grated garlic, 1 tablespoon of chili powder, ½ teaspoon of rosemary powder, and salt and pepper to taste.

grilled pigs' feet

This unusual dish is simple to prepare at the last minute if the pigs' feet have already been cooked and stored in the refrigerator. When you shop for pigs' feet, look for the long ones. They are not always easy to find. (In New York you can buy them in Chinatown.) Allow one per serving.

Wrap each pigs' foot in cotton material and tie securely, to keep the skin from breaking during the long cooking process. Put them in a large kettle with 2 cloves of garlic, an onion stuck with cloves, a bay leaf, salt, a little vinegar and water to cover. Bring it to a boil, turn down the heat and let the kettle simmer for about 5 hours. Remove the pigs' feet, unwrap them and put them in a bowl. Pour the broth over them and let them chill.

When you are ready to grill them, dip each one in beaten egg and then roll in crumbs. Grill over charcoal until nicely browned and crusty and heated through. Serve with a devil sauce, fried potatoes and watercress without dressing. You'll find this a delicious dish.

ham steak

Old-fashioned smoked ham gives you the best ham steaks. Have them cut ¾- to 1-inch thick. Don't cook ham steak too fast, as the slower cooking makes it tender and brings out the smoky flavor. Grill the steaks over hot coals until they are brown on the outside and the fat is crisp. Serve with eggs— fried or scrambled.

E

grilling
and
broiling
fish

pan-fried fish

Small fish are excellent pan-fried or sautéed. Clean them, roll them in flour and pop them into a skillet with plenty of bubbling butter. (Remember to mix a little oil in with the butter.) Or you can use bacon fat. Cook the fish gently over a medium heat until they are brown, turn them gently, season with salt and pepper, and brown on the other side. Test for doneness with a fork. Serve with lemon and melted butter.

VARIATIONS:

1. When the fish is done, remove it to a hot platter. Add a handful of chopped parsley to the pan and a lump of butter. Boil it up and pour over the fish. Serve with lemon wedges.
2. Remove the fish to a hot platter and add half chopped parsley and half chopped chives to the pan with the butter. Proceed as above.
3. Remove the fish to a hot platter and add the parsley and butter and ¼ cup of dry white wine to the pan and proceed as above.
4. Fry 4 or 5 strips of bacon in the skillet. When it is crisp remove the bacon, pour off some of the fat and use the amount necessary to pan-fry the fish. Serve the fish garnished with the bacon crumbled into small pieces.

lobster

Broiled lobster is an ever-popular dish along the Atlantic seaboard. It is an easy dish to prepare at an outdoor grill. The most important item besides the lobster is a good sharp kitchen knife or, better yet, a cleaver. Hold the lobster belly-downward (it must be a live lobster, of course), and kill it with a jab of the knife at the base of its head. Turn over and cut down the middle from the head to the tail, using a heavy knife and hammering it if necessary to cut through the shell. Split the lobster right through the back, shell and all, leaving it in two halves. Take out the dark vein running through the middle, the spongy matter (the lungs) and stomach. The green liver and the coral, if any, are good eating.

Brush the lobster halves on the flesh side with plenty of melted butter and season to taste with salt and pepper. Place them flesh side to the flame, about 4 inches from the heat, and broil. Small lobsters take a little more than 12 minutes, large ones about 18 minutes. Serve with small bowl of melted butter and lemon wedges.

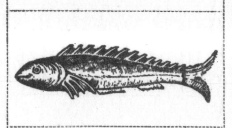

lobster with herbs

Half-way through the broiling process sprinkle the lobster flesh with chopped parsley and chives.

rock-lobster tails

If live lobster is not available in your neighborhood, you can broil the frozen South African lobster tails—actually a crayfish—in the same way as a split live lobster.

grilling
and
broiling
franks

frankfurters

Try some of the following suggestions for sprucing up the popular but too-well-known hot dog.

1. Cut a deep slit in one side of each frankfurter, insert some sharp cheddar cheese, and wrap the frankfurter with a strip of bacon to hold it together. Fasten with a toothpick, and grill.
2. Pan-grill thick slices of beefsteak tomatoes, grill frankfurters and serve each one on top of a tomato slice.
3. Heat frankfurters or knockwurst over hot coals. Cut them into bite-size pieces, insert a toothpick in each one, and serve with a large bowl of hot barbecue sauce for guests to dunk their portions into. This is good as a hot snack with all types of cocktails.
4. Mix up your favorite biscuit or bread dough. Roll it out about ½-inch thick. Cut it in strips as wide as the length of the frankfurters and long enough to go around once and lap over. Roll each frank in a piece of the dough, arrange these on a greased baking sheet and bake in a moderate oven until the dough is cooked through.
5. French fashion: Spread a French roll with garlic butter to which you have added some chopped chives and parsley, add a grilled frankfurter and a slice of cheese. Wrap the whole thing in a piece of foil and heat until the cheese melts. Have a bowl of hot barbecue sauce for everyone to dunk his serving in.

F

summer drinks

bloody mary

A fine pick-up for the morning after, a delightful drink before lunch or dinner.

For each drink, use 2 ounces of vodka, 3 ounces of tomato juice, juice of 1 lemon, a dash of Worcestershire sauce, a dash of Tabasco, and a pinch of salt. Shake the ingredients together in a shaker with cracked ice. Strain into a large cocktail glass and dust with paprika or celery salt.

golden screw

For each drink, use 2 ounces of vodka and 3 ounces of orange juice.

Shake together with cracked ice. Strain into a chilled glass. This is an excellent accompaniment for Sunday morning brunch.

hawaiian cooler

For each drink, use 2 ounces of vodka, 2 ounces of pineapple juice, and the juice of ½ lime. Shake together with cracked ice and strain into chilled glasses.

martini and gibson

The Martini and the Gibson are good in all seasons of the year, and are probably the most popular American cocktails.

For each drink, use 2 ounces of gin or vodka, ¼ to ½ ounce of dry vermouth, and plenty of ice. Stir vigorously with a spoon until thoroughly chilled and blended. Strain into a chilled glass. For a Gibson, add a cocktail onion; for a Martini, a twist of lemon peel or an olive.

If you are going out into the country or to the beach to have your outdoor meal, mix your Martinis or Gibsons, chill well and carry them in a thermos jug. Leave in very little, if any, ice—to avoid diluting the mixture.

vodka or gin and tonic

Summer drinks with quinine water have had quite a vogue lately. Try several different brands of tonic water to decide which one you like, as they vary considerably in flavor. For each drink, use 2 ounces of gin or vodka, cracked ice, a slice of lemon or lime, and tonic water to taste. Pour the gin or vodka into a tall glass filled with cracked ice or ice cubes. Add the slice of lemon or lime and pour in tonic water to taste. Mix with a swizzle stick.

tom collins

The Collins can be made with almost any liquor. For each drink, use 3 ounces of gin, vodka, rum, or whiskey, juice of 1 lime or 1 lemon, ½ teaspoon of sugar or more, to taste.

Put the ingredients into a shaker with cracked ice and shake vigorously. Pour, ice and all, into a tall chilled glass. Add a splash or so of soda, garnish with a slice of lemon or lime.

planter's punch

For each drink, use 3 ounces of Jamaica rum, 1 ounce of lime juice, 1 teaspoon of sugar or sugar syrup. Pour into a 12-ounce glass filled with ice, add a dash of Angostura bitters and a little water to taste.

dark rum cocktail

For a large group, use 1 fifth of Jamaica rum, 1 cup of lime juice, ½ cup of honey or maple syrup. Blend these ingredients thoroughly and taste to see if you need any more sweetening or any additional lime juice. Pour into cocktail glasses filled to the top with finely crushed ice.

This cocktail can be made in large quantities ahead of time and kept in a pitcher or jug. Simply pour it into the ice-filled glasses as needed.

whiskey sour

For each drink, use 2 ounces of whiskey (Bourbon, rye or a blend), juice of 1 lemon, sugar to taste (¼ to 1 teaspoon). Put in a shaker with cracked ice and shake well. Strain into a whiskey sour or cocktail glass, add a squirt of soda and a slice of lemon or a half slice of orange, and a maraschino cherry.

Make sours of rum, gin or vodka in the same way.

white wine cassis

Crème de Cassis is a syrup made from black currants and it goes very well in summer drinks. To a good glass of well chilled white wine add 1 tablespoon Crème de Cassis, or more to taste.

G

THE FINE ART OF DRINKING

"I am consoled for not having lived ninety years back;"
Dr. Johnson once said to a convivial friend, "in fact, for
not having lived in any period but the present. And the
consolation for having renounced all the glories of the
past is, simply, one glass of your ancestral wine."

Perhaps this is an overstatement. To by-pass all ancient charms, to forego the bacchanals and saturnalias and the sound of soft Hellenic idylls quaintly chanted over cups of Chian and Pramnian, is sacrifice indeed — given a choice in the matter. But Johnson's intent is clear: fine wine is an end in itself, a private world, a potable portal to portable dreams.

Wine is more than an alcoholic beverage. It is a living organism. It grows, breathes, matures; and, like a woman, has its youth, its triumphal years, and its dowager dignity. Again, wines unfavored by fortune seldom develop virtues; when the vintage is poor, the spirit is lacking. Yet wines at their best have much in common with the grand beauties of history and legend, the Diane de Poitiers, the Lady Hamiltons, the finely drawn nymphs of Fragonard and Boucher. They create subtleties of emotion, flashing webs of imagery, a singing in the sails that is not of the wind.

Wine is a creation whose virtues are not grasped at first tasting. In fact, the reverse is true; the initiation is apt to be disappointing, an experience which has its parallel in other places. Excellences of this kind are savored only after experience and sophistication. It is necessary, it seems, to bring sensitivity, and an element of æsthetic maturity to the art of drinking. As with painting, music and the hunting of Snarks, appreciation of distinction hinges on knowing *what* to look for — as well as *when* to look for it, and *where,* and *how.*

A few examples will make this clear. Newcomers to the arts look for all-over impressions, not design and detail . . . which alone convey fine imagery. Musically naive people prefer brass to strings and fortissimo to tonal design. They miss entirely the small inventions, the delicacy of line, and the melodic program which contribute the essential greatness to the pattern and which communicate a variegated round of pleasure to the knowing listener. And so with wines. The average American's first preferences in wine will run to types overpoweringly sweet . . . Muscatel, Sauternes, Barsac, Haut Sauternes. Or, at best, Champagne, whose cost appeals to his sense of conspicuous waste, and whose sparkle bears a comfortable resemblance to ginger ale.

Compare, if you will, his reaction to a great Claret, such as Chateau Margaux. Here there is no sweetness; the flavor is inclined to be tart, to pucker the tongue. The novice wrinkles his nose, empties the glass at a single draught, and hopes that, in reward for his silence, the gods will make him speedily drunk.

But Clarets do not speak under these conditions. No more would you expect pleasantness from a Beethoven quartet played in rush hour on the subway shuttle between Times Square and Grand Central.

Fine Clarets and Burgundies are distinguished by extreme subtleties of fragrance and flavor. They must be served in prime condition, at the proper temperature, and in combination with a kind of food which harmonizes with their tonal pattern. Spiced food or acid salad dressing, for example, will drown out both bouquet and overtones of flavor. Smoking, while drinking, kills the wine's fragrance, and, to a marked extent, desensitizes the palate. Almonds, roquefort cheese, and certain other foods, on the other hand, enhance the quality of the wine, accenting the intangibles.

"Wine is the king of liquids," said the celebrated epicure, Brillat-Savarin, "and it carries exaltation of the palate to the furthest degree. "As long as the wine is retained in the mouth one has an agreeable but not complete perception of its flavor. It is only at the moment that one ceases to swallow that one can really taste, appraise and appreciate the quality peculiar to each kind of wine. A short interval is necessary before the gourmet can say, *It is good!* or *passable!* or *bad!;* *By Jove, it's Chambertin!* or *Good Lord, it's Suresnes!*

Now, about mixed drinks. In spite of a lot of nonsense that has been written on the subject, mixed drinks and fine wines are not incompatible. Each has its own function, place and special requirements. If both are to be served in the course of an evening's entertainment, it is well to see to it that a reasonable interval separates them. If cocktails are served before dinner, let at least half an hour pass between the last cocktail and the first wine. It is also a good practice to serve, in the interim, food that will neutralize the strong or sweetish flavor of the cocktails; almonds or other nuts or cheese canapés are perhaps best for this purpose.

A second point to keep in mind is timing. A good evening, in gourmet terms, is an evening in which alcohol works its civilizing effects slowly and magically, with no sharp peaks and no sudden drops. Too strong drinks served too quickly defeat their purpose: they give everyone a sudden lift, then drop them, an hour later, sodden, depressed and sleepy.

Civilized drinking calls for mild, pleasant drinks, each leading to the next in piquancy, flavor and effect, building slowly to a grand climax . . . shortly before departure time. *Result: a pleasant sense of elation deftly sustained;* an undimmed awareness of distinctions and quality; and a continued pageant of pleasantness and charm.

The Wines of France

The education of an epicure consists, in a large measure, of a grasp of the subtleties and classifications of French wines. *Le fin gourmet,* it has been said, knows not only flavor distinctions of each French vintage and vintage year, but even the first names of the men who tread the grapes.

The most that can be done in this condensed space is to arrange and discuss the main French wines by types and sub-types. The following generalities will contribute a basic orientation.

There are two major wine-producing regions of France . . . Bordeaux and Burgundy. Most of the wines prized in history have been grown in one of these regions. Bordeaux red wines, which are invariably dry, are *Clarets,* a term which refers specifically to the red wines of Médoc, Saint-Emilion and Pomerol. The four greatest names in Clarets, and by some considered the greatest of all wines, are:

CHATEAU MARGAUX

CHATEAU HAUT-BRION

CHATEAU LAFITTE-ROTHSCHILD

CHATEAU LATOUR

Bordeaux white wines vary from moderately dry to extremely sweet. The regional types are roughly as follows:

GRAVES	*moderately dry*
BARSAC	*moderately sweet*
SAUTERNES	*sweet*
HAUT SAUTERNES	*extremely sweet*

Graves are dry enough to be served with fish, but they are not as dry as white Burgundies, Rhine or Moselle wines. Sauternes are far too sweet to be taken in quantity. They are sweet because of the laborious methods by which they are made, being pressed from special bunches of grapes which are left on the vine until evaporation has concentrated their sugar content. Haut Sauternes are made from the most shrunken of the late-picked grapes. They are naturally more expensive than other wines because of the additional quantity of grapes required to produce a given unit of juice. The most famous of all Haut Sauternes is Château Yquem.

BURGUNDY

Burgundy is stronger, heavier in body, richer than Bordeaux. It is sometimes called the wine of kings and the king of wines. Unlike Bordeaux wines, Burgundies are never château-bottled. To know Burgundies, it is necessary to be familiar with the names of all the major communes and vineyards, and this is no inconsiderable undertaking. Among the more famous commune names in red Burgundies are:

GEVREY-CHAMBERTIN	POMMARD
VOUGEOT	VOLNAY
NUITS-ST. GEORGE	PULIGNY-
ALOXE-CORTON	MONTRACHET
BEAUNE	VOSNE-ROMANEE

Commune name is no guarantee of vineyard quality. There are superior and inferior vineyards in every commune. Only experience can teach the wine-taster the fine points of Burgundies.

Virtually all of the subdivisions of the Burgundy wine region produce white wines of distinction and character. The most famous of the white Burgundy are the following types, each represented by a number of noteworthy vineyards:

CHABLIS	PULIGNY-MONTRACHET
MEURSAULT	POUILLY
CHASSAGNE-MONTRACHET	

Sparkling Burgundy. The Burgundy region utilizes the Champagne process to produce a type of sparkling wine not altogether unlike Champagne. White, rose and red wines are variously bottled as Sparkling Burgundy.

Champagne . . . *wine of romance*

Champagne is the most festive of all wines, and the one wine traditionally associated with gaiety and high charm.

Its invention, if invention it was, is attributed to a certain Dom Pérignon, one-time cellarer at the Benedictine Abbey of Hautvillers, a spot lying in France somewhere between Ay and Epernay. The good Dom somehow capitalized on a peculiar phenomenon of nature — the fact that if sugar is added to wine after its fermentation has been completed, and the wine then sealed tightly in bottles, a second fermentation occurs within the bottle. Result: natural carbonization, fizz and sparkle. The Dom, it might be added, is also credited, incorrectly, with the invention of the bottle cork.

Champagne, unlike other French wines, is seldom the product of a single vineyard. It is almost invariably a composite of wines produced in the many vineyards of the official Champagne district of France.

NOTE ON AMERICAN CHAMPAGNE

In spite of the traditional reputation of French Champagne, it is to be observed that Champagne of extraordinary quality and delicacy is produced in this country, particularly in the vineyards of upper New York and California.

Dosing. All Champagne, up to the time of shipment, is *vin brut,* that is, natural, dry wine But it so happens that few Champagne drinkers like a natural wine; the markets of the world demand Champagne in varying degrees of sweetness. A syrup composed of pure cane sugar dissolved in old wine is added to each bottle in doses automatically measured to the Champagne type to be produced. Each bottle, after dosing, is re-corked, re-wired and labeled. Only the most delicate wines can be shipped as *brut,* or natural.

Label Types. There is considerable latitude in the meaning of relative sweetness labels as used by various shippers. In general, however, they can be interpreted as follows:

Brut	Extremely dry	.5 to 1.5% sweetening
Extra Sec	Medium dry	1.5 to 3% sweetening
Sec	Medium sweet	5 to 7% sweetening
Demi Sec	Sweet	5 to 7% sweetening
Doux	Extremely sweet	7% or more sweetening

On Modern Ways of Serving Wines . . .
and a few hints
for added convenience

ALL DRY WHITE WINES should be chilled.
Tradition calls for *cellar temperature.* Translate this as about a half hour in the refrigerator.

SWEET WHITE WINES are traditionally served at room temperature.
You will find, however, that chilling is much more to the American taste. Chilling will take the cloying effect out of the sweetness.

IF SEVERAL WINES are served during a meal, the sequence should ascend in order of strength and body. Light wines should come before heavy wines, white before red, dry before sweet.

SPARKLING WINES should be served thoroughly chilled. Proper service calls for the use of a wine bucket. In the era of the ice cube, however, it is not usually practicable to garner enough cubes to fill a bucket. Best procedure is to count on the refrigerator for the actual chilling; use the bucket only as an extra fillip.

DO NOT CHILL a dry red wine, Port or Sherry.

NEVER UNDER ANY provocation put ice in the wine itself. The only exceptions are *spritzes* (wine and soda) and special long drinks.

THE BOUQUET OF A CLARET or Burgundy is improved if the bottle is uncorked about an hour before serving.

OLD RED WINES (containing sediment) should be handled gently. The bottle should not be shaken for at least one day before serving. After uncorking, the wine should be decanted or served from a *cradle.*

IN OPENING CHAMPAGNE, it is customary to wrap a napkin around the bottle as a precautionary measure; glass pressure may cause the bottle to shatter.

IN POURING WINE, etiquette requires that the host's hand be placed over the upturned label.

The Fortified Wines

Sherry, Port and Madeira differ from so-called table wines in that they are fortified with brandy. In addition, each is processed in special and traditional ways to create the subtleties and distinctions which have placed them in the roster of great wines.

PORT . . . "A DRINK FOR MEN"

Port is defined by English law as *a fortified wine produced in the delimited Douro region (of Portugal) and shipped through the Bar of Oporto.* Wines of similar type, but produced elsewhere, cannot be sold in England or the United States under the unqualified name *Port*.

During the past two centuries, Port has become associated with England rather than the country of its origin; it has become, in fact, as distinct an English institution as fox hunting, roast beef and cricket. Dr. Johnson spoke of it as *our noblest legacy . . . a drink for men*. In less restrained moments he sang its praises as *the unsounded purple sea of marching billows, deep-sea deep*.

"It has not," said that remarkable scholar Dr. George Saintsbury, *"the almost feminine grace and charm of Claret or the immediate inspiration of Champagne. But it strengthens while it gladdens as no other wine can; and there is something about it which must have been created in pre-established harmony with the best English character."*

There is more to this than a literary flourish. The first Port wines imported to England were harsh *natural* wines. And despite the fact that a trade treaty between England and Portugal made Port wines available at extremely low prices, they found few takers. After years of trial and error, the British shippers finally hit on the idea of adding brandy to the wine before all the grape sugar had fermented out. The result was a sweeter wine with more alcohol to the flagon.

The Port Process. Wines destined to become Ports are allowed to ferment naturally for two or three days. The fermentation is carefully watched. When in the opinion of the vineyard owner the proper amount of unfermented sugar remains in the *must*, the wine is run off into casks containing sufficient brandy to raise the alcoholic content to 20 percent, automatically checking fermentation. The unfermented grape sugar remains in the wine as sweetening. Thus, Port is invariably sweet.

There are four types of red Port: Vintage, Crusted, Ruby and Tawny. There is also a white Port.

Vintage Port is a wine of any exceptional year, bottled two or three years after the vintage. There are usu-

ally not more than three exceptional years in a decade.

Vintage Port is generally exported in casks and bottled abroad by the buyer. The bottle customarily carries two dates — the year of vintage and the year of bottling.

As years pass, Vintage Port throws off a heavy deposit, consisting chiefly of calcium tartrate and coloring matter. The deposit forms a solid crust on the side of the bottle. Once disturbed, the crust does not re-form as a solid, but remains in suspension, clouding the wine. For this reason, Vintage Port, once bottled, is seldom re-shipped and little of it reaches the American market.

Crusted Port is similar in type to Vintage Port, differing only in that it is not necessarily the product of an exceptional, or *Vintage* year and, consequently, is sold at a lower price.

Ruby Port is a blended Port, matured in the wood rather than in the bottle. The production of Ruby Port in some ways resembles the making of Sherry: Wines are drawn from various classified piles of casks to effect a blend conforming to the shipper's standards of body and flavor. As many as thirty or more wines may be combined to produce a single blend.

As with Vintage and Crusted Ports, Ruby Port throws off a sediment. Much of this, in the cask, tends to remain suspended in the wine. To clarify the wine, casks are *fined* at least twice a year. Fining consists of settling out the sediment with a chemical agent or, in the case of finer wines, with the white of eggs.

The fining process settles out not only the sediment of the wine but some of the coloring matter. As a result, the more a wine is fined, the lighter it will become in color. An old wooded Port, consequently, is paler than a young one. This special quality of paleness in Port is called *Tawniness*.

Tawny Port is, roughly, a grown-up Ruby Port. It is usually a blend of a number of well-matured Ruby Ports. It is more delicate than Ruby, slightly less sweet and without the latter's fruitiness.

Great Port Vintages

1904
1908
1912
1917
1920
1924
1935

SHERRY . . WINE OF WIT

Every reader of Shakespeare is familiar with *sherris-sack*, the wine praised by Falstaff. "It ascends me into the brain," said Falstaff; "dries me there all the foolish and dull and crudy vapors which environ it; makes it apprehensive, quick, forgettive, full of nimble, fiery and delectable shapes; which, delivered o'er to the voice, the tongue, which is the birth, becomes excellent wit."

Sack is probably a derivative of the Spanish *seco*, dry, which means that the phrase *dry sack*, so popular with

English playwrights, is a classic of redundancy.

Popular in England since Shakespeare's time and developed by British shippers who today own most of the Sherry stocks in Spain, Sherry owes its name to England, being the consequence of the English pronunciation of *Jerez* or, more correctly, Jerez de la Frontera, a town near the southern tip of Spain.

Like most European wines, Sherry is produced from grapes grown in an officially delimited area. Yet, unlike most other wines, Sherry does not derive its quality solely from the combination of gifts of nature and a vintner's skill. Sherry results from a unique and almost century-consuming process. A fine Sherry can only be developed by a shipper owning large stocks of old wine.

HOW SHERRY ACQUIRES ITS INDIVIDUALITY

Wine destined to become Sherry is an unknown quantity; no one can tell whether it will mature dry or sweet, pale and delicate, or deep-colored and full bodied. The juice from a single vat of grapes, run off into separate casks and allowed to ferment, produces at the time of *falling bright* (separation of the precipitate, or lees, from clear wine) a variety of descendants; the contents of each cask develops its own unpredicted distinctions and individuality.

After *falling bright*, casks are sampled by expert tasters, classified and marked; the wine in each is then dosed with brandy and the casks left unstoppered in the open air. It is at this point that a mysterious Sherry transformation occurs; instead of turning to vinegar, as any other wine would if left so long exposed to air, wine in these casks acquires a special scum, (microorganisms known as *mycodermi vini*) which converts it to Sherry. This conversion, which is actually a second fermentation, is called, poetically, *La Flor*, the flowering. The wines again acquire individual differences, requiring new classification.

The Solera System. Sherry *cellars* are always above ground; they are basically stockpiles lying in gardens and are called *bodegas*. Each *bodega* contains stacks of specially classified casks, the *soleras*.

Anyone who wants a clear understanding of the significance of quality in Sherry must grasp the full meaning of a *solera*, which is both a system and a pile of casks. The word is derived from the Spanish *suelo* (base).

Most soleras consist of about a hundred casks, piled in tiers under a shed. The lowest tier contain the oldest wines, the tier above that the wines next in seniority, and so on, to the top.

The solera casks have a special relationship to one another — a cascading relationship. As a given amount of wine is drawn off for bottling from casks of the lowest tier, these casks are replenished from the next tier above. The top tier is refilled from reserve stocks in the *criadera,* or outside *nursery* pile. Not more than half the wine from any lower tier is drawn off in a single year.

❦ ❦ ❦

Sherry is produced and bottled in many types. Those commonly shipped to this country, however, are usually limited to five specific types:

MANZANILLA	*Pale, extremely dry, light bodied, with a crabapple flavor. (This is technically not a Sherry, since it is produced from wines grown outside the legally defined area.)*
FINO	*Pale, extremely dry.*
AMONTILLADO	*Moderately pale, moderately dry, characterized by a nutty flavor.*
AMOROSO	*Golden, medium dry.*
OLOROSO	*Rich, soft, mellow, sweet.*

Cognac ... *the soul of wine*

Cognac, which is properly a brandy, that is, a potable spirit obtained as a distillate of wine (or a fermented mash of fruit), is customarily ranked with the greatest of wines. It is properly considered the only fitting climax to a dinner at which great wines are served.

Although all Cognacs are brandies, all brandies are not Cognacs. The term is restricted to brandy produced from grapes grown in the Charente district of France, a name whose renown has been eclipsed by the name of its product. A pleasant story is told in this connection. A certain Bishop of the Charente was once dining, in Rome, in the company of a group of cardinals. The conversation

turned to dioceses. "What diocese is yours?" the bishop was asked.

"I am Bishop of Angoulême," he replied, and observed a circle of disinterested faces. "I am also Bishop of the Charente," he added. His answer was received in silence; none of the cardinals had heard of the Charente. "In short," the good Bishop added, ironically, "I am Bishop of Cognac."

"Ah, Cognac!" The assembly answered to a man, "What a superb Bishopric!"

❦ ❦ ❦

Cognac production was first begun in the Sixteenth Century. Possibly it was the result of an effort to produce a concentrate of wine for shipment. It was thought by some that a concentrate would travel better than wine, retain its quality longer, and would require only the addition of water to acquire, once again, the virtues of its original state.

It so happened that the overseas and colonial markets which received the distillate enjoyed the spirit as it was; thus Cognac came into being as a spirit in its own right.

COGNAC CLASSIFICATIONS

A Frenchman, it has been said, is never so happy as when classifying something. Cognacs, like the great French wines, have been graded in terms of the localities in which they have been produced. The official Cognac region has been divided into sub-districts, and these listed in terms of the excellence of the brandy they yield.

The area called Grande Champagne, whose soil contains in places as much as 75% chalk, produces the ideal Cognac, unequalled in delicacy and perfume.

Petite Champagne, the second district, forms a half moon around the Grande Champagne. The soil here is deeper and richer. The Cognac of Petite Champagne is excelled in finesse only by that of Grande Champagne.

The third region, the smallest of the Cognac districts, is known as the Borderies. It lies north and west of the town of Cognac. A surface layer of clay here, over the chalk, gives the Cognac of the Borderies a special flavor and vitality rather than delicacy.

The remaining districts are Fins Bois, Bons Bois, Bois Ordinaires and Bois Communs. In these the percentage of clay in the soil is greater, and the brandies produced are less distinctive.

The Stars and Letters on a Cognac Bottle

THE STARS ON A COGNAC LABEL have no special significance. Their presence is merely traditional, and derives from an old superstition — the notion that years of comets produce superb brandies. According to legend, the first star appeared on Cognac in the comet year 1811, and was used by one shipper as a mark indicating extraordinary quality. The following year was again an outstanding year and was indicated by a second star. A succession of good years increased the number of stars to five, at which the shipper fortunately decided to call a halt.

The letters stand for English, not French, words. They symbolize quality terms, as follows:

E	Especial	S	Superior
F	Fine	P	Pale
V	Very	X	Extra
O	Old	C	Cognac

Some Facts about Age in Cognacs

Cognac, it has been said, is like a woman. She is at her best between the ages of 25 and 40.

MATURING TAKES PLACE in casks made of a special oak obtained from the forests of Limousin. It is said in the Charente that Cognac owes all its color and half its taste to the wood in which it is matured.

As Cognac matures, it absorbs tannin from the wood, grows more acid and loses alcohol (by evaporation). Cognacs are distilled with an alcoholic percentage of 70; after ten years in the cask this percentage may have fallen to 60, in thirty years to 50.

Cognac does not age in the bottle. One of the great myths of the liquor business is the myth of Napoleon brandy. Not only are most bottles sold as such out-and-out frauds, but if a bottle of brandy of this age were available, it would be no better now than at the time it was put in glass. And if a brandy were kept in the cask for a century and a half, it would today be nothing more than thin, acid, watery stuff.

Armagnac

Armagnac, which is a grape brandy similar in many respects to Cognac, is produced in the Department of Gers, southeast of Bordeaux. Differences in the distillation process and in the type of wood used for the casks in which aging occurs account for the flavor differences between Cognac and Armagnac. The latter is drier and harder than Cognac and is a favorite of many connoisseurs.

Marc Brandies

The popular strong drink of France is not the relatively expensive grape brandy of Cognac or Armagnac, but brandies distilled from the left-overs of the wine press. These distillates are produced in many parts of France, particularly in Burgundy. They are known as *Eau de Vie de Marc* or simply *Marc* (pronounced *mar*). The Marc brandies of Italy are usually called *Grappa*.

American Brandy

Brandy of exceptional quality is now being produced in the United States, chiefly in California. Although the American industry was compelled to start, literally from scratch, after Repeal, ample stocks of fine, mature domestic brandy are now available. Like Armagnac and other grape brandies, American brandy has its own distinctive quality and flavor, and has established its special place in the repertoire of fine spirits.

The Gin Story

Gins came into existence in the Seventeenth Century as a result of a popular demand for strong spirits pleasant to drink, yet moderate in price. Earlier crude distillates, made chiefly from wine, were harsh and bitter. Experiment proved that the addition of a strong flavor made the alcohol less difficult to swallow. Juniper was finally hit on as the ideal flavor, one acceptable to the broadest market. The name is derived from the French for juniper berry — *Genievre*.

The general acceptance of gin in England is attributed to the tax policy of Queen Anne. Anxious to bolster the home spirits industry, she put a staggering tax on imported wines and liquors. Soldiers who had acquired abroad a taste for juniper-flavored spirits found, on their return, that domestic gin was the only drink available at a price they could afford. Gin thus became England's standard Jacobin drink, acquiring popularity and non-aristocratic associations in an inverse ratio.

This fact is reflected in a famous English tavern sign, which reads:

> *Drunk for a penny,*
> *Dead drunk for two pence.*
> *Clean straw for nothing.*

In time the art of fine gin making was learned in England and the crude spirit first known became one of the fine spirits of the world — a distillate made by master distillers according to secret formulas.

TYPES OF GIN

There are, basically, only two types of gin: English or London Dry gin, and Hollands gin, otherwise known as *Schiedam* (from the town where it was first made) or as Geneva (from the French *Genievre*). So-called *Sloe Gin* is not a gin at all, but a liqueur flavored with sloeberry. Old Tom gin is simply English gin dosed with sweetening syrup.

sloeberry. Old Tom gin is simply English gin dosed with sweetening syrup.

ENGLISH GIN

English gin is produced from a mash consisting of about 75% corn, 15% malt and 10% other grains. After fermentation, the wort, or beer, is distilled and rectified to produce a high-proof, relatively pure spirit. This, in turn, is diluted and redistilled in the presence of juniper berries and other ingredients, including, usually, coriander seed, cardamon seed, angelica root, anise seed, caraway seed, bitter almonds, cassia bark, calamus, fennel, orris root, licorice and orange peel.

HOLLANDS GIN

Hollands gin is made from a barley malt with no other grains added. The juniper berry and other flavoring agents are ground up in the original mash and fermented with it. It is distilled at an extremely low proof (94 to 98 degrees), with the result that a large percentage of the basic flavoring material passes over into the distillate. The consequence of the distilling process is that Hollands gin acquires such a pronounced flavor of its own that it is not satisfactory as a mixing agent in cocktails, the juniper taste drowning out all others.

Hollands gin should be drunk straight or with bitters. In the East Indies the custom is to swish bitters inside a glass; then, after emptying, to fill the glass with Hollands. Served in this fashion, Hollands makes an excellent apéritif.

Rum, Rumbustion and Rumbullion

Rum is produced today wherever sugar cane grows. Technically, it is any alcoholic distillate produced from the fermented juice of sugar cane, sugar cane molasses, or any by-products of the versatile cane. Rum's name is one of the standard mysteries; some derive it from *rumbustion*, which was an early name for this potent drink. Others consider it a shortened form of *rumbullion*. Webster endorses the latter.

For many centuries rum was associated with seafaring, both as a barter item and a drink sailors found to their liking. The indirect result has been the development of the rum industry along almost all of the main sea routes of the western world. Today rum is found in three main types:

1. *The dry, light-bodied, brandy-like rums of Cuba, Puerto Rico, Haiti, and Santo-Domingo.*

2. *The sweetish, rich, full-bodied rums of Jamaica, Martinique, Demerara, Barbados, and the Virgin Islands.*

3. *Aromatic, Batavia Arak rums from Java.*

This classification cannot be taken as hard-and-fast. Many of the areas listed above produce rum of several types, and to some extent the gradings tend to overlap.

Each general type of rum exhibits special flavor qualities; in the making of fine rum cocktails it is usually important to stick to the type of rum specified by the standard recipe.

FROM INDEX OF AMERICAN DESIGN,
COURTESY THE MACMILLAN CO.

NOTE ON AGE IN SCOTCH

A Scotch whisky of great age is not necessarily better than one bearing no age statement on the label. The quality of Scotch depends basically on the quality of whiskies in the blend, and on the delicacy and finesse of the blend — as well as on proper aging. An inferior blend will never become a good whisky — no matter how long it is aged.

NOTE ON THE "E" IN WHISKEY

All American, Canadian and Irish whiskey is spelled with the e. Scotch and Scotch type are spelled without the e.

Scotch Whisky

The term whisky, which is probably a derivation from the Gaelic *Uisgebeatha* (in Scotland, *Uisgebaugh*), meaning water of life, has a venerable history; it is intertwined with the legends and song of both Scotland and Ireland, although it is in Scottish writings . . . particularly Scott and Robert Burns . . . that its special lore has passed to this country.

There are four types of Scotch malt whisky: Highlands, Lowlands, Campbeltown and Islay (pronounced eye-lay). Each has its individual character and flavor. A fine liqueur Scotch is usually a blend of all four, together with a percentage of grain whiskies.

Five distinct steps are involved in the production of a fine Scotch: malting, mashing, fermenting, distilling, maturing and blending.

Malt is germinated grain. The process of malting consists of sprinkling barley for three weeks with warm water, causing the grain to sprout. The process converts some of the barley's starch into diastase.

The green malt is then *kilned,* that is, dried out over a peat fire. The peat smoke swirls around the sprouted barley, giving it the characteristic flavor which distinguishes all Scotch.

Mashing consists of mixing the dried malt with water until a thick wort has been produced. Yeast is then added to the wort and fermentation begun. When fermentation is completed, the liquid is known as *beer.*

At the proper moment, the beer is *distilled.* The proof of the resulting whisky is reduced by the addition of spring water, preferably water that has passed through red granite formations and peaty soil.

Scotch whisky is matured in sherry casks. It is blended after three or four years and again casked — after blending — for further aging.

The significant difference among Scotch blends is the proportion of the four types of malt whiskies. Highland malts are considered the finest and are the most costly. These whiskies are light in body and flavor, with a not-too-pronounced flavor of smoke. Also light are the lowland malts. The heavy, smoky and pungent whiskies are generally from Campbeltown and Islay.

Irish Whiskey

Irish whiskey exists in two basic types: that of Northern Ireland, which is made entirely from barley malt; that of Eire, which is distilled from mashes containing wheat, rye oats and other grains, as well as both malted and unmalted barley. In general, Irish resembles Scotch, but is without the characteristic smoky taste of Scotch. The flavor difference is due principally to the fact that, unlike Scotch, the Irish malt is not *smoke cured.* North Ireland Malt whiskies are sometimes blended with grain whiskies, although straight barley malts are common. Most Irish is aged seven years or more before shipment.

American Whiskey

Whiskey was an important part of the economy of the early colonial settlers, in many cases being actually used as a form of money. When, in 1791, the Federal government in George Washington's presidency levied a tax on whiskey, a minor insurrection occurred, later known as the Whiskey Rebellion, and many of the distillers from Pennsylvania migrated to territory which included what are now the states of Kentucky and Indiana. In the southern part of Indiana and in Kentucky they found ideal water for whiskey production.

The first Kentucky whiskey was made from corn ground in the mill of Elijah Craig in Georgetown, Bourbon County. The whiskey was called *Bourbon County Whiskey.* Bourbon soon became a standard word, as did the name Bunkum County in North Carolina. (*Bunkum* came to mean nonsense when a certain North Carolina Congressman from Bunkum county made long, windy speeches in Washington to impress the people back home. On such occasions other Congressmen would walk out, saying *That's just for Bunkum.*)

The continued production of whiskey in Kentucky, Southern Indiana and Pennsylvania, however, is not just a result of historical accident. The water in these areas passes through one of the main limestone formations in the U. S., and acquires the calcium content considered ideal for whiskey making.

THE MAKING OF AMERICAN WHISKEY

All types of American whiskies, without exception, go through five basic processing steps:

1. The grain, whatever mixture it happens to be, is ground to a meal.

2. The meal, together with water and a small amount of malt, is cooked, forming a *wort.*

3. Yeast is added to the wort, and the wort is fermented, forming a *beer.*

4. The beer is distilled in a double column, or *patent* still, producing raw whiskey at 160° proof.

5. Proof is reduced to 100-103° by the addition of pure well water, and the whiskey thus cut put in new, charred white oak barrels to mature.

SWEET MASH AND SOUR MASH

These are terms used to describe the two different yeasting processes used in the production of American whiskies. A sweet mash is created with a freshly developed batch of yeast alone as the fermenting agent. A sour mash is the result of a mixture of some of the leftover mash from each preceding batch (as well as fresh yeast) with each new batch of mash. The sour mash process is primarily used in the making of Bourbon whiskies.

TYPES OF AMERICAN WHISKEY

Type is a way of classifying whiskey. It is no indication of quality. There are good and inferior whiskies of all types. Whiskey types are defined by the Federal Alcoholic Administration as follows:

1. *Straight whiskey.* An alcoholic distillate from a fermented mash of grain distilled at not exceeding 160° proof and withdrawn from the cistern room of the distillery at not more than 110° and not less than 80° proof.

2. *Straight Rye Whiskey.* A straight whiskey distilled from a fermented mash of grain, of which not less than 51% is rye grain.

3. *Straight Bourbon Whiskey* (and straight corn whiskey). A straight whiskey distilled from a fermented mash of grain, of which not less than 51% is corn grain.

4. *Blended Whiskey* (or *Whiskey—a Blend*). A mixture which contains at least 20% by volume of 100% proof straight whiskey and, separately or in combination, whiskey or neutral spirits, if such mixture at the time of bottling is not less than 80° proof.

5. *A Blend of Straight Whiskies* (or Blended Straight Whiskies). Mixtures of only straight whiskies.

Canadian Whiskies

Canadian whiskies are for the most part rye whiskies, although some Bourbon is also produced in Canada. In general, however, Canadian whiskies are lighter in body than American ryes and Bourbon, the reason lying in certain technicalities of production. The whiskies are distilled at a higher proof than American, and evaporation losses are compensated for by the addition of neutral spirits. Canadian whiskies are bottled in bond at 90° proof; American bottled-in-bond whiskies are 100° proof.

Types of Mixed Drinks

Tradition has established a variety of types of drinks, assigning to each its proper glass and form of service. Following is a description of the types and official forms of the mixed drinks which have become standard in America:

Drink	Ingredients	Glass	Ice
COBBLER	Port or Sherry, Curaçao or sugar, brandy, fruit	Water goblet	Cracked or shaved
COCKTAIL	Various	Cocktail glass	Ice in shaker only
COLLINS	Gin or Rum, lemon juice, sugar, fruit, soda	Highball glass	Cracked
COOLER	Port or light wine, sugar syrup or Grenadine, ginger ale or soda	Highball glass	Cracked
CRUSTA	Port or Sherry (or Brandy), peel of half orange or lemon, lemon juice, Maraschino, Angostura bitters. (The distinguishing feature of a Crusta is that the entire glass is lined with the fruit peel; edges are frosted with powdered sugar)	Wine glass	Ice in shaker only
DAISY	Gin, etc., raspberry syrup, lemon juice, fruit, soda	Highball glass, or special stein	Cracked
EGG NOG	Whiskey, Brandy or Rum, egg, milk, sugar, nutmeg	Cup or highball glass	Ice in shaker only
FIX	Port or Sherry, or hard liquor, lemon, sugar, plain water, fruit	Highball glass	Shaved
FIZZ	As above, but with soda instead of plain water	Highball glass	One cube
FLIP	Port, Sherry or Madeira, sugar, egg; sometimes nutmeg	Large wine glass	Ice in shaker only
HIGHBALL	Whiskey, Rum or Brandy, ginger ale or soda	Highball glass	One cube
JULEP	Whiskey, sugar, mint (glass frosted with powdered sugar)	Highball glass or tankard	Shaved
RICKEY	Gin, lime, soda	Highball glass	One cube
SANGAREE	Port, lemon slice, sugar, fruit, nutmeg	Highball glass	Cracked
SLING	Gin, fruit juice, cordials	Highball glass	Two cubes
SMASH	Port, Sherry, or liqueur, lump sugar, mint, fruit	Old Fashioned	One cube
SOUR	Whiskey, Brandy or other liquor, lemon juice, sugar, soda, fruit	Delmonico, or wine glass	Ice in shaker only
SWIZZLE	Rum, or other liquor, sweetening, soda	Highball glass	In pitcher
TODDY	Rum, lemon slice, sugar cloves, hot water	Coffee cup or special Toddy glass	None
TOM AND JERRY	Jamaica rum, beaten eggs, sugar, hot water	As above	

IF YOU LIKE A MANHATTAN . . .
1 part Italian Vermouth
1 part French Vermouth
4 parts Scotch whisky
A dash of Drambuie

IF YOU LIKE A MARTINI . . .
1 part Amontillado Sherry
5 parts gin
2 or 3 dashes of Pernod

IF YOU LIKE AN OLD FASHIONED . . .
Pour into each glass 1 to 2 spoonsful of sugar syrup (you'll find this much superior to lump sugar, which generally never gets completely dissolved). Add 1 to 3 dashes Angostura bitters. Stir to blend thoroughly. Add about 1 oz. whiskey and stir again. Add 1 to 2 large cubes of ice. Fill glass almost to brim with whiskey. Add several dashes of Liqueur Strega and a twist of lemon. Decorate with a Maraschino cherry.

IF YOU LIKE A DAIQUIRI . . .
1 part Orgeat or Crème d'Ananas
2 parts citrus juice (juice of 1 lemon to that of 3 limes)
8 parts Cuban rum

(Shake vigorously — with plenty of finely crushed ice; strain into chilled and frosted cocktail glass)

Liqueurs . . . *the perfect finish*

Liqueurs were originated in the Middle Ages, chiefly by alchemists in the search for an elixir of life. Some were developed as aphrodisiacs and love potions, others as medicines. Monasteries undertook the development of cordials thought to have curative virtues.

Technically, a liqueur, or cordial, is an alcoholic beverage prepared by combining a spirit (usually brandy) with flavoring agents and sugar syrup.

There are two basic types of liqueurs: (a) natural-colored fruit liqueurs which are made by infusing a fruit (such as apricots) in brandy; and (b) colorless or plant liqueurs, which are made by a combination of maceration and distillation.

It is illegal in this country to use the word brandy on a label unless the product contained in the bottle is distilled from a fermented mash and contains less than $2\frac{1}{2}\%$ of sugar.

In Europe the word brandy is used loosely; and the terms Apricot Brandy, Peach Brandy, etc., are applied to products which, by American laws, are *liqueurs*.

FRUIT LIQUEURS

Fruit liqueurs are made by steeping whatever fruit is used six to eight months in brandy (usually at 120 to 130° proof). During this period, the brandy absorbs the color, aroma and flavor of the fruit. The product, with other additions, is sweetened, aged further and bottled.

PLANT LIQUEURS

Plant liqueurs are produced from plants, seeds, roots,

and herbs, and, unlike fruit liqueurs, are distilled. Usually the ingredients are softened by soaking in water (24 to 48 hours), then placed in brandy. The resulting batch is then distilled in a pot still. The distillate obtained contains the desired flavor, but is generally both colorless and dry, requiring artificial coloring and special sweetening. Fine plant liqueurs, such as Green and Yellow Chartreuse, Benedictine or Vieille Cure, are then aged in special old vats, many of which have held the same liqueur for generations and which, together with so-called secret formulas, constitute the most precious possession of a manufacturer.

FASHIONS IN LIQUEURS

There was a time when it was fashionable for women to drink liqueurs rather than whiskey, gin and brandy. In past years there were as many liqueurs as there are cocktails. Every small town pharmacist in Europe concocted his own liqueur mixtures. Large manufacturers celebrated every important national event with the production of a new cordial. At the turn of the century there was scarcely a restaurant proprietor in France who did not include at least fifty liqueurs in his wine list.

Modern taste, however, has reduced the number of liqueurs in common use almost as drastically as it has the list of ordinarily accepted cocktails. The liqueurs most often served today are a few plant liqueurs prepared from secret formulas, such as Vieille Cure, Green and Yellow Chartreuse and Benedictine; fine non-secret plant liqueurs such as Crème de Menthe and Crème de Cacao; a few standard fruit liqueurs, such as Apricot, Peach and Cherry Heering; and the three best-known orange-peel liqueurs: Curaçao, Cointreau and Grand Marnier. An exception to the above classifications is Drambuie, made from Highland malt whisky and honey.

END

Some Little-known Facts
about Mixed Drinks

THE TIME-HONORED EFFECTS of drinks are created by the alcohol they contain, not their flavor nor mixing ingredients. Nevertheless, there is a special chemistry involved in mixing. Unaged cocktail bases, such as gin or vodka, take effect more quickly than mellowed bases like Cognac or old whiskey. Dry drinks pack a quicker punch than sweet. Italian vermouth will take effect more slowly than French.

The *sleepers* however, are drinks made with eggs, milk or cream. These are the velvet gloves which hide alcohol's mailed fist. They mute out the harshness and bitterness of cocktails and slow down the system's response. But the response comes nonetheless; and when it does, it comes with the fury of long pent-up power. The alcohol eventually reaches the bloodstream and, once there, it is the same alcohol that might have arrived via an undisguised Martini — only it usually arrives in larger quantities, because the initial blandness of the drink has apparently justified more frequent refills.

ANTOINE'S
Some Simple Don'ts

Roy Louis Alciatore is the son of the son of the man (see daguerreotype above) who started Antoine's Restaurant in New Orleans. The proprietor of such a restaurant, and such a tradition, must be not only a philosopher of food; he must be arbiter as well. Roy Alciatore has written a pamphlet on the subject of what *not* to do while dining out. Having learned from said pamphlet that eating is one art, dining quite another, Gentry takes pleasure in passing on to you the best of Mr. Alciatore's advice.

"Mais apres tout, si on sait ce qu'on ne doit pas faire pour bien manger, on sait aussi ce qu'on doit faire."

1 Don't drink a gin fizz or any thick or sweet drink right before a meal. If the dinner is to include fine wines, what is more logical than to have an appetizer of such wines as French vermouth, dry sherry, Dubonnet, or a combination of these wines? Don't have your *aperitif* immediately before dinner; 15 minutes or better should elapse between the *aperitif* and the first dinner course. The serving of hors d'oeuvres with the *aperitif* is criminal, and by taking the edge off the appetite defeats the purpose for which the *aperitif* was intended.

2 Don't just drop into a restaurant and order a meal. Go to the restaurant of your choice and make all of the arrangements with the proprietor or headwaiter a day or two in advance. Order your wines, too, in advance, so that they may be brought up from the cellar to acquire the proper temperature or to be cooled to the right degree.

3 Don't let your guests do the ordering. When entertaining guests in a restaurant it is meet and proper

that the host should do the ordering . . . . uniformity in ordering assures the success of the party.

4 Don't make the mistake of ordering too many things. A few selected dishes are better than a great number chosen haphazardly.

5 Don't order wines yourself if you know nothing about them. Ask the waiter or wine steward, who is trained in such things, to select a wine suited to the type of food you have ordered. Ask to be shown the bottle before it is opened to satisfy yourself that it is the wine you ordered. To order a sweet wine like a sauterne with fish is unpardonable. Sauterne is a dessert wine, and if it is good sauterne it is always sweet. There is no such thing as a *dry* sauterne.

6 Don't brand yourself as a rank plebeian by seasoning your food before tasting it. Many a chef's brain child has been smothered with condiments, when it should have been showered with compliments. If you are in a good restaurant, the food will be properly seasoned before it leaves the kitchen.

7 Don't go into a first-class restaurant and ask for a glass of wine. Remember that the best wines are shipped in bottles, and that consequently no self-respecting restaurateur will jeopardize the reputation of his house by serving wines from jugs and barrels. Nor is it reasonable for you to expect a restaurateur

to open a good bottle of wine just for the purpose of serving one or two glasses out of it.

8 Don't hesitate when visiting a restaurant for the first time to try the specialties for which the house is famous.

9 Don't demand music with your meals. Table conversation is the only suitable accompaniment of good food. Dinner dancing is an abomination and holds no place with the bon vivant.

10 Don't go to a first-class restaurant if you are in a hurry. If you cannot spare the time, you are better off at the corner drug store, where they will dish you out an already prepared sandwich in short order.

11 Don't go to a first-class restaurant to look for bargains in food. A good restaurant caters to a clientele of epicures who are far more concerned with the quality of the food than with the price.

12 Don't exercise patience with an insolent or careless waiter. He is a disgrace to the profession, and the sooner he is reported to the manager, the better it will be for everyone concerned. On the other hand, a careful and solicitous waiter earns and deserves a tip, or *pourboire*, for his services.

13 Don't hesitate to make a complaint if your food is not what you expect it to be. Substitutions and exchanges will gladly be made in an effort to repay you for the inconvenience and delay thus caused you.

14 Don't make the mistake of ordering a good meal and then expecting to enjoy it with ice water as a beverage.

15 Don't judge or misjudge a restaurant by its appearance. Many are the misguided restaurant owners who place greater emphasis on the decor than on the food and cuisine. Inversely, you will also find that excellent meals are to be had in dubious attics and unpretentious cellars.

16 Don't go into a first-class restaurant to order only a cup of tea or a plate of ice cream. Tea rooms for tea, and ice cream parlors for ice cream, and good restaurants for skillfully prepared food.

17 Don't go into a restaurant if you wish only to drink. Go to a bar or cocktail lounge instead. A restaurant's "raison d'être" is the serving of food, and drinks are served only as an accompaniment to food.

18 Don't change your order after it has once been definitely given. Once your order reaches the kitchen, the chef immediately begins the preparation thereof, and should the order be changed then, the first article ordered usually becomes a total loss for the house.

19 Don't bring your own wines or liquors into a restaurant where liquor is sold. It is as bad as bringing your own food.

20 Don't order an old and expensive wine with a plain and ordinary dinner. Rare old wines should be drunk on special occasions when the menu warrants a good bottle.

And now we have come to the point when it is time to say, "Garcon, l'addition s'il vous plait."

Roy Louis Alciatore
Proprietor, Antoine's Restaurant, New Orleans, La.

CHRISTMAS DINNER

Menu and recipes chosen by Luchow's, New York's grand old German restaurant.

Herring Salad

4 salt herrings	dash of black pepper
6 boiled potatoes	1 teaspoon sugar
3 apples	½ teaspoon dry mustard
4 sour dill pickles	½ cup olive oil
2 cooked beets	½ cup wine vinegar
boiled veal knuckle	1 cup stock or bouillon
1 green pepper	6 fresh lettuce leaves
½ onion	3 tablespoons capers
	3 hard-cooked eggs

Rinse herrings, drain, cover with cold water and let soak overnight. Drain, remove skin, cut fillets from bones. Dice fillets fine.

Peel and dice potatoes; peel, core, and dice apples; dice pickles, beets, meat, green pepper, and onion. Combine all with fish in a shallow dish. Sprinkle with pepper, sugar, and mustard. Pour oil, vinegar, and stock over all. Cover and let chill in refrigerator. Serve on crisp lettuce garnish with capers and hard-cooked egg quarters or slices. Serves six.

Double Consommé

3 pounds beef	½ small carrot
1 pound soup bones	1 stalk celery
1½ teaspoons salt	1 small piece kohlrabi
4 quarts water	1 sprig parsley
½ small onion	1 tomato, quartered

Boiled vegetables such as 3 or 4 small potatoes, 6 small carrots, and 3 or 4 small turnips.

Wipe meat with wet cloth. Rinse bones and place in kettle with salt, vegetables, and water. Bring slowly to boil, then boil one hour. Skim top. Add beef. Cover and let boil slowly 2½ to 3 hours. Lift meat out and place in deep tureen; keep meat warm. Strain stock, and reheat clear soup. Pour soup over meat and cooked hot vegetables. Serves six.

Roast Watertown Goose with Apple Stuffing

1 twelve-pound	½ onion, sliced
fat young goose	6 peppercorns
4 cups water	¼ pound butter
	2 tablespoons flour

Have goose cleaned and drawn, the wings, neck, head, and feet chopped off. Wash goose inside and out, drain. Cover with cold water and let soak 15 minutes. Drain, pat dry. Rub with salt inside and out. Fill with apple stuffing and place in baking pan. Add water, onion, and peppercorns. Roast in moderate oven (325°F.) 15-20 minutes per pound. When water has boiled down, baste frequently with butter which has been browned. Remove goose to warmed platter. Place pan on top of range. Stir flour into fat. Add 2 cups water. Stir and let boil 2 or 3 minutes, until smooth and slightly thickened. Serve with goose. Serves six.

Apple Stuffing

1 cup well browned, diced,	1 cup sugar
white bread croutons	1 cup goose fat
2 cups green apples diced	½ cup white raisins

Cook apples, raisins and sugar with one cup of water. While still hot, mix with croutons and goose fat. Stuff goose with mixture before roasting or, if you prefer, steam mixture for serving separately.

Red Cabbage

1 head red cabbage,	salt and pepper
sliced thin	¼ pound butter, or
2 onions, sliced	chicken or bacon fat
2 apples, cored and sliced	4 medium-size ham
½ cup red currant jelly	knuckles
1 bay leaf	3 ounces vinegar

Mix red cabbage with onions, apples, currant jelly, bay leaf, salt, and pepper. Put butter, chicken, or bacon fat in heavy casserole with tight-fitting cover; add red cabbage, ham knuckles, ¼ cup water. Bring to a boil and cook slowly 2½ hours. Add vinegar at the last minute. Remove bay leaf and serve.

Plum Pudding

¼ pound bread flour
½ pound sugar
½ pound seedless raisins
½ pound Sultana raisins
½ pound currants
¼ pound candied orange
  and lemon peel, shredded
¼ pound soft bread crumbs
½ pound suet (chopped
  as fine as possible)

3 ounces almonds (blanch
  and then shred before
  adding to mixture)
juice and skin of 1 lemon
4 eggs beaten lightly
½ teaspoon salt
¼ teaspoon nutmeg
¼ teaspoon cinnamon
¾ cup French Brandy
1 dash of clove
1 cup milk

Mix all ingredients well and put in buttered mold, cover with buttered muslin or paper. Put cover on tight. Steam over low fire four to five hours. Unmold and serve hot with Hard or Brandy Sauce.

Hard Sauce

½ cup butter
½ cup superfine sugar

¼ oz. rum
⅛ cup heavy cream

Mix all ingredients in bowl and beat for ten minutes. Cool in refrigerator. Yields 1½ pints which serves from eight to ten persons.

Brandy Sauce

½ cup fruit juice
  (peach or apricot preferred)
½ cup brandy

Heat fruit juice, add brandy. Serves 10

NEW YEAR'S SUPPER

Menu and recipes chosen by Cafe Nicholson, one of midtown New York's elegant dining places.

MENU

***Broiled Veal Kidney
with Sauce Béarnaise***

Endive Salad

Snowball   Demitasse

Broiled Veal Kidney, Sauce Béarnaise

1 large veal kidney per person
melted butter
salt and pepper

Wash kidneys, split each in half but do not sever completely. Butter slightly on both sides to prevent curling, season with salt, pepper and any other seasoning according to taste. Place over portable charcoal broiler, or on the grate in the fireplace. Cook on both sides (the cut side first) for either rare, medium, or well done as desired. Overcooking tends to toughen kidneys, so well done is not advisable. Serve with Sauce Béarnaise.

Sauce Béarnaise

4 sprigs of tarragon,
  chopped
a little chervil
6 crushed peppercorns
2 chopped shallots

2 tablespoons white wine
2 tablespoons vinegar
2 egg yolks
½ pound melted butter
lemon juice

Reduce the chopped tarragon, chervil, peppercorns, shallots, white wine and vinegar until you have quite a thick sauce. Cool. Mix a tablespoon of water with the egg yolks, and add to thick sauce. Beat well over very low heat. Add the melted butter gradually, stirring constantly. Place dish with the sauce in hot water pan and heat well. Strain through cheesecloth, add a little lemon juice, a little more chopped tarragon, and a bit of salt to taste, and serve.

Endive Salad

1 large endive per person   garlic
canned roasted pimento   salt and pepper

Split endive in half for individual salads. Top with a half roasted pimento. Pour juice from the can of roasted pimento over endive. This will suffice for salad dressing, with seasoning of garlic, salt and pepper to taste.

Snowball

Bittersweet chocolate sauce
vanilla ice cream
shredded cocoanut

For each guest fill the bottom of an individual silver goblet or large crystal sherbert glass with bittersweet chocolate sauce. Take a scoop of vanilla ice cream in the shape of a snow ball, and roll it in shredded cocoanut. Place snowball carefully in the chocolate sauce and serve immediately.

For the holidays Gentry presents a rare but superb recipe for

PRESSED DUCK

Canard à la Presse is a gourmet favorite at la Tour d' Argent, the Parisian restaurant known for its fine preparation of duck. This specialty is interpreted here for Gentry readers by Antoine Becco (picture at right), head of l'Escoffier, at the Beverly Hilton Hotel, Beverly Hills, California.

Take a fine duckling six weeks to two months old, hang it until strangled, pluck, dress, singe and draw it. Put the liver aside, taking care to remove the gall bladder. Truss the duckling for roasting on a spit (of apple wood) over a hot fire for about ten minutes.

While the duckling is roasting, pass the liver through a very fine sieve and blend some foie-gras with it, adding some butter, ground pepper, a little nutmeg, a touch of Cayenne pepper, paprika and salt. Mix all together until you have a smooth paste.

When the duckling is roasted, remove the legs and divide the drumstick from the upper leg; rub these in salt and pepper and spread mustard thickly over all. These four pieces are called *Hell-fire* and should be grilled about twelve minutes over the live coals.

Remove the skin and slice the breast, arranging the slices on an oval platter. Leave a space for flaming with good brandy which is sprinkled from a spoon.

Split the carcass and press it to collect the blood.

Beat up the livers and a glass of aged port with a small whisk in a chafing dish, adding the blood in a slow trickle, ending with three or four drops of lemon juice and the residue of the flaming. Do not allow to boil. Season to taste.

Pour this sauce over the slices only; serve the *Hell-fire* separately in paper ruffles with potato chips.

At gala dinners this dish is often rounded off with a *Trou Canard:*

In a cocktail glass place
    1 cube sugar
    2 drops Orange Bitters
    1 apple quarter soaked in Angostura,
      on a toothpick
Pour over them
    1 glass Calvados

Drink without stirring and chew apple quarter to enjoy its liquor content.

La Tour d'Argent is one of the oldest and most celebrated restaurants in Paris. It is situated on the top floor of a building on the Quai de la Tournelle and commands a view across the city which can be enjoyed from an open air terrace in the summer. The restaurant is famous for its duck dishes, and each patron who orders duck is handed a slip stating the number (in series commencing in the year 1880) of the duck being served to him, the current numbers being in the region of two hundred thousand. The illustration at right shows the type of press used in the preparation of Pressed Duck.

Illustration courtesy *Paris Cuisine*, Little, Brown and Company.

A Handy Guide to Nogs, Grogs and Punches

NOGS

While there are numberless formulas for the preparation of egg nogs, and varieties of opinion as to how best to concoct them, there are some fundamental procedures that can be followed with assurance. Without doubt, the egg yolks should be beaten until they are light and frothy; the necessary sugar added by beating into the yolks. The egg whites must be beaten separately until almost stiff, poured on top of the mixture, and blended by folding in. This is a process of cutting, dipping and folding over with a knife. Never place ice in the egg nog itself; cool by packing the bowl with crushed ice or placing it in a refrigerator. A short stay in the deep freeze will also be an effective chiller, but beware of leaving the egg nog in too long.

Pendennis Club Egg Nog

This is one of the simplest, also the richest, of egg nogs. It is admirably suited to the taste of those who believe that an egg nog should show a relationship to zabaglione and syllabub.

1 dz. egg yolks	1 lb. pwd. sugar
1 bottle bourbon	2 qts. heavy cream

Mix the sugar and whiskey and allow a couple of hours for complete blending. Beat egg yolks to a froth, meanwhile adding the sweetened whiskey. Let this mixture stand for several hours. Whip the cream until stiff, and fold this into the egg and whiskey mixture.

Gentry Instant Egg Nog

Here is an egg nog which can be prepared quickly, and with a minimum of effort. Blended to a base of French ice cream, it is self-chilled and ready for serving the moment the liquor and ice cream are mixed.

> 2 ounces Jamaica rum
> ½ to 1 bottle bourbon
> 2 quarts French vanilla ice cream

Stir until mixture is creamy. Serve in champagne glasses. Add dash of powdered nutmeg.

Baltimore Egg Nog

This is a thinner and more distinctly flavored egg nog. Its appeal lies in its light body and sweet fruit flavor.

1 dz. eggs	½ pt. Jamaica rum
1 lb. pwd. sugar	½ pt. peach brandy
1 pint brandy	3 pints milk
	1 pint heavy cream

Beat the sugar into the egg yolks, Slowly stir in the liquors. Add milk and cream. Finally fold in stiffly beaten egg whites.

GROGS AND TODDIES

There is an interesting history behind the term, grog. It is an honored tradition to issue a ration of rum to sailors in the British navy. In 1740, a penny pinching admiral, Edward Vernon, issued an order requiring that this rum be diluted with water. Since Vernon's nickname was Old Grog, this diluted brew was referred to as grog. In America the term has come to designate a hot drink, made of rum and water to which lemon and sugar are added, which is practically synonymous with a toddy.

New England Hot Grog

The familiar New England hot grog is made as follows:

> 1 jigger Jamaica rum
> 1 tsp. sugar syrup
> 1 tbs. lemon juice

Stir in a highball glass or large mug. Add hot water and a twist of lemon peel. Hot tea can be used instead of water. A variation known as Black Stripe calls for molasses in place of sugar.

Grog and other hot spirituous drinks have many pleasant and medicinal uses. They are unsurpassed for counteracting chills after winter sports or a cold drenching, they are helpful in allaying the discomforts of a head cold, and they are excellent promoters of sleep.

Hot Toddy

A standard recipe for this cold weather favorite follows:

1 oz. sugar syrup	1 dash cinnamon
3 ozs. hard liquor	1 dash nutmeg
	1 thin slice lemon

Mix in tall highball glass or goblet, and fill with hot water. The nutmeg is usually dusted over the top of the toddy.

PUNCHES

Although punch is now a typical American institution, associated with church sociables and college dances, it is an ancient drink whose name derives from the Hindustani. The word punch is derived from a term meaning five, which characterized the number of ingredients blended in the mixture. Modern punches, however, contain as many liquors and flavoring elements as taste permits.

Dragoon Punch

According to bartenders' legend, this is the old-time cavalryman's answer to the Artillery Punch. Blended to a base of ale and porter, it is said to transport guests to the high places at the pace of a dragoon's gallop.

3 pints porter	½ pint sweet sherry
3 pints ale	½ pint sugar syrup
½ pint domestic	3 pints Champagne
brandy	3 lemons, thinly sliced

All ingredients, with the exception of the Champagne, are blended in the punch bowl. Immediately before serving, ice and the Champagne are added. The mixture retains the sparkle of the Champagne when prepared in this manner.

Young People's Punch

½ pint sugar syrup	4 ozs. pineapple
½ pint lemon juice	juice
1 pint orange juice	2 ozs. Maraschino
4 ozs. Curaçao	2 bottles red wine
	2 qts. club soda

Mix all ingredients except the club soda some time before serving. Pour in punch bowl over a large piece of ice. At the last moment add the soda. If greater strength is required, add a jigger of brandy to each serving.

A night of good drinking
Is worth a year's thinking.
Charles Cotton: c. 1665

They that drink longest live longest.
Scottish Proverb

When the arm bends the mouth opens.
Danish Proverb

There comes a night
When we all get tight.
American Proverb

Drunk for a penny, dead drunk for tuppence, clean straw for nothing.
*Old sign on a
London liquor shop*

When everybody says you are drunk go to bed. *Italian Proverb*

It is a bad man who remembers what went on at a drinking bout.
Greek Proverb

Carefree and drunk. *Securus et ebrius.*
Latin Proverb

A bumper of good liquor
Will end a contest quicker
Than justice, judge or vicar.
R. B. Sheridan

Who drinks will drink again.
French Proverb

Drinking a little too much is drinking much too much. *German Proverb*

Drink? Die! Drink not? Die anyhow!
Therefore, drink! *Bavarian Proverb*

What a man says drunk he has thought sober. *Flemish Proverb*

A drunken man thinks the sea is only knee-deep. *Russian Proverb*

Drink! for you know not whence you came, nor why:
Drink! for you know not why you go, nor where. *Persian Saying*

It's all right to drink like a fish —
if you drink what a fish drinks.
Mary Pettibone Poole

No man is drunk so long as he can lie on the floor without holding on.
Obscure Saying

Nogs Grogs, Punches . . . continued

Stirrup Cup

Here is a punch which is customarily mixed in the glass, in individual portions:

1 part brown sugar dissolved in water	4 parts pineapple juice
2 parts lime juice	12 parts Jamaica rum

Serve in a tall glass partially filled with cracked ice. Decorate glass with lemon peel twisted into a spiral.

Tom and Jerry

The name *Tom and Jerry*, supposedly a compound from the nicknames of two old-time bartenders, is familiar to all who are partial to traditional yule drinks. A Tom and Jerry is a variety of hot egg nog. Although all recipes call for a base of rum, this base is blended either with brandy or bourbon. The quantities for punch bowl servings are indicated below.

1 dz. eggs	1 tbs. allspice
½ lb. sugar	1 tbs. cinnamon
4 ozs. Jamaica rum	1 tbs. ground cloves

Beat egg yolks and whites separately, the sugar and spices with the yolks. Rum is added to the mixed yolks; the beaten whites are then combined with the yolks. This forms a basic mixture, which is ladled out as required. For each serving ladle a portion of this base into a large mug, add two ounces of bourbon (or brandy), and fill mug with boiling water or hot milk. Dust with ground nutmeg.

Applejack Punch

One of the most inexpensive of the potent punches, it is recommended for large gatherings, where heavy traffic is expected at the punch bowl.

8 ozs. Grenadine	1 pint orange juice
1 pint lemon juice	2 bottles applejack
	2 qts. ginger ale

All ingredients except the ginger ale are blended an hour or so before serving. The ginger ale and ice are added at the last.

Wassail Recipe

1 dz. eggs	2 tsps. ginger
4 bottles Sherry or Madeira	6 whole cloves
2 lbs. sugar	½ tsp. mace
1 tsp. pwd. nutmeg	6 allspice berries
	1 tsp. cinnamon

Mix the dry ingredients in a half pint of water, add the Sherry or Madeira, and let the mixture simmer over a slow fire. Beat the egg yolks and whites separately and add these to the hot brew. Before serving, add several baked apples and a half bottle of brandy for a final fillip.

Artillery Punch

Named for the devastating effect of its salvos, this mixture is a famous black tea-base punch. It is a dry mixture, free from the cloying sweetness which has often classified punch as a drink to accompany afternoon tea and angel cake.

1 qt. strong black tea	½ pint gin
1 bottle rye	½ pt. domestic brandy
1 bottle red wine	1 jigger Benedictine
1 pt. Jamaica rum	1 pint orange juice
½ pint lemon juice	

If the above mixture is found to be too dry, add sugar syrup to taste.

Fish House Punch

Perhaps the most potent of punches is believed to have originated around 1732, at the famous State in Schuylkill Club, in Philadelphia. There are many recipes for this non-carbonated mixture, all variations on a rum and Cognac base. One of the most acceptable is the following:

¾ lb. loaf sugar	1 btle. Cuban rum
1½ pts. lemon juice	1 bottle Cognac
1 btle. Jamaica rum	3½ pints water
	4 ozs. peach brandy

Note: A special sequence is to be followed in mixing these ingredients. Sugar, as all chemists know, does not dissolve readily in alcohol; the sugar consequently, should be stirred in the water until dissolved, then mixed with lemon juice, producing a warm lemonade. Liquors are then added. The mixture must stand for several hours to blend properly and ripen. Before serving, a large block of ice is placed in the bowl, and the mixture is poured over it and stirred until sufficiently cool.

To heighten the joys of the holiday season come some recipes from The Old Publick House in New England, where they have a way with good food and good cheer.

Buttered Rum with Hot Cider

1 tsp. maple sugar or brown sugar	1 pinch cinnamon
	2 cloves
1 butter ball (marble size)	slice of lemon
	1½ oz. Jamaica rum

Combine ingredients in mug or glass and fill with hot cider. Serve immediately.

Sillabub (*Our Old Grog List Spelling*)

½ cup brandy	1 cup sherry
sugar, milk,	1 cup port
cream, nutmeg	

Mix the sherry, port and brandy. Pour in punch bowl. Fill with rich milk and add sugar to taste. Mix these ingredients well. Pour on thick cream and dust with nutmeg. This should be at room temperature when served.

CHAMPAGNE LORE

More champagne is served at the holiday season than any other period of the year. Here are some points to keep in mind: Always keep champagne lying on its side to keep the cork moist and to preserve the sparkle of the wine. Chill before serving to about 45 degrees. Avoid overchilling as this impairs the subtleties of the vintage. A good way to achieve the right temperature is to place the champagne in the refrigerator for two or three hours or place it in an ice bucket with crushed or chopped ice for 20-30 minutes.

Because the wide saucer-shaped glass in which champagne should be served tends to allow the wine to become warm, the glass should never be filled more than three-quarters full and then frequently freshened. While opening the champagne bottle, wrap a napkin around the neck. It may be very fine and festive to have the cork popping about the room but it may cause damage or leave a mark on your ceiling. The napkin also prevents spilling over your clothes.

Lemon Champagne Punch

1 bottle Champagne	1 pint lemon ice

Place lemon ice in punch bowl and pour chilled champagne over it. Serves 10.

Fruit Champagne Punch

juice of 2 oranges	1 cup rum
juice of 2 lemons	1 cup of pineapple juice
½ cup sugar	2 bottles Champagne

Mix in order named in large punch bowl with block of ice. Serve in punch glasses with fresh strawberry and slice of pineapple. Serves 18.

Nectar Champagne Cup

1 pineapple cut in slices	4 oz. curacao
12 slices of cucumber rind	1 quart bottle club soda or seltzer
1 box of strawberries	
1 bottle Champagne	

Stir slowly in punch bowl with block of ice. Serves 12.

A Gourmet's Wine Chart

Foods and wines should be chosen to complement each other. Gentry recommends:

With foie gras:
> *Any light Champagne.*

With oysters and other seafood:
> *A dry white wine: Muscadet, Alsace, or Pouilly.*

With grilled fish:
> *All dry white wines.*

With fish and sauce dishes:
> *A white wine of fuller body: Cramant, Meursault, Chablis, Bordeaux Blanc sec.*

With crayfish and lobsters:
> *Mellower white wine: Bordeaux Blanc, Anjou, Vouvray or Champagne brut.*

With entrees:
> *Moderate red wine: Bourgueil, Bordeaux and Bourgogne Rouges ½ corsés.*

With roasts or grills:
> *Limpid red wine: Beaujolais, Côtes-du-Rhône, Tavel Bourgogne and Bordeaux plus corsés.*

With game:
> *A great red wine: Bordeaux, Bourgogne.*

With processed cheese:
> *Limpid red wine: Beaujolais, Côtes-du-Rhône, Tavel Bourgogne and Bordeaux plus corsés, or a great red wine: Bordeaux and Bourgogne.*

With fresh cheese:
> *Light red or white wine: Chinon, Coteaux du Loir.*

With soft, more fatty cheeses:
> *Light red wine: Fleurie.*

With side-dishes and desserts:
> *The great sweet white wines: Grand Bordeaux, Blanc Rochecorbon, Monbazillac.*

With fruit:
> *Champagne.*

Cooking with Beer...

Beer is finding its way among culinary props in the kitchen. Already enjoying a reputation as a good mixer, it is now striving for recognition as a recipe ingredient. According to the Ballantine Beer Company, who cooked up the recipes listed below, its use lends piquancy to the menu. Those who tend toward expanding waistlines should probably approach the subject with some caution. Bon appetit and cheers!

Beef and Beer Stew

3 tbs. fat	¼ tsp. thyme
1½ lbs. beef stew	2 tsp. salt
meat, cubed	sprig celery
2 tbs. flour	¾ tsp. sugar
1½ cups water	12 small white
1 12-oz. bottle	onions
beer	4 medium pota-
½ bay leaf	toes halved
8 small carrots	

Melt fat in large skillet. Dredge meat in flour; brown in fat. Add liquids and seasonings. Cover tightly; simmer one hour or until tender. Add peeled vegetables, and simmer additional half hour. If desired, pan gravy may be thickened with flour. Four to six servings.

Epicurean Shrimp

1 12-oz. bottle beer	2 slices lemon
¼ cup chopped	1½ lbs. raw shrimp
onion	2 tbs. butter
1 clove garlic	2 tbs. flour
1 tsp. salt	1 8-oz. can tomato
¼ tsp. thyme	sauce
½ bay leaf	½ tsp. sugar
sprig parsley	1 cup cooked rice

Bring beer, onion, seasoning, parsley, lemon and bay leaf to boil in saucepan. Add cleaned and shelled shrimp. Simmer 5 minutes. Strain liquid. Melt butter in separate pan; blend in flour. Gradually add tomato sauce, sugar, shrimp and liquid; bring to boil, stirring. Serve on cooked rice. Four to six servings.

Steak Surprise

1 2-inch porter-	4 tbs. butter
house steak	1 tsp. Worcester-
malt vinegar	shire sauce
olive oil	2 tbs. flour
1 lb. fresh	2 cups beer
mushrooms	¼ tsp. dry mustard
salt and pepper	

Rub steak with vinegar and oil; season on both sides and let stand at room temperature an hour. Broil to desired degree of rareness, searing 1½ minutes on each side at 550°, then dropping heat to 375°, and turning once. (Broil at lowered heat 6 minutes on each side for rare; 8 minutes for medium; 10 for well done.) A few minutes before steak is ready, sauté sliced mushrooms in butter, season with mustard, salt and pepper, add flour, stirring well. Drain fat from steak juice in broiler pan and with beer add to mushrooms. Stir well, bring to boil, pour over sliced steak on hot platter and serve at once. Serves four to six.

Bacon Fondue

8 slices white bread	½ tsp. dry mustard
3 tbs. butter	dash Tabasco
8 thin slices sharp	salt and pepper
cheese	1 12-oz. bottle beer
3 eggs	½ lb. bacon
1 tsp. Worcestershire sauce	

Remove crusts from bread; spread slices with butter. Arrange bread and cheese slices alternately in greased 8-inch casserole. Beat eggs well; add seasoning and beer. Pour into casserole. Bake in moderate oven (350°) 40 minutes, or until well browned. Top with crisp bacon. Four servings.

Swiss Steak with Rice

2 lbs. round steak	1 bay leaf
cut 2 in. thick	1 tsp. Worcester-
1 cup flour	shire sauce
2 tsp. salt	1¼ cups cooked rice
dash pepper	1 cup stale warm
6 onions	beer
¼ cup fat	2 cups cooked
1 cup water	string beans
butter	

Pound meat thoroughly. Rub flour and seasonings into the meat. Brown sliced onions in fat. Remove onions and brown meat in same pan. Cover meat with onions and water, add bay leaf and Worcestershire. Bake in slow oven (325°) for 2 hours. Top with rice, pour beer over all. Cover and bake until meat is tender. Serve with buttered string beans. Serves four to six.

Welsh Rarebit

1 tbs. butter	½ tsp. grated
1 cup beer	horseradish
1 lb. grated	2 tsp. dry
Cheddar	mustard
2 egg yolks	½ tsp. salt
¼ tsp. Cayenne	¼ cup milk
pepper	dash paprika
2 tbs. Worcestershire sauce	

Melt butter in chafing dish or double boiler; add beer and stir. Add cheese, melting very slowly, stirring steadily. When liquid is smooth, add egg yolks mixed with seasoning and milk. Stir quickly until thickened. Pour over the soft side of half-toast with crust removed in individually heated servers. Sprinkle with paprika and serve immediately. Serves six.

Veal Breast Caprice

3 lbs. breast	2 cloves
of veal	pinch of grated
3 tbs. butter	nutmeg
2 tbs. flour	1 sliced Spanish
1 tsp. salt	onion
¼ tsp. pepper	1½ cups beer

Have butcher remove bone and roll veal. Soften butter, together with flour, salt and pepper, and rub on meat. Place on rack in open roasting pan and sear in hot oven (475°) until lightly browned. Add cloves, nutmeg, onion and beer. Cover pan and reduce oven heat to 325°. Bake an hour and a quarter. Six servings.

Beef Tongue with Beer Sauce

3 to 4 lbs. beef	1 tsp. seedless
tongue	raisins
soup greens	1 tsp. chopped
2 cloves	almonds
4 peppercorns	grated lemon peel
1 tbs. butter	1 small bay leaf
1 tsp. powdered	1 cup beer
sugar	salt

Cover tongue with cold water and simmer with coarsely chopped soup greens (1 onion, 2 celery stalks, 3 sprigs parsley, 2 carrots) cloves and peppercorns, in covered kettle about 3½ hours. Remove from heat and let stand in liquid until cool. Save liquid; remove skin and fat from tongue and cut in ½ inch slices. Melt butter, add sugar and let brown. Add 3 cups strained tongue liquid and bring to boil. Add raisins, almonds, lemon peel, bay leaf and beer. When simmering, add sliced tongue, and bring to a boil. Salt to taste. Serve part of sauce in gravy bowl. Six to eight servings.

GENTRY CHART OF FAMOUS ELIXIRS

Name	Country	Source or Chief Ingredients	Color and Taste	How and When Served	Remarks
ADVOCAAT	Holland	Eggs and brandy.	Yellow and sweet.	Between meals and as nightcap; cold or room temperature.	*Wonderful combination food and tonic. Try it for a quick energy pick-up.*
AKVAVIT	Denmark	Spirit distilled from potatoes; flavored with caraway seed, cardamom, orange and lemon peel.	Yellow.	Very cold as a liqueur.	*The "whiskey" of Scandinavia; can be served whenever "hard" liquors are called for. It is customarily not sipped but, like vodka, downed at a single swallow.*
ANISETTE	U. S. and Europe	Brandy liqueur flavored with aniseed.	White with anise flavor.	As after-dinner liqueur.	*Try a dash in your Dry Martinis for a distinctive effect.*
APPLEJACK	U. S.	Brandy distilled from apples.	Brown.	Neat, in highballs, or as base for mixing.	*For a variation in cocktails try a Jack Rose Deluxe: 1 part Grenadine, 2 parts lemon juice, 8 parts Applejack. Shake with cracked ice; strain. Add twist of lemon.*
ARMAGNAC	Gers, France	Grape brandy.	Golden, dry.	As after-dinner liqueur; room temperature.	*Similar in type to Cognac, but slightly drier in flavor, Armagnac owes its distinction to a special distillation process and the type of wood used in the aging casks.*
BATAVIA ARAK	Java	Rum distilled from Javanese molasses and red rice.	Pale and dry, with strong aroma.	In cocktails, punches, highballs.	*The basic ingredient of Arak Punch — commonly known as Swedish Punch.*
BENEDICTINE	Fecamp, France	Plant liqueur made by steeping herbs and fruit peels in Cognac.	Golden; spicy and sweet.	As after-dinner liqueur.	*A traditional after-dinner drink is B & B — 1 part Benedictine, 1 part Cognac. The letters "D.O.M." on the Benedictine label stand for "Deo Optimo Maximo," "To God, the Best, the Greatest."*
CALVADOS	Normandy, France	Apple brandy distilled from apples grown in the department of Calvados in Normandy.	Brown; dry and fruity.	As after-dinner liqueur or use as a cocktail base.	*Perhaps the greatest of the apple brandies.*
CHARTREUSE	Spain	Plant liqueur made according to a secret formula of the Carthusian Fathers.	Yellow or green; spicy and sweet.	As after-dinner liqueur.	*Green Chartreuse is decidedly more potent than Yellow — 110° proof as against 86°. It is also drier and more aromatic.*
CHERRY HEERING		A rich liqueur made from wild, black cherries in a base of grape brandy.	Dark red; sweet.	As after-dinner liqueur.	*The finest of all cherry liqueurs.*

Name	Country	Source or Chief Ingredients	Color and Taste	How and When Served	Remarks
COGNAC	Charente, France	Grape brandy.	Golden, dry.	As after dinner liqueur, in high-balls, and as cocktail base.	Ordinary Cognac is traditionally served in pony glasses. old Cognac in large "snifters."
COINTREAU	Angers, France	Brand name for one of the finest Triple Secs — a white Curaçao, usually distilled at 80° proof.	White; sweet orange flavor.	As after-dinner liqueur, and cocktail ingredient.	The official Side Car cocktail recipe calls for 1 part Cointreau. 2 parts lemon juice, 8 parts Cognac. Shake vigorously with cracked ice.
CREME DE CACAO	U. S. and Europe	Liqueur flavored with cacao and vanilla.	Chocolate colored, chocolate flavored.	As after-dinner liqueur or cocktail ingredient.	Flavor base of the Alexander cocktail: 1 part Crème de Cacao, 1 part cream, 4 parts gin. Shake with cracked ice.
CREME DE CASSIS	France	Liqueur flavored with black currants.	Red, with sweet, currant flavor.	Extremely cold in mixed drinks.	For a mild, long drink, try a Vermouth-Cassis: 1 pony Crème de Cassis, 1 jigger French Vermouth, 1 cube ice. Stir in tall glass with soda.
CREME DE MENTHE	U. S. and Europe	Brandy liqueur flavor obtained from several varieties of mint, chiefly peppermint.	Green or yellow.	Chilled as an after-dinner liqueur, or frappé over crushed ice.	Flavor base of the Stinger cocktail: 2 parts white Crème de Menthe, 1 part lime juice, 6 parts brandy. Shake with crushed ice; strain into chilled, frosted glass.
CURAÇAO	U. S., West Indies, and Europe	Brandy liqueur flavored chiefly with the dried peel of the green oranges from the island of Curaçao.	Orange in both color and flavor.	As after-dinner liqueur or mixed drink ingredient.	In the Curaçao cocktail, the usual proportions of sweet and sour are reversed. The recipe: 2 parts Curaçao, 1 part lemon juice, 6 parts whiskey. Stir with cracked ice. Add twist of lemon peel.
DANZIGER GOLDWASSER	Danzig	Liqueur made chiefly from orange peel and other spicy herbs. Flecks of genuine gold leaf are added, though this in no way contributes to flavor or effect.	White and sweet.	At room temperature as after-dinner liqueur.	One of the oldest liqueurs in existence — a descendant of the elixirs of medieval alchemists.
DRAMBUIE	Scotland	Liqueur compounded from Scotch whisky, honey, and special herbs.	Golden; sweet and spicy.	As after-dinner liqueur.	An ideal flavor addition to any sweet cocktail made with a Scotch whisky base.
DUBONNET	France	Sweet red wine flavored with aromatic herbs.	Red and sweet.	Thoroughly chilled as an appetizer, or use as flavor base in mixed drinks.	Dubonnet can be served whenever Port or Sherry is in order. Dubonnet cocktail: 1 part Dubonnet, 1 part gin. Stir with cracked ice. Add twist of lemon peel.
GRAND MARNIER	Cognac, France	Brand name for an exceptional Curaçao.	Orange in color and flavor.	As after-dinner liqueur or as flavor base in all cocktails calling for Curaçao.	Perhaps the finest of all orange-flavored liqueurs. Blends perfectly in all cocktails of the "sour" type. A "must" for crêpes suzettes.

Name	Country	Source or Chief Ingredients	Color and Taste	How and When Served	Remarks
KIRSCHWASSER	U. S. and Europe	Brandy made from the distillation of fermented cherries.	White with dry, bitter almond flavor.	At room temperature as after-dinner liqueur.	*A good Kirschwasser cocktail is the Swiss Special: 1 part gin, 1 part Kirschwasser, 2 parts rye. Add 1 or 2 dashes sugar syrup. Shake with cracked ice. Float ½ teaspoon of Grand Marnier on each.*
KÜMMEL	U. S. and Europe	A spirit liqueur flavored chiefly with caraway seed.	White, with pronounced caraway flavor.	Cold as liqueur after coffee.	*One of the best Kümmel cocktails is the Tovarich: 1 part Kümmel, 2 parts lime juice, 8 parts Vodka. Shake well.*
PRUNELLE	France	Liqueur made from plums.	Brown, with sweet, plum flavor.	At room temperature as after-dinner liqueur.	*A pleasant plum liqueur, not to be confused with plum brandies — such as Quetsch or Slivovitz.*
QUETSCH	Alsace, France	Brandy made from distillation of fermented plums.	White and dry.	As after-dinner liqueur.	*This is a true brandy, not a liqueur; it can be used whenever Cognac is in order.*
SAKE	Japan	Special type of rice beer.	White and dry.	Slightly warmed during dinner.	*You will find Saké more palatable when its flavor is disguised. Try it with bitters.*
SLIVOVITZ	Hungary, Central Europe, U.S.	Brandy made from distillation of fermented plums.	Brown and dry.	Like whiskey, or as after-dinner liqueur.	*Slivovitz has not as yet found its way into the official pages of cocktail literature.*
SLOE GIN	England and U.S.	Liqueur flavored with sloeberries — fruit of the blackthorn tree.	Reddish; sweet and astringent.	At room temperature as after-dinner liqueur; as flavor base in mixed drinks.	*Base of the Sloe Gin Fizz: juice of one lemon, 1 teaspoon sugar syrup, 2 jiggers Sloe Gin. Shake with crushed ice; strain into chilled 8-oz. glass. Fill with soda.*
STREGA	Italy	Highly aromatic liqueur made with Italian herbs.	Golden; sweet.	At room temperature as after-dinner liqueur.	*A perfect finish to an Italian dinner.*
SWEDISH PUNSCH	Sweden	Liqueur made with Java rum. (See Batavia Arak)	Yellow, with sweet rummy taste.	Chilled as after-dinner liqueur.	*An interesting Swedish Punsch cocktail is the Doctor: equal parts lemon juice, Swedish Punsch and Gin. Also known as the Greta Garbo.*
TEQUILA	U. S. and Mexico	Spirit distilled from fermented pulp of the century plant.	Pale, dry.	Straight.	*Prepare yourself for spontaneous combustion.*
VERMOUTH	France; Italy; U.S.	Wine in which aromatic herbs have been steeped.	Dry or sweet.	Chilled as an apéritif, or use as cocktail base.	*French Vermouth is the standard base for Dry Martinis; Italian, for Manhattans.*
VODKA	U. S. and Russia	Whiskey distilled chiefly from wheat.	White, dry.	Thoroughly chilled.	*Russians traditionally drink Vodka throughout a meal. This practice is recommended however, only if you have steel innards.*

Appetizers

FROM CHINA

Crab Meat and Pork

1½ pounds pork, ground	2 teaspoons salt
¼ pound cooked or canned crab meat	½ teaspoon pepper
	1 teaspoon sugar
½ cup chopped mushrooms	1 cup cornstarch
	2 eggs, beaten
½ cup chopped canned water chestnuts (optional)	2 tablespoons water
	Fat for deep frying

Combine the pork, crab meat, mushrooms, water chestnuts, salt, pepper, and sugar in a chopping bowl. Chop until well blended and very fine in texture. Shape into 1-inch balls. Dip each ball in cornstarch and coat well. Combine the eggs and water and dip each ball in the mixture. Heat the fat to 360° and drop the balls into it. Fry for 15 minutes. Drain well. Serve with sliced cucumbers. These little balls are excellent as hors d'oeuvres; spear each one with a toothpick and a thin slice of cucumber.

FROM RUSSIA

Eggplant Caviar

1 large eggplant	3 tablespoons vinegar
1 small onion, sliced	1½ teaspoons salt
2 tomatoes, peeled	½ teaspoon pepper
1 slice white bread, trimmed	2 teaspoons sugar
	4 tablespoons salad oil

Wash the eggplant and cut off the stem. Place the eggplant on a baking sheet or wrap it loosely in aluminum foil. Bake in a 325° oven for 1 hour. Cool for 30 minutes. Peel and set aside. Place the onion in a chopping bowl and chop fine. Add the tomatoes and eggplant and chop fine. Pour the vinegar on the bread, soaking it well. Add to the eggplant with the salt, pepper, sugar, and oil. Continue chopping until well blended. Correct seasoning; the mixture should be fairly spicy. Chill for at least 1 hour. Serve with slices of thin pumpernickel bread.

To Drink With Appetizers:

with Crab Meat and Pork — Hong-Kong gimlet; with Eggplant Caviar — Vodka.

Soups

FROM SPAIN

Gazpacho

2 onions, chopped	2 teaspoons Spanish paprika
2 cloves garlic, minced	
4 green peppers, chopped	⅓ cup olive oil
	⅓ cup wine vinegar
5 tomatoes, chopped	1½ cups water
2 teaspoons salt	1 cucumber, peeled and sliced very thin
½ teaspoon pepper	

Combine the onions, garlic, green peppers, and tomatoes. Force through a sieve or purée in an electric blender. Add the salt, pepper, and paprika. Add the olive oil gradually, beating steadily. Add the vinegar and water and stir well. Correct seasoning. Place in the refrigerator to chill for at least 2 hours, using a wooden or glass bowl; do not use a metal bowl. Add the cucumber slices before serving. Slices of toast rubbed with garlic may be served with the *gazpacho*.

This dish may be served as either a cold soup or as a salad, though it will be quite a wet salad. When *gazpacho* is served, no other soup or salad is necessary.

FROM MALAYA

Chicken Liver and Pea Soup

1 pound pork and several pork bones	1 teaspoon powdered ginger
2 quarts water	1 No. 1 can green peas, drained
2 teaspoons salt	
½ pound chicken livers	1 tablespoon soy sauce
½ cup chopped mushrooms	½ teaspoon pepper

Combine the pork, bones, salt, and water in a saucepan. Bring to a boil and cook over medium heat for 2 hours. Strain the stock and reserve it. Chop the liver coarsely. Place liver in a saucepan with the mushrooms, stock, ginger and green peas. Cook over low heat for 10 minutes. Add the soy sauce and pepper. Bring to a boil and remove from heat. Serve very hot. The pork may be used for another dish, or served separately.

Note: If desired, 2 cans of beef or chicken consommé and 3 cans of water may be used instead of making a pork stock.

Seafood

FROM TURKEY

Swordfish on Skewers

1½ pounds swordfish	1 teaspoon salt
2 tablespoons olive oil	1 tablespoon lemon
¼ teaspoon paprika	juice
2 tablespoons finely grated onion	10 bay leaves

Wash and dry the fish. Remove the skin carefully and cut into 1½-inch cubes. Combine in a bowl the olive oil, paprika, onion, salt, lemon juice, and bay leaves. Stir well. Place the cubes of fish in it and see that each piece of fish is coated with the mixture. Marinate in the refrigerator for a least 5 hours, overnight if possible. Divide the fish in six parts and place pieces carefully on skewers. Broil in 450° oven for 6 minutes on each side. Serve with the following sauce:

6 tablespoons lemon juice	½ teaspoon salt
4 tablespoons olive oil	1 tablespoon chopped parsley

Combine the lemon juice, olive oil, salt, and chopped parsley. Stir all together. Serve at room temperature in a sauceboat.

Note: If swordfish is unobtainable, fresh tuna or halibut may be substituted.

FROM JAMAICA

Codfish Fritters

1 pound salt cod	3 eggs, beaten
1 onion, chopped fine	¼ cup flour
½ tomato, chopped	3 tablespoons butter
1 clove garlic, minced	

Soak the cod in cold water overnight, or at least 3 hours. Drain completely. Place in a saucepan with water to cover and cook for 40 minutes. Additional water may be required. When cooked, remove the bones carefully. Mince fine with a fork. Add the onion, tomato, and garlic and mix. Beat the eggs and add. Mix well. Form into small fritters.

Dip each fritter in flour. Heat the butter in a frying pan and fry the fritters until golden brown on both sides. In Jamaica, this dish is served with boiled green bananas or with fried plantains. However, it may be accompanied by French fried potatoes. Small fritters make very good hot hors d'oeuvres.

To Drink With Seafood:

with Swordfish and Codfish — French white wines such as Alsace, Pouilly, Chablis, Graves;
with Curry — French red wines; Burgundy or claret, or Italian wine, Chianti.

FROM SINGAPORE

Lobster Curry

3 cups milk	2 tablespoons curry powder
2 cups fresh or dried grated coconut	2 tomatoes, chopped
¼ pound butter	2 tablespoons flour
5 onions, chopped	1 cucumber, peeled and cubed
2 cloves garlic, minced	Meat from 2 boiled
⅛ teaspoon cumin seed	lobsters or 1 pound
2 teaspoons powdered ginger	lobster meat, cubed
Dash of cayenne	2 tablespoons lemon juice
2 teaspoons salt	1 tablespoon plum jam

Combine the milk and coconut in a saucepan. Bring to a boil, remove from the heat, and soak for 30 minutes. Press all the milk from the coconut, discard the pulp.

Melt the butter in a saucepan and add the onions and garlic. Sauté for 10 minutes, stirring frequently. Add the cumin seed, ginger, cayenne pepper, salt, curry powder, and tomatoes. Cover and cook over low heat for 10 minutes, stirring frequently. Add the flour, stirring constantly. Add the coconut milk slowly, stirring steadily until the boiling point is reached. Add the cucumber and lobster meat and cook over low heat for 15 minutes. Mix the lemon juice and jam together and add to the lobster mixture. Correct seasoning. Mix well. Serve hot, with boiled rice.

Note: Singapore is famous for the fieriness of its curries. Additional curry powder may be added if desired.

FROM ITALY

Shrimp in Wine Sauce

2 pounds shrimp, shelled and cleaned	½ teaspoon pepper
	Dash of cayenne
½ cup flour	pepper
½ cup olive oil	1 tablespoon chopped
½ cup dry white wine	parsley
2 teaspoons tomato paste	1 scallion (green
4 tablespoons warm water	onion), chopped
1 teaspoon salt	2 teaspoons lemon juice

Wash and drain the shrimp. Roll them in the flour. Heat the olive oil in a skillet. Add the shrimp and brown on both sides. Drain the oil but reserve it. Add the wine to the shrimp and cook over low heat until the wine is absorbed.

Combine the reserved olive oil, tomato paste, water, salt, pepper, and cayenne pepper in a saucepan. Cook over low heat for 5 minutes. Pour this sauce over the shrimp, add the parsley and scallion, and cook for 5 minutes. Remove from the pan, add the lemon juice, and serve.

Entrees

FROM JAPAN

Beef Sukiyaki and Soy Sauce

4 tablespoons sesame oil or salad oil	1 cup sliced celery
2 pounds sirloin steak, cut into strips, ½ inch by 2 inches	1 cup sliced, canned bamboo shoots
½ cup stock or ½ bouillon cube dissolved in ½ cup boiling water	½ pound mushrooms, sliced thin
¾ cup soy sauce	1 cup shredded spinach
¼ cup sugar	4 scallions (green onions), sliced
1 tablespoon sherry	1 pound vermicelli, boiled and drained
3 onions, sliced thin	

Heat the oil in a large frying pan. Add the meat and brown on all sides. Combine the stock, soy sauce, sugar, and sherry in a bowl. Add half of this mixture to the meat, reserving the balance. Push the meat to one side of the frying pan. Add the onions and celery and cook over low heat for 3 minutes. Add the remaining stock mixture, bamboo shoots, mushrooms, and spinach. Cook over low heat for 3 minutes. Add the scallions and cook for 1 minute. Place the vermicelli on one side of a platter and the sukiyaki on the other side and serve immediately.

FROM GREECE

Lamb and Artichokes

¼ pound butter	1 bay leaf
3 pounds lamb, cut into 1-inch cubes	4 cups boiling water
2 onions, chopped	6 artichokes
2 cloves garlic, minced	3 eggs
2 teaspoons salt	2 tablespoons lemon juice
1 teaspoon pepper	12 ripe olives

Melt the butter in a saucepan. Add the lamb and brown well on all sides. Add the onions, garlic, salt, pepper, bay leaf and boiling water. Cover and cook for 40 minutes, stirring occasionally.

Remove the largest outside leaves of the artichoke. Cut off and discard the top third of the artichoke. Cut the balance of the artichoke in half and add to the lamb. Cover and cook over low heat for 45 minutes. Beat eggs and lemon juice together in a bowl. Add 1 cup of the gravy from the saucepan very gradually to the contents of the bowl, beating steadily. Return this mixture to the saucepan, beating constantly. Add the olives. Cook over low heat for 5 minutes but do not allow to boil.

To Drink With Entrees:

with Sukiyaki — Saké;
with Lamb — Greek or New York State red wine;
with Goulash — Tokay;
with Chicken — Rhône wine or Burgundy.

FROM HUNGARY

Hungarian Beef Goulash

6 tablespoons butter	3 pounds beef (cross rib, chuck, etc.)
5 onions, chopped	1 can tomato sauce
2 tablespoons Hungarian paprika	1 clove garlic, minced (optional)
2 teaspoons salt	½ cup sour cream
½ teaspoon pepper	

Melt 4 tablespoons of the butter in a heavy saucepan. Add the onions and sauté for 15 minutes, stirring frequently. Remove the onions and set them aside. Combine the paprika, salt and pepper. Cut the meat into 2-inch cubes and roll in the mixture. Melt the remaining butter in the saucepan. Add the meat and brown well on all sides. Return the onions to the saucepan. Add the tomato sauce and garlic and stir. Cover and cook over low heat for 3 hours, stirring occasionally. Add the sour cream and stir. Heat but do not allow the mixture to boil. Serve hot.

FROM INDIA

Chicken Korma

2 3½-pound frying chickens, disjointed	2 onions, chopped fine
1 cup buttermilk or yogurt	½ teaspoon powdered ginger
4 cloves garlic, minced	2 cloves
4 tablespoons butter	1½ teaspoon salt

Clean the chicken parts carefully and place in a large bowl. Mix the buttermilk or yogurt with half the garlic and pour over the chicken. Marinate at room temperature for 2 hours, basting frequently. Melt the butter in a casserole or heavy saucepan. Add the onions, remaining garlic, the ginger, cloves, and salt. Sauté over low heat for 5 minutes, stirring frequently. Prepare either of the following mixtures. The following Indian *korma* mixture will give a superior flavor.

Indian Korma Mixture	Simple Korma Mixture
2 tsps. ground coriander	1 tablespoon imported Indian curry powder
2 tsps. ground almonds	1 teaspoon ground almonds
¾ tsp. ground turmeric	
¼ tsp. ground cumin seed	
⅛ tsp. pepper	
⅛ tsp. dried ground chili peppers	

Add either mixture to the onions and stir well. Cook for 5 minutes, stirring frequently. Add the chicken and its marinade. Cover and cook over low heat for 1½ to 2 hours, or until chicken is tender, stirring occasionally. Serve with boiled rice.

Round-The-World Recipes . . .

FROM FRANCE

Veal and Mushrooms

½ pound butter	2 egg yolks
3 onions, sliced thin	3 tablespoons heavy
2 tablespoons flour	cream
1 cup chicken stock or	24 mushrooms, stems
1 cup canned con-	removed
sommé	12 slices veal (¼ inch
½ cup milk	thick)
1 teaspoon salt	1 3-oz. can pâté de foie
⅛ teaspoon pepper	gras

Melt half the butter in a saucepan. Add the onions and cook over very low heat for 15 minutes; do not allow them to brown. Sprinkle with the flour and mix well. Gradually add the stock and milk, stirring constantly until the boiling point is reached. Add the salt and pepper. Cover and cook over very low heat for 40 minutes, stirring occasionally. Force the mixture through a sieve. Beat the egg yolks and cream together in a bowl. Gradually add the sauce, beating constantly to prevent curdling. Reheat but do not allow to boil.

Melt 4 tablespoons of the butter in a skillet. Add the mushrooms and sauté for 5 minutes, stirring occasionally. Melt the remaining 4 tablespoons of butter in a skillet. Add the veal slices and sauté for 5 minutes on each side. Spread the pâté de foie gras on 6 of the veal slices and cover with the remaining 6 slices.

Place the veal in an ovenproof dish that may be brought to the table. Arrange the mushrooms around the meat and pour the sauce over it. Place under the broiler until delicately browned, about 5 minutes. Serve directly from the dish.

Salads

FROM TURKEY

Fruit Salad with Ginger-Brandy Dressing

2 teaspoons powdered	1 cup fresh or canned
ginger	pineapple, cubed
½ cup brandy	1 cup strawberries,
2 oranges, peeled and	halved
sliced thin	

Dissolve the ginger in the brandy. Combine the oranges, pineapple, and strawberries in a bowl. Pour the brandy over the fruits, basting them for a few moments. Cover the bowl and chill for 3 hours. Arrange the salad on lettuce leaves and serve.

Note: Any combination of three fruits may be used with ginger-brandy dressing for an unusual fruit salad.

FROM ITALY

Green Salad with Anchovies and Capers

½ cup chopped green	2 scallions (green
pepper	onions), sliced
½ cup chopped red	6 radishes, chopped
pepper	1 teaspoon chopped
2 teaspoons chopped	anchovies
parsley	2 tablespoons capers
½ cup chopped fresh	½ teaspoon salt
tomatoes	¼ teaspoon pepper
2 tablespoons chopped	3 tsps. wine vinegar
celery	½ cup olive oil

Combine the green pepper, red pepper, parsley, tomatoes, celery, scallions, radishes, anchovies, capers, salt, and pepper in a bowl. Add the vinegar, mixing lightly. Add olive oil gradually, mixing thoroughly.

For a Party

FROM SWITZERLAND

Cheese Fondue

1 clove garlic	2 teaspoons potato flour
½ cup white wine	2 tablespoons kirsch or
¼ pound Gruyère cheese,	dry sherry
grated	12 slices toast

Rub an earthenware casserole or chafing dish with the garlic, then discard it. Pour the white wine into it and cook over medium heat for 2 minutes. Add the grated cheese and bring to the boiling point, stirring occasionally. In a cup, mix the potato flour and *kirsch* or sherry to a smooth paste and add to the cheese mixture, stirring occasionally for 3 minutes, or until the mixture is thick. Cut the toast into 1-inch strips. Bring the casserole to the table and place the toast strips around it. Each guest dips a strip of toast into the *fondue.*

FROM SCOTLAND

Scotch Shortbread

½ pound sweet butter	1 cup sifted cake flour
1 cup confectioners'	2 tablespoons cornstarch
sugar	

Combine the butter and sugar together on a board. Blend together with the hands. Sift the flour and cornstarch together and gradually work it into the previous mixture until well blended. Preheat oven to 425°. Butter an 8-inch square pan and dust lightly with flour. Pat the dough into the pan with the hands, as this dough cannot be rolled. Prick the top with a fork in several places. Bake in a 425° oven for 5 minutes; then reduce the heat to 350° and bake 10 minutes longer, or until lightly browned. Cut into squares immediately.

To Drink At a Party:

with Cheese Fondue — Swiss white wine or Kirsch; with Shortbread — fruit punch or Scotch.

From: THE COMPLETE ROUND-THE-WORLD COOKBOOK, by Myra Waldo. Copyright 1954 by Myra Waldo Schwartz, reprinted by permission of the author and Doubleday & Company, Inc.

THE SLIM GOURMET IS BORN

From "Physiologie du Gout" by Brillat-Savarin . . . drawing by Bertall, engraving by Ch. Geoffroy.

Report on 365 days in which the author lived the life of a Slim Gourmet, lost 80 pounds and enjoyed every day of his epicurean diet.

By Martin Lederman

It all started on April 1st, 1952, when my scales showed a stripped-down weight of 250 pounds, and I decided that something had to be done about it. The doctor, after a thorough check-up, found that I was organically in fine shape, but advised me that a loss of 40 to 50 lbs. would improve my health.

He knew that I had been on a slimming diet once before, that he could refrain from giving me too detailed advice.

Instead, he put a good medical text on reducing in my hand. "You can follow the advice of this book," he said, "It is sound."

I followed the prescription. I counted calories. I weighed the portions served me — to the great annoyance of waiters, cooks, and hostesses. I even lost a few pounds from my persistent embarrassment.

However, I was not happy. And the ghost of this learned author with his recommendations, prescriptions, and portions pursued me in my dreams. In these I found myself enjoying the pleasures of the table only to be reminded of my diet by the sudden appearance of a stern mentor who removed everything I liked from my plate.

The book was trustworthy and sound; the author spoke

the truth — but not the whole truth. He took a stand against so many things I had been accustomed to enjoy. And his insistence on boring menus, calorie-poor foods, and abstinence from so many good things was more than I would be prepared to follow, even for the sake of health and the promise of an Adonis-like figure.

I decided at last to work out my own salvation. As if I had been bitten by a new hobby-horse, I began the study of everything I could find on the subject of nutrition, the problem of overweight, and the methods of therapy.

Many of these books were written either by authors of the Salvation Army Convert type, who condemned with conviction what they had adored until yesterday; or they were the ones of the *Slimming Clown Variety,* who coined at least a dozen corny slogans on every page to bully the reader into a veritable slimming binge. Both neglected a very important aspect — the psychology of the patient, who was not a dummy, but a living and usually quite individualistic human being.

One evening I looked at the bottom of the bookcase which contained my new nutrition library. I had stored there a collection of books describing the enjoyment of food and drink, and a considerable array of cook books. "Here you are," I said to myself, "trying to make cottage cheese replace the protein of a Cassoulet Toulousain, and longing for the pleasures of a four-course dinner at the Pavillon. You are an incurable gourmet who dreams of sauces and Crepes Suzette when he orders hard-boiled eggs and salad without dressing, who is a slave to the delights of the French, Virginia, Italian, and New Orleans Kitchens — who is, in short, beyond hope and repair."

The thing to do, at least so it seemed to me that memorable evening, was to build a bridge connecting these two desires, to find a way to reduce which would not deprive me of all the pleasures I had hitherto enjoyed and which had caused my girth to spread like the proverbial chestnut tree.

I decided from this way of looking at my problem that I had to get a new idea of the quantity of my food intake. As I needed, instead of my customary 5000 calories, only 2500 calories per day, I concluded I would have to eat exactly half the portions I had considered as normal.

Yet, I reasoned, that should not be so difficult for the true gourmet. We know that the second helping or the second glass never equals the first in taste.

✓ ✓ ✓

The law for the gourmet (the first I wrote down on that memorable evening, when I discovered the Slim Gourmet) is:

Utilize all your faculties of enjoyment from the first bite! Eat with all your senses! Leave quantity eating to the food barbarians. Stress quality!

The second law for the new gourmet is this:

Don't cocktailize food. Look for the enjoyment of natural taste in all foods.

The Slim Gourmet is only a natural consequence of a thorough dedication to these basic principles, as I proved to myself by shedding 80 pounds from April of 1952 (when I discovered the laws) to April 2, 1953, when this piece is being written.

When I look back on my self-transformation from a 250-pound food lover to a 170-pound Slim Gourmet, I do not remember that I suffered for even one single day the hunger pangs or attacks of self-pity that are said to be the companions of the weight reducer.

The more I became convinced that my findings and laws were better than past practices and superior to the way of life I had led before, the more enjoyment and pleasure I derived from the new food philosophy.

Every day I discovered a new world. At every meal I could read better in the book of Nature's variety and add new enjoyments to the traditional table pleasures which I learned to despise as the early Christians must have despised the cult of Jupiter Capitolinus.

Of course, I acted very rationally in the matter of calorie restriction and balanced meal composition. Not for nothing had I read the multitude of books on modern nutrition. However, it was not the fact that I restricted my daily allowance to 2500 calories, which had pride of place; it was the selection of *what good things I could eat* that kept my mind and interest busy.

Eating with all my senses made me soon enjoy small portions only; and deep soup plates or a host's too generous carving became dinner-mares to me. Though politeness prevented my protesting, I developed, as a self-defense against gargantuan portions, the fortitude of character to leave whatever was too much on the plate; and even a 20-year-old whiskey was left in the glass when it had been refilled without my express wish. After all, I rationalized, is self-destruction the aim of good manners?

On the basis of my alcoholic inventory, I propose the following resolutions for the Slimming Gourmet: *1.* I will remain a social drinker — and will not under any provocation drink alone. *2.* There is no wine which I cannot enjoy fully without refilling my glass. *3.* The only other drinks I will allow myself are Scotch, Bourbon, and Cognac — and even these I will limit to jigger portions — one per day. *4.* Cognac aged less than thirty years, and whiskey less than eight, do not tempt me; I will drink these only when my gourmet requirements have been met — and that is so seldom that my quantity restrictions are almost superfluous.

The most divergent habits are followed in the number and composition of our meals. Some nations and some people like a heavy breakfast; others, a late and full dinner; still others prefer that lunch be their main meal. My experience with myself, my family, and my friends taught me that these habits have so many roots in education, tradition, working hours, and psychological disposition, that it would be very wrong to make people conform to a general description. If you like a good breakfast, have it. If you cannot sleep without an icebox-raid, raid it. If you want to load your system at lunch with what others eat only at dinner, why shouldn't you?

The Slim Gourmet believes in free choice of his individual ways. It is not when he eats that makes him a gourmet, it is not how he composes his food, but rather

THE SLIM GOURMET'S 10 TRICKS OF THE TRADE

1. *Take it easy.* Dieting is easier when done slowly. It took me some time to learn how. The first 8 weeks I lost 2 pounds a week and felt less well than now, when I lose (while eating well and working hard) a pound every two weeks.

2. *Time is what counts.* Even a daily caloric deficit of only 300 calories (equal to 2 highballs or one average restaurant dessert) makes you lose 28 pounds in a year.

3. *Don't be a fanatic.* It is better not to tell hostesses about your dieting. Slim Gourmets can practise their art in secret. After all, there are people in everybody's circle of friends who eat very little and get away with it.

4. *Don't go hungry to the table.* If you feel you have too much appetite before a meal, a cup of coffee or tea or tomato juice first helps greatly.

5. *Don't be stingy with sleep.* When slimming, you must give your body an extra hour of sleep, or at least relaxation.

6. *Don't neglect your appearance.* This is valid for women and for men. You have to look well; otherwise your friends take visible loss of weight for impairment of health and urge you to stop reducing. Hearing such advice twice can make the firmest determination falter.

7. *Read and re-read calorie charts.* Read these until you know calorie values as well as Toscanini knows the nine Beethoven Symphonies.

8. *The first dish in restaurants must be something served quickly.* It can be consommé, half a grapefruit, tomato juice, or oysters. Never order anything which takes 20 minutes to serve. Only one person in a million will have the fortitude, while waiting, to ignore the roll and butter so easy to reach and so wrong to eat.

9. *Drink beer in wine glasses, wine in cognac glasses, cognac in liqueur glasses.* It is mostly the first sip that makes us happy. So why not restrict the quantity?

10. *Never wear too-big clothing.* Oversize garments make people pity the slimming gourmet. Buy the right size shirts, or have new collars made when your shirt collar shows that your weight is dropping off.

EDITORS' NOTE: *The author has in preparation a comprehensive guide to successful dieting — the 25 Secrets of the Slim Gourmet. We will be glad to forward to him any inquiries from readers relative to the Slim Gourmet system which he has originated.*

how intensively he eats and how little he consumes that makes him slim.

I reproduce here what I ate yesterday, after a year's experience and experiment:

		CALORIES
BREAKFAST:	Chemex-filtered jet black Coffee	—
	Eggs Slim Gourmet, consisting of:	
	½ hard boiled egg with red caviar	45
	½ hard boiled egg with chopped olives	40
	½ deviled egg with cottage cheese and shrimps (only the white of the eggs)	50
	1 slice bread and butter	100
LUNCH:	1 McIntosh Apple with a dash of Cognac	125
	Whole Maine baby lobster with asparagus salad and 1 roll	400
	Turkish coffee with sugar	40
DINNER:	Madrilene en gelee	25
	Sweetbreads on ham, braised with capers, and baked potato	300
	1 glass of Claret	75
	2 Fresh peaches on a bed of lady fingers with wine sauce	175
	Coffee	—
SNACK:	½ triangle of American Camembert on a cracker	100
		1475 calories*

*A word on the calorie deficit. My normal daily allowance is around 2500 calories (height, 5 feet 8 inches; white collar type of sedentary work; little sport). At present I plan my food around 1500 calories and take occasional temptations into account (40-year-old brandy or some cocktail snacks) which may add 2000 calories per week. That brings me to a daily average of about 1800 calories, which makes me lose a pound per week. A little calorie deficit should always be maintained, if only to make a reserve for the inevitable accounting mistakes that creep in.

There is no law as to what Slim Gourmets should eat. There is only a law as to *how to eat* . . .

eat with all the senses!

And — whatever the Slim Gourmet eats must be better than what he ate before. If he likes eggs boiled 3½ minutes, they should be exactly 3½ minutes, and let him eat in peace (no morning paper next to the plate), at the right temperature and with little salt — with his taste-buds, eyes, and all his other senses.

Living according to one's habits of eating, upgrading the quality and reducing the quantity, searching for the best natural tastes and no cocktailizing of nature's gifts into non-recognition, eating with all one's senses and choosing one's food with discrimination . . . this Slim Gourmet program entails no asceticism, no suffering, and need not awaken the self-pity of reducers, which makes it so difficult to live with them. The only effort essential for the Slim Gourmet's way is the mastering of the nutritional A B C and of the Slim Gourmet's tricks of trade, which are set out on the opposite page for the benefit of all future Slim Gourmets. **END**

SPORTS

5

It's a curious juxtaposition: *Gentry*'s published life span occurred during the golden age of America's Favorite Pastime. Mickey Mantle and Willie Mays were household names and regarded as national heroes. No red-blooded and skinned-kneed American boy raised during this era will ever forget his fond or scarring memories playing in Little League, yet the magazine gave surprisingly short shrift to baseball—probably for two reasons.

William Segal was more of a globalist than a populist, and despite the ubiquity of baseball diamonds from Philly to Fresno, the game was still a sport unique to the United States. The term "World Series" sounded swell, but no translation was needed to read the scoreboard, since no other country has ever participated. Most important, baseball is a team sport and Segal, though an enthusiastic and adept sportsman, confined his skills and acumen to games where an athlete could shine and feel fulfilled as a solo.

Consequently, *Gentry* not only focused on sports where man is either pitted against the elements, the clock, or other individuals, but did so with a singular goal—to achieve personal excellence. In a winter issue, the head of the Aspen Ski School presents a schuss-by-schuss guide, examining the combinations of speed and technique necessary to "win" any of the following three categories of ski competition: slalom, downhill, and jumping. One may be taken in by the majestic array of masts and rigs in a summer feature on sailing, but the article was designed for the man seriously in the market for a ketch, a sloop, or a schooner. The story is markedly precise about how much headroom is required for cabin comfort, the depth at which each keel must sit in the water, and exactly how much footage a one-man crew can manage.

Segal's love of water extended to fly casting, too. It's not exactly clear how one is supposed to follow the moment-to-moment changes in flexing the wrist, tightening the elbow, and adjusting the arc of the arm if you are standing knee-deep in a stream with one hand on a fishing reel and the other on the line, but you may never encounter a more detailed breakdown to the art of fly casting. Catching fish doesn't even enter into the equation: The goal is simply to cast with grace.

And since grace was the unexpected yet essential touchstone in *Gentry*'s pursuit of athleticism, no team sport was hailed as highly desirable, not even the one that now transfixes a majority of American males each weekend. In fact, in a world where most men still use the word to refer to the game of soccer, *Gentry* dutifully but mechanically analyzed "How to Look at a Football Game" as if no American male had ever seen, let alone participated, in a high school scrimmage; played touch football at a family picnic; or spent New Year's Day eagerly awaiting the kickoff at the Rose Bowl.

Rather, the game the *Gentry* man was born to hold in highest regard is golf, for the game is the crystallization of so many markers of affluence and ambition. The setting is as elegant as a mansion's manicured gardens. The clothes are eye-catchingly sporty. Despite the obvious skill required, the sport is played at one's leisure. Best of all, it's an all-for-none and one-against-all competition that fittingly ends at a country club. Could any sport be more perfectly devised? If you read the recollected rhapsodies re-creating the most memorable victories of four of history's greatest golfers—Ben Hogan, Byron Nelson, Gene Sarazen, and Bobby Jones—the answer would seem to be no. But the magazine provides its own novel and upstaging pinnacle. All you need is eight acres of unused land and a checkbook full of ready cash handy. It is doubtful that even the most golf-obsessed *Gentry* readers ever took up the challenge to "Build Your Own Golf Course," but the feature may be the most remarkable the magazine ever produced, because not only is the project audacious in both its engineering and originality, but the fantasy realized by its execution would be singularly glorious. Let Kevin Costner build his cute baseball diamond in the cornfield. According to *Gentry*, your very own golf course is the ultimate field of dreams.

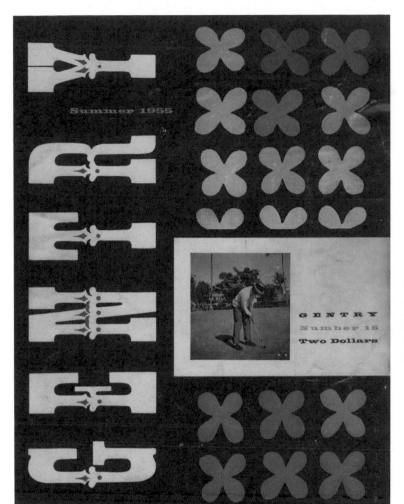

**CLOCKWISE,
FROM TOP LEFT:**

Gentry, Number Fifteen,
Summer 1955; Number
Thirteen, Winter 1954–55;
Number Twenty-two,
Spring 1957.

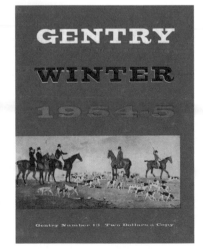

TOWARD A PORTRAIT
OF SUGAR RAY ROBINSON

by **CHANDLER BROSSARD**

You ask yourself, Why is he so different from the

others? Why was he the champ among champs? He wasn't

that much faster, or stronger, or smarter. What is

the subtle X of his identity?

AT THE coroner's inquest, the District Attorney of Cleveland looked very sternly at him. "Mr. Robinson," he said, in the manner of a man about to reveal a great discovery, "isn't it true that you had Mr. Doyle in trouble in the third round?"

Ray shifted in his chair and looked bored. "Yeah, that's right." He paused. "It's my business to have people in trouble."

Biggest gate he ever had up to fighting Kid Gavilan in Philly was $27,000, and after he'd been fighting for 10 years too, as the best there was. Nobody went to see him because the other guys just weren't in the ring. It was just a question which round Daddy-O would decide to put the man away in. In the Philly fight with the Kid, he made—hold on now—$40,000. Fort Knox and all that.

He made $750,000 out of the second Turpin fight.

"Sometimes I wish I were a psychologist or something like that."

Because there was so absolutely little competition among the welters, of which he was top banana, he often fought middleweights or even, if need be, light-heavies.

In the ninth round, Artie Levine, leading middleweight contender and weighing about 165 to Ray's 145, brought one up from the freezer and Ray was down, actually out. Ref counted to nine, Ray got up, instinct driving now, and finished the round by making the ref carefully wipe all resin from his

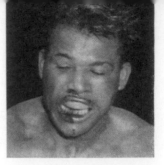

gloves and asking him to examine his glove strings, which he insisted were coming loose.

"Ray," George Gainford said back in his corner, "you're losing this fight."

"Don't depress me, man. Tell me something I don't know."

In the tenth round, Ray knocked middleweight Artie Levine out.

"The trouble with you is you're right-hand happy," Gainford said one day in the very beginning, when Ray was still in the amateurs (90 bouts, 80 knockouts, 60 in the first round). So Big George tied Ray's right behind his back and for a long time made him do it all with the left. Result: best left in the world.

"Come on, George man. Untie my right, huh?"

"They ain't gonna fight no benefits for Ray Robinson," said he. He put his dough in a bar, barber shop, beauty shop, apartment houses, cleaning place, lingerie shop. The latter began as a present to his wife Edna Mae to keep her busy.

"You know, I was never so surprised as when I found out what that little ol' shop was grossin' per week."

"Yeah?"

"Yeah nothin'. You know damn well I took it away from Edna Mae."

As he was training for his championship bout with squat, powerful middleweight champ Jake LaMotta: "I'm not in shape yet. I'm kinda glove shy."

"My head don't feel like you're glove shy," said his sparring partner, and quit after three rounds.

"Don't rub no sweatin' cream down there. I don't want to lose no weight down in that area."

"Why should I slip you a fin? Man, I had to fight for this f..... money. You want a fin, you go out and fight for it."

His first bid for the middleweight championship came when he fought Steve Belloise, then the number-one contender. Belloise outweighed him 10 to 15 pounds, outreached him and was generally considered to be a man rough in the extreme. For the first three rounds it was even fighting. Then in the fourth and fifth, Belloise began chasing Ray. Ray looked off balance and confused as Belloise was the insistent aggressor. It looked like Ray might be taken. In the next round, Ray knocked Belloise out with one punch, a right cross.

"Actually, it was an overhand right in response to his left lead," Ray explained precisely.

"What was the matter with you in the fourth and fifth rounds, Ray?"

"Nothing. I was just changing my style. Like a transition, you know what I mean?"

Later, in Belloise's dressing room as he left, beige beanie on head and beige Cadillac waiting outside:

"Stevie boy, you all right?"

"Ray, you're the greatest."

There is a man named Joe Roach. Thin, tall, quiet, a professional Negro golfer. He is quiet, tender, strong, and likes his own identity very much. Ray is with him 20 hours out of the 24. He is on Ray's payroll.

As he turns around and walks a step or two he says to Ray: "Wait'll that man on the fairway gets out of the way before you tee off."

No response, but obedience.

"I think an eight iron is right for this, don't you?"

"Uh huh," says Roach, and measures the distance for himself.

There was a young flashy welter named Chico Vejar. He hit you several times while you were deciding whether to jab him or hook him.

"You want to be champ, Chico? Well, you got to do it all the way. You can't do no messin' around. It's really tough, boy."

Chico is now unranked.

"Did you see my brother when you were in Paris, Ray? I asked him to call you. He knows a lot of interesting people."

"Don't send no men to me when I'm in Paris. I don't want to see no men there—just women."

"Here's what happened, and I don't mean to put Turpin down, 'cause he's a good fighter. Not a real good fighter, but a real tough fighter. You know. Well, the referee before the fight took me aside and said, Now you can't do this and you can't do that and if you do this it's against the rules. I said, What will happen if I do this, like, you know, a kidney punch or something like that? And he said, I won't take the championship away from you but I will take your purse. Well I said, to hell with that. Who's gonna come all the way to England to lose $200,000? Would *you*? Hell no, you wouldn't."

He stepped on the scales and he weighed 152 when he was supposed to weigh just 147.

"Ray, we could take the championship away from you right here. You know that."

"Uh huh."

"But if you make this a nice fight and don't knock this boy out, we won't."

After the fight, which went the distance: "That was the hardest fight I ever had."

"What do you mean?"

"That boy didn't know how to fight at all."

"Do you think you can hurt this man? He's a heavyweight, you know."

"I can hurt any man I hit right."

A certain party was sitting in Ray's, uptown. This was just after the LaMotta fight which Ray won in the thirteenth when it was clear that LaMotta would be killed before he fell down and Ray's hands were visibly bleeding from under his gloves. Ray came in with his white polo coat on and a large black hat. He was walking slowly with a certain gentle sway in his walk.

"Ray, that was a terrific fight, man. Did you get my telegram? We sent you a telegram telling you we were with you. Did you get it?"

"Yeah, I got it." He begins to walk away. He has big gloves on. "You really want to see me killed, don't you? That's why people watch fights."

The gloves, of course, were to hide his smashed hands.

"Danielle Darrieux is over there, Ray. Wouldn't you like to dance with her?"

"If she wants to dance, let her come over here."

"Roach, what you eatin'? Is that mackerel you eatin' with those grits? Gimme some, just a taste."

He wakes up in the middle of the night. In Denver. He turns over. "Roach, let's go outside and see what's happening in this town."

"I'm tired."

"Come on, man. I can't sleep."

"Ask Edna Mae."

"She's sleeping. Come, man."

Roach left Ray for six months. His girl friend in Chicago said, Come on out here, honey, I want to see you. This car is for you. In that six months Ray had four fights. Two of the men never fought again. One man's eardrums were permanently smashed. He knocked them all out within three rounds. He knocked one man out in two minutes of the first round, though this was supposed to be a 15-round championship fight. The man's name was Sugar Costner.

"Ain't no sugar but one, and that's me."

In the twelfth round of the fight with Maxim—the heat was hallucinatory—he began to reel around like a man in a dream. He was ahead, 11 rounds to one.

"I'll bet you that if they took his urine specimen now, it would have blood in it," said Dr. Nardiello.

He knocked Bobo Olson out in the third when Olson made a jewel-like mistake. He got into a body-punching contest with Ray, stepped back, and as he usually does after such a bout, tapped his gloves together. Ray hit him with a left hook and he did not get up.

"It ain't how hard you get hit, it's the way you feel about gettin' hit. That's what counts."

"After Tiger Jones beat me a lot of people said, Ray, you're through. Give it up. You'll get hurt. I took a long walk and I asked God if I was through and He said 'No, Ray, you are not through.'"

"Why do you have a fuchsia-colored Cadillac?"

"See this tie?"

"Yes."

"Well, my wife gave it to me. I like the color. So one day I went down to the Cadillac people and I said, Make me a car this color and I showed them the tie. I think a car ought to be pretty."

Marciano had Joe Louis against the ropes in the eighth. He hit Louis with a left and Louis fell back into the ropes and began to go down. Ray ran to the ring. "Get up, Joe! Get up!" He began to cry.

"You want to know how to tell if a boy can be a good fighter? Well you just watch a boy, any kid, and watch him if there is a fly in the room. If that boy without even knowing it watches that fly like out of the corner of his eye all the time, well that boy can be a good fighter. You know what I mean?"

"Tell me, Ray," began the sports broadcaster, "was that a knockdown or a slip when Rocky hit you in the second round?"

"All I know is he hit me one helluva punch on the back of my head and then I was on my knee."

"Then it wasn't a slip?"

"I wouldn't exactly say so." He grabs the mike: "Joe Louis! Meet me under the archways!"

Could have been Achilles calling Hector.

"What kind of a punch was that that you knocked Rocky out with, Ray?"

"Well, I started a left hook going, then in the middle of it I saw Rocky drop his left a little, so seeing my opportunity I shifted it to a right, and it was too late for him to do anything—I mean, adjust himself to it."

"Mr. LaMotta, what would you say is the best way to fight Ray Robinson?"

"Keep on coming in and crowd him. Don't let him get set for those combination punches."

"Combination punches?"

"Yah. Left hook, right cross, left hook. He's the best combination puncher in the business. If you ever let him get started on a combination, it's goodbye Daddy."

"How many times did you and Ray fight?"

"Six times."

"And what . . ."

"He won five."

"I begged Joe to quit fightin'. I said Joe if you need money, if that's why you go on fightin', I'll give you every cent I make this year. You can have it. But don't go on fightin'. 'Cause you are too old."

"Roach, let's go back to Paris. People like each other in Paris."

"Man, I ain't in no kinda condition."

"Oh?"

"Yeah. My fightin' weight's 150 and I weigh 152. I'm outta shape. I feel slow."

In the fourth round of his championship fight with Villemain, a fight broke out among the spectators near Ray's corner. He started to watch it as the bell rang. He thought it might be some friends of his. Villemain came across the ring to him and Ray maneuvered him so that he could continue to watch the fight. The crowd loved it.

"Roach, did you take those ribs to Momma?"

"Joe Louis! Meet me under the archways!" ◆

SKI RACING

THE PICTURE SERIES ON THE FOLLOWING PAGES IS DESIGNED TO
ANSWER THE OFT-ASKED QUESTIONS, WHAT IS DOWNHILL RACING?
WHAT IS SLALOM RACING? THE MOST IMPORTANT TECHNICALITIES
AND SLALOM GATE COMBINATIONS ARE RECORDED IN THE PICTURE
SEQUENCE ESPECIALLY PREPARED BY MR. FRED ISELIN, INTERNA-
TIONALLY KNOWN AUTHORITY ON SKIING AND CO-DIRECTOR OF THE
ASPEN SKI SCHOOL IN COLORADO. . . . . . . PLEASE TURN THE PAGE

Photographs by Pat Henry

PART I

DOWNHILL SKI RACING

Downhill ski racing has become one of the most exciting sports, not only for the participant but for the spectator as well. During an international or great national ski event the downhill course is lined on both sides with thousands of spectators awaiting the thrills which inevitably accompany a downhill race. For here is one of the few sports where human beings, without the help of mechanical force, achieve speeds up to eighty miles an hour.

Most of the ski-minded public has the impression that ski racing is for youngsters only up to twenty years of age. The fact is, however, that in competition a racer in his thirties has the greatest chance to rank in the first five. Neither is ski racing a matter of dare-deviltry as many people assume. Experience is far more important to a racer than all the daring in the world. And this can be acquired only through years of active racing. — FRED ISELIN

Pertinent Information
ABOUT
Downhill Courses
and Racing Rules

For international downhill racing the course should be at least two to three miles long and with a minimum altitude difference of 2500 feet.

For a ladies' downhill course, 1500 feet altitude difference (vertical drop) is required. The ladies' downhill course is usually shorter.

To make the downhill course fit for racing and training, the course has to be stamped and packed in sufficient width to make it safe for highspeed skiing (75 to 100 feet).

The course should be marked very clearly with the marking flags.

There are three types of flags to mark a course:

1. Red flags placed on the side of the course are direction flags. These should be placed every 30 feet.
2. Yellow flags are placed to indicate dangerous points along the course.
3. A pair of blue flags are used as control gate. Control gates are placed to prevent the racers from taking too great risks and are usually placed to bring the racers over a particular section of the course in order to prevent accidents.

The downhill race is purely a race against time. Style or form during the race in no way counts for or against the skier.

The only penalty during a downhill race is disqualification. A racer is disqualified . . .

If he enters the race under false premises

If he should be late at the start or fail to return to the start after having *jumped* the go signal

If he breaks his speed with his poles

If he fails to finish the race at least on one ski

If he has been seen training on a closed course or if he has been seen rearranging markings or improving the course to his own advantage

If he does not let pass a competitor who overtakes him

If he receives assistance

If he fails to pass the finish line with both feet

If he does not pass through all the control gates.

SKI RACING DOWNHILL

THREE OF THE IMPORTANT AND MOST FREQUENTLY USED

STRAIGHT RUNNING DOWNHILL POSITIONS ARE ILLUS-

TRATED. THESE ARE ALSO CALLED SCHUSS POSITIONS.

THE VERTICAL, HIGH POSITION. Good on bumpy and rough terrain (weight in center, knees slightly flexed).

THE EXTREME FORWARD POSITION. Favorable for steep but smooth slopes (the weight is forward on the toes; hands well in front of knees; good control of skis in this position).

THE CROUCHED-SITTING POSITION. Used mostly on flat, gentle, downhill slopes (weight on heels; skis run more freely with weight off front part of skis; wind resistance is at minimum).

PREJUMPING

TO LEARN PREJUMPING YOU MUST BE A GOOD SKIER. A SENSE OF TIMING IS VERY IMPORTANT. IF YOU JUMP TOO EARLY YOU WILL NOT FLOAT OVER THE BUMPS; IF TOO LATE YOU WILL HAVE A WRONG JUMP BECAUSE YOU WILL FLOAT DOWN AND LAND PERHAPS IN FLAT TERRAIN.

Back view: Shows that racer took off approximately 50 feet before edge of bump.

APPROX. 40 FT.

CORRECT JUMP

EDGE

PREJUMPING

OVER A DROP-OFF OR BIG BUMP

INCORRECT JUMP

PREJUMPING

OVER SEVERAL SMALL BUMPS

Here skier approaches a drop-off or bump and is ready to plant poles for take-off.

Racer *takes off* and floats over bump. Note crouched position which skier assumes while he is in the air.

Today's downhill courses with great terrain variations and bumps require good prejumping techniques. The racer, who is approaching a bump or a drop-off at high speed, is jumping off the ground before reaching the edge of the bump to avoid great jumps which involve losing time and make for risky and difficult landings (see diagram opposite). The prejumping is mostly done with the help of ski poles. Depending on the skier's speed in approaching a drop-off or bump, he might take to the air 40 to 60 feet before the edge. Instead of a jump, the skier tries to float as low as possible above the ground, keeping the skis parallel with the contour of the terrain. Pole work in prejumping is important.

Skis are parallel to slope. Crouched position is maintained during the flight to lessen wind resistance.

. . . Landing is smooth and in crouched position.

CROSSING A GULLEY AT HIGH SPEED. At right, skier has high position before reaching the transition point of gulley, to be able to absorb shock. One ski (feeling ski) well ahead; both poles ahead, to be used as brace on gulley's counterslope edge, which is the edge of far side of gulley. A flag marks the beginning of the slope of the gulley. At left, skier reaches top of gulley's counterslope. Poles are planted as brace Quick, extreme crouching of the racer will prevent risky and time-losing jump. He tries not to take off. If he does, he keeps in crouched position, as in the prejump landing.

WAXING. On flat race stretches, where wax plays a major role, the racer makes use of his wax technique. Top racers often wax each ski differently, or use a different wax on each ski depending on snow conditions on a long downhill race course. Picture shows skier with his weight completely on one ski as wax on his other ski seems to be slow.

SKATING STEP. This is often of use for quick starts or to gain speed on flats. The body should be kept low, as shown in photograph.

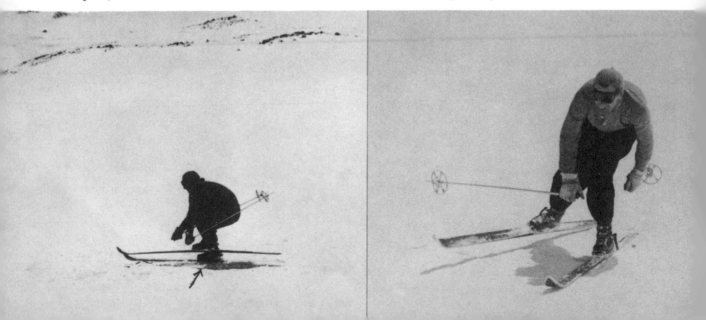

PART II

SLALOM SKI RACING

To the average observer a slalom race is not nearly so spectacular as a downhill race. The slalom race might be compared to a horse show in Madison Square Garden while the more exciting downhill race might be compared to the Kentucky Derby. As a matter of fact, skiing a slalom is much more difficult than downhill racing and is rightly regarded in ski circles as the height of achievement. Slalom is not only a matter of speed but a combination of speed plus technique. Controlled by pairs of flags or so-called gates, an international slalom course has up to fifty gates. The chart and photographs on the following pages record and describe some of the famous gates in slalom ski-racing.

Information

ABOUT

Slalom Courses and Rules

A slalom course is indicated by pairs of flags called *gates*, through which the skier must pass. Usually the slalom course is run twice, with the total time of two runs determining the winner.

The vertical drop or altitude difference in a slalom race should be at least 800 feet.

The snow for the course should be hard and is usually footpacked in order that all competitors have as nearly as possible the same conditions.

In order to give the first contestant a fair chance, two or three non-contestants should open the slalom course.

A pair of matching poles with the matching flags (blue, red or yellow) form a gate.

No consecutive gate may be of the same color.

The width of a gate must be at least 3 meters, or approximately 9 feet.

The distance between gates requires a minimum of 75 centimeters, or approximately 2½ feet.

The complete slalom course has to be set at least one hour and a half before the race, to give the racer a chance to *study* the course. Contestants are not allowed to ski through the gates before the race.

A slalom course will not exceed a total of 50 gates.

A time penalty of 5 to 10 seconds will be counted against a racer who passes the line between the poles with only one leg.

The disqualification rules are the same as for the downhill race, except for the rule which forbids the racers to train on the slalom course or ski through a gate or alongside the slalom course for practice.

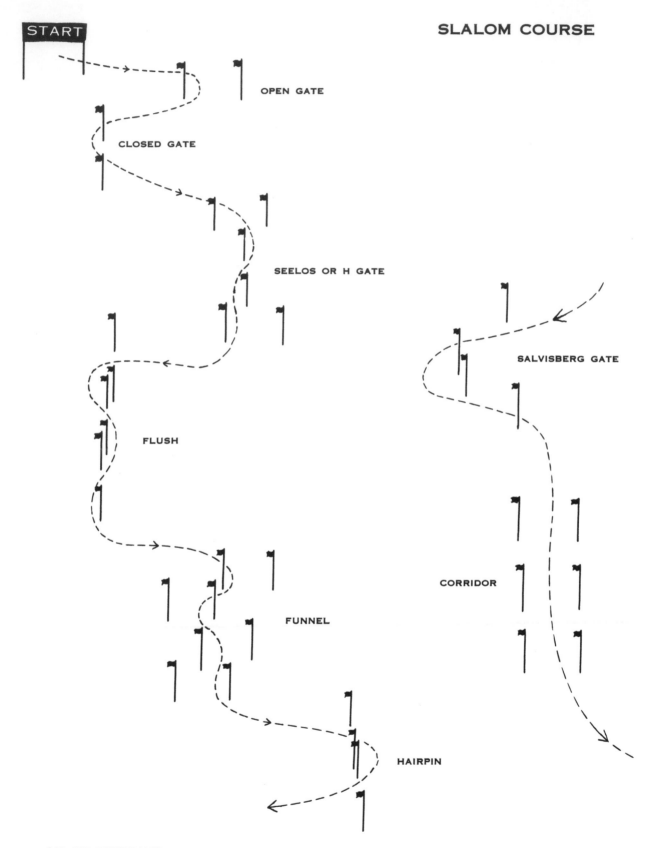

SLALOM COURSE

START

OPEN GATE

CLOSED GATE

SEELOS OR H GATE

FLUSH

SALVISBERG GATE

FUNNEL

CORRIDOR

HAIRPIN

SKI RACING
SLALOM

CLOSED GATES: Set at vertical line to slope.
International rule: Gate width 3 meters.

OPEN GATES: Set at horizontal line to slope.

SEELOS COMBINATION. Two open gates and one closed.
Named after the famous slalom champion Anton Seelos.

FLUSH. Several closed gates one after the other in the fall line of the slope. Skier *comes out* of third flush gate. Keeps weight forward. Pole work is important. Most racers use *ruade* type turn going through a flush (ruade means kick with heel).

FUNNEL. A row of open gates, preferably four or more, which are set in a zigzag manner.

HAIRPIN. Two closed gates set one above the other. This gate combination requires making a very sharp turn.

SALVISBERG. Variation of regular hairpin but with two middle flagpoles set to one side.

PENALTIES

PENALIZATION. Only one ski passed between the two flags. A time penalty is the rule for this.

NO PENALIZATION. Racer hits pole with shoulder and breaks pole down. Racer is not penalized for this.

DISQUALIFICATION. Racer *missed* gate; did not ski over line between flag poles.

END

The New Tennis

By Elwood Cooke

All sports have changed in the last twenty years. Like everything else, they have been modernized. Old standards are constantly being shattered. The results show vast improvements on old records.

While the records show that track, swimming, baseball, golf . . . all of which are *measurable* sports . . . are changing radically both in methods and goals, tennis, like boxing, is one of the sports that cannot be measured by records or comparisons. It is impossible to see how the great Bill Tilden would fare against the Budges and Kramers. Obviously, there will be staunch defenders of both sides, the old versus the new. But as a tennis player who has competed with nearly all the leading amateurs and pros, it seems obvious to me that tennis is advancing like all other athletics.

The style of tennis has changed. In the golden days of Lacoste, Johnson and Tilden, endurance, groundstrokes and legs were the answer. The opponent was maneuvered by placement, varying slices and spins, until an error was extracted. There were exponents of the volley, but not until the last ten years has volleying become the basis of winning tennis.

Don Budge, in my opinion the greatest player of them all, did a great deal to revolutionize the game. He began to advance to the net at every opportunity. So great was Budge in all departments of the game, that nearly every shot he hit was a virtual approach to the net. No opponent was able to be crafty or clever against Budge. He wouldn't allow it, by his sheer power.

Players began to imitate his style, but unfortunately there has never been another Budge. Today, players attempt to make every shot an approach, but few of them devote the time and work necessary to develop good enough groundstrokes to execute the theory. As a result, they have had to lean more heavily on brilliant volleying. Budge was a great volleyer, but he didn't have to be. His approach shots were so formidable that the return was always a *set-up*. Players of today, because of their weakness off the ground, have had to become expert volleyers. Frank Sedgman, the current champion, tries to make every shot a volley. He volleys from all over the court, never allowing the ball to bounce when he can avoid it.

Gone is the classic groundstroke, the point that lasts for ten minutes. Now, a point is won or lost in a matter

Picture Sequence of the Service

LINING UP BODY POSITION FOR SERVICE.

FORWARD PRESS, WEIGHT ON LEFT LEG, SWAY BACKWARD TO RIGHT IN ORDER TO GIVE SERVICE RHYTHM. BALL AND RACQUET GO UP TOGETHER.

WHILE BALL GOES UP, TIME IS ALLOWED TO MAKE CIRCULAR MOTION WHICH ENABLES YOU TO ACCELERATE SPEED OF RACQUET HEAD.

T*he* **S***ervice.* The object of the service is to extract a weak return from the opponent.

The slice service is most simply accomplished. Facing the net, the ball is thrown slightly forward, and to the right. The racquet is swung across, and slightly behind the ball, from right to left. This imparts a spin that makes the ball bounce high and to the left.

The American twist service is the most difficult as well as the most effective. Standing sideways to the net, foot forward, the ball is thrown over the left shoulder, and the racquet brought up and over it. This imparts a spin that makes the ball bounce high and to the right. Both of these services travel slowly, allowing plenty of time for the server to come to the net.

The flat service is hard to control. It is designed to win the point outright. Power is the keynote. Facing the net, the ball is thrown high in the air, and directly in front. The racquet comes down on the ball. Height is essential. The higher the ball when struck, the greater the accuracy.

POINT OF CONTACT IS MADE WITH ARM FULLY EXTENDED IN ORDER TO BRING GREATEST LEVERAGE DOWN ON BALL.

WEIGHT OF ARM, SHOULDER AND BODY HAS NOW PASSED THROUGH THE BALL.

RECOVER AND GET INTO READY POSITION AS QUICKLY AS POSSIBLE FOR OPPONENT'S RETURN.

READY POSITION THE RACQUET IS ON ITS WAY BACK . . . . . . INTO HITTING POSITION

of seconds. The service is the biggest weapon. Players invariably follow their serves into the net.

One cannot compare the old with the new. Equipment is different today; gut is faster, more tightly strung; the balls are better and more easily controlled. Tennis is a new game today.

THE NEW VOLLEY

The volley consists of hitting the ball before it reaches the ground. Obviously the closer you are to the net, the more decisive will be your volley. But remember that the closer you are to the net, the greater the vulnerability to the lob.

The volley is a full stroke with little backswing. To volley successfully you must make your shot in about half the time you have to make a groundstroke. First, you are close to the net, and the distance traveled by the ball is much less; secondly, the ball is not allowed to bounce, therefore its speed is greater. You have too little time for a backswing.

It is not necessary to put the ball away on the first volley. Years ago, when a player came into net, he did so only to put a ball away. He would stand almost on top of the net, coming in when it was safe to take this *put away* position. Today, players have found that they can maneuver an opponent from all over the court with the

volley until they feel safe in closing into net for the kill. In defending against this, many an opponent will hit a soft shot that bounces at your feet as you come in. It is impossible to put such a shot away. You must make an approach volley, hitting the ball to a spot where the opposing player will have difficulty passing you as you come forward to close in.

WHEN AN OPPONENT IS AT NET

When it is obvious that an opponent will rush the net on a given shot, there are three alternative shots you may make.

The passing shot. This is dangerous· and should be attempted only when there is sufficient time to aim the ball. It is a normal groundstroke hit down the line or cross-court, out of reach of the net man.

The lob. This is basically a defensive shot. The ball is hit high over the opponent's head, the deeper the better. It forces the opponent to make an overhead smash. If the ball is lobbed deeply enough you will usually have time to get into position for any return.

The soft passing shot. Until recently, this was almost exclusively a doubles shot. Now it is used continually against net rushers. The ball is hit softly and short, forcing the volleyer to take the ball below the level of the net. It puts the volleyer on the defensive.

WEIGHT OF BODY THROUGH BALL   . . . BEGINNING OF FOLLOW-THROUGH   THE FINISH.

The **F**orehand. The forehand is usually the most aggressive groundstroke. It is the basis of the back court game. The majority of shots are taken on the forehand.

In hitting a forehand the difficulty most often encountered is the back swing. All types of complex theories have been developed, but actually it's simpler just to remember the following:

Take the racquet back as soon as possible. The racquet should be kept on the same plane as the ball. You will find that your weight rests on your right foot.

Keep your eye on the ball. This cannot be overstressed.

Pivot the weight from the right to the left foot, and step in the direction you are aiming. Let the natural forward movement of your shoulders swing the racquet. You will find it travels on almost a straight line.

THE EASTERN FOREHAND GRIP

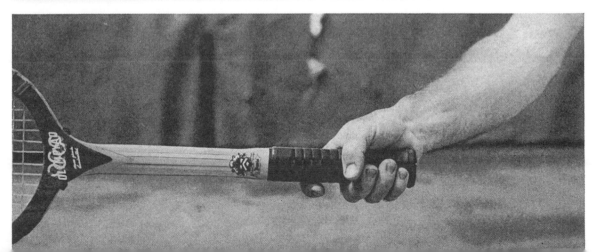

READY POSITION   RACQUET BACK   GETTING INTO HITTING POSITION

The Backhand. The backhand in years gone by was virtually a defensive shot. Today if a player expects to achieve the top he must be able to hit aggressively from both sides. The backhand, like the forehand, is hit well in front of the body with the arm fully extended at the point of contact with the ball.

Take the racquet back quickly, so that you are waiting for the ball, and as nearly as possible on the same plane as the ball.

Keep your eye on the ball.

Pivot weight from the left foot to the right, and step in the direction you are aiming the ball. The natural shoulder pivot swings the racquet.

✓   ✓   ✓

Tennis is not so hard to master as most teachers would have you believe. The new tennis is tending towards the simple way to do things. Remember that the idea is to control the play and end up with the ball back one time more than your opponent. Don't try winning points the hard way from the back court. Put all the pressure on your opponent by going to the net on a good approach shot. It is the other fellow who then has to make a perfect passing shot or lob. — ELWOOD COOKE

THE EASTERN BACKHAND DRIVE
WITH THUMB OF HAND EXTENDED
ALONG THE RACQUET

POINT OF CONTACT   BODY WEIGHT SHIFTS FORWARD THROUGH BALL   FOLLOW-THROUGH

"After a reverential cheer at the final green, the
crowd dispersed, awestruck, realizing that
they had witnessed something they had never seen before,
and would never see again."

THE FOUR FINEST ROUNDS OF GOLF

by GENE GREGSTON

Brash young golf reporter goes way out on limb,

courageously names the four top rounds

of all time. You may agree, or violently dissent, but you'll find

it tough to keep his choices off any list of the

immortal achievements in golf

HUNDREDS of fine golf rounds have been recorded in the long, sparkling history of the game.
And no one knows how many more great perform-
ances have been turned in by unknown golfers in
the relative obscurity of a small course or a local
tournament. It may be foolhardy, then, to attempt
to pick the four greatest rounds ever played.

Yet there are some that beg for consideration—
rounds which are especially meritorious on the
basis of competitive conditions, dramatic setting
and contribution to the history of the game itself.

There was Francis Ouimet's 72 which beat the
great British professionals, Harry Vardon and
Ted Ray, and won the play-off for the United
States Open championship in 1913. That victory
by the young amateur brought golf's light from
under the bushel of Britain and entrenched the
sport in America. There was Ben Hogan's closing
67 in the 1951 U.S. Open at Oakland Hills; Bobby
Jones's opening 68 at St. Andrews in his second
British Open conquest; Mike Souchak's 60 in the
1955 Texas Open, which included a nine-hole score
of 27 that contributed to a new PGA record of

257 for 72 holes. There was the course-record 71
fired by the incomparable Babe Zaharias in the
1954 USGA Women's Open at Peabody, Mass.
There was Byron Nelson's 1945 streak, when he
won 18 tournaments and established a PGA record
with an average of 68.33 strokes per round. And
no one could criticize the choice of any one of a
dozen rounds by the inimitable Walter Hagen.

But, with all due respect, I haven't picked any
of these.

Immediate dissension is anticipated. What
standard have I contrived that permits me to omit
any, let alone all, of these high moments in the history of the game? Simply this: each of the four
rounds I *have* chosen was not only a display of
superior shotmaking but also an integral part of a
more important and dramatic achievement. Each
of them in its own way represents a milestone in
the history of golf. True, there have been better
scores. In fact, the four players involved here have
all scored better—but neither they nor any other
golfers have ever played finer rounds under competitive pressure.

1   BOBBY JONES
at Sunningdale, England, 1926

Jones's greatest round was not shot while he was winning any of his 13 national championships, but in the very first qualifying round in the preliminary to his first British Open victory.

Qualifying tests for that meet were played at the Sunningdale Club course in Surrey, not far from London.

So incredible was his performance in that first qualifying round that Bernard Darwin, renowned British golf chronicler, reported:

"After a reverential cheer at the final green, the crowd dispersed awestruck, realizing that they had witnessed something they had never seen before, and would never see again."

Jones's score was composed of nine-hole cards of 33–33, four under the par of 70 and six under fours. He used 33 strokes from tee to green and 33 putts, his game being so steadily superb that his card showed neither a two nor a five. Observers noted but a single deviation from perfection in the entire round!

It came at the 13th hole, a par three of 175 yards. There, Jones's tee shot rolled into a bunker. But the 24-year-old Georgia youngster calmly chipped out dead to the pin for his three.

The late O. B. Keeler, the famous Atlanta *Journal* writer who reported all of Jones's national championships as well as his infrequent failures, wrote of that 66:

"There have been lower scoring rounds; Bobby himself had scored better, but this card of 66 was played with a precision and freedom from error never attained before or after by the greatest precisionist of them all; incomparable in steadiness of execution."

And if it ranks as the best round by "Emperor" Jones, it definitely belongs on any list of the finest ever played.

2   GENE SARAZEN
at Fresh Meadow, Long Island, 1932

Bobby Jones, commenting on the 1932 U.S. Open at Fresh Meadow, has called Gene Sarazen's last round "the finest competitive exhibition on record."

As he was leaving his house that morning to drive to the club, Sarazen suddenly sensed that he'd forgotten something. Rushing back into the house and up to his bedroom, he grabbed a gabardine jacket from the closet. It was the same jacket he had worn when he had received the British Open championship cup a few weeks earlier.

The jacket came through magnificently. Sarazen not only carded a 66 for the final 18, but he played the last 28 holes in 100 strokes!

He later recalled that an important change in his mental outlook may have been instrumental in his amazing stretch drive. He started the last day playing with what he termed "timidity," but soon realized he was so far off the pace that caution was foolish. After a birdie deuce on the ninth hole of the third round, Sarazen scored a three-under-par 32 on the back side, putting him four under par for those 10 holes.

That afternoon he began with a par and a bogey five—but that was the only break in his inexorable rhythm. He birdied the third, fourth, sixth and ninth holes to turn with a 32—a score of 64, incidentally, for the middle 18 holes of his closing rush. He added a 34 on the final nine for his fourth-round 66.

The magnitude of Sarazen's feat is best illustrated by his position as he started those last 28 holes: he was seven strokes behind the leader. Yet he not only erased that deficit but won by three strokes. A total of 10 shots gained in 28 holes!

3

BYRON NELSON

at Augusta, Georgia, 1942

Another remarkable rally occurred in the 1942 Masters play-off.

Byron Nelson had defeated Ben Hogan in both play-offs in which the two famous Fort Worth professionals had engaged—first for the caddy championship of Glen Garden Country Club when they were 15 years of age, again in a Texas Open at San Antonio.

In that '42 Masters tournament Ben came from eight strokes back at the halfway mark to tie Byron at 280 at the end. The next day brought a memorable match. The war was to foreclose on the tournament until 1946; almost all of the people who were "somebody" in golf were in the gallery.

Nelson's sensitive stomach reacted as usual to this situation, and on the morning of the match he was violently ill. On the first tee he began by slicing his shot into the woods. He took a horrendous six strokes on the hole while Ben seized a two-shot advantage with a par four. At the fourth, Hogan increased his margin to three strokes with a par three when Nelson scored a bogey four. Both had birdied the par-five second hole.

They halved the fifth. Then, on the next eight holes, Nelson uncorked some of the grandest competitive golf he or anyone else ever played. On those eight holes—six to thirteen inclusive—Nelson was six under par! In the process he wiped out Hogan's three-shot edge and took a three-stroke lead of his own. Nelson won with a 69 to Ben's 70 over the par-72 Augusta National course.

Nelson himself has said that round represents the best golf he ever played, and veteran observers describe the match as one of the greatest play-off duels in the annals of the game.

4

BEN HOGAN

at Carnoustie, Scotland, 1953

But Hogan was to have his day.

He has called his own fourth-round 67 in the 1951 U.S. Open at Detroit his greatest single round of golf, but I'd choose the last round of his successful bid for the British Open title, when he shot a course-record 68 over the bleak links of Carnoustie and completed the "triple sweep" of 1953—Masters, U.S. Open and British Open.

The critical British audiences couldn't contain their enthusiasm for the performance. That 68, classic that it was, gave Ben the triumph by four strokes with a score of 282. He had put his—and America's—golf reputation at stake; he not only protected it, but enhanced it. The tournament captivated the U.S. public as had no other golf event since Jones's time.

The British measure performance against level fours, or 72. But par for Carnoustie was generally conceded to be about 73 or 74. Hogan shot his 68 with the help of a perfect hit and one near miss.

The perfect hit occurred on the fifth hole when Ben chipped from the fringe of a bunker into the cup—for a birdie three. It boosted him into the lead for the first time.

The near miss took place at the 10th tee:

"As I was taking my stance on the tee, out of the corner of my eye I saw this big black dog walk across the tee about ten yards in front of me. I thought I saw him walk into the crowd, but as I hit a full driver the dog walked back. My ball didn't miss him two inches. If it had hit him, it probably would have killed the dog and could have messed up my score pretty badly."

This 68 was the second-best 72-hole score ever posted in a British Open, eight shots better than the previous four-round record at Carnoustie. ◆

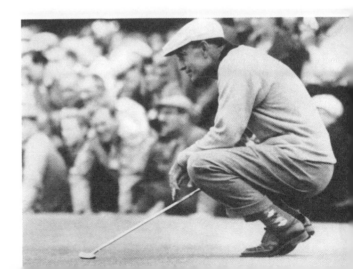

Yale Bowl. Ewing Galloway Photo

HOW TO LOOK AT A FOOTBALL GAME

AN EXPLANATION OF THE STRATEGY AND TACTICS WHICH GIVE FOOTBALL THE EXCITEMENT
AND LOGIC OF CHESS AND THE DYNAMICS OF AN ARMY IN COMBAT . . . BY MIKE WEISS

Whether you are huddled behind the goal-posts in some wind swept stadium, or scrouged down in your easy chair at the fifty-yard line of your television set, there are times when you are often bewildered, confused and dismayed at the vocal information that comes over the loud speakers. Even the experts often are!

It is a far cry from that early day when an intrepid Princetonian picked up a football and, contrary to convention, started to run with it to the present complicated patterns of today's game.

In the days of the Poes, Kings, Ames and Heffelfingers, seven huskies locked legs on a line, and four mammoths started a simple direct assault. It was simply lug, tug, push, shove and haul until the ball was advanced ten yards in four downs, or vice versa . . . but you, kind reader, are seeing football refined and complicated some decades later.

Button-hooks, mouse-traps, T's, naked reverses . . . it sounds like a bewildered hardware dealer staging a strip tease instead of football. Until you understand the jargon, the patterns of various plays refuse to reveal themselves.

To the football afficionados, the unfolding of these

series of patterns is as thrilling and beautiful as the spectacular solo which usually climaxes a deliberately planned sequence of plays. There is something akin to the ballet in the progressive building up of various themes and rhythms of the attack. If you miss these, you miss the greatest of football's spectator joys.

Then again, the analogy may be drawn that football is like chess, a deliberately pre-conceived method of attack and defense, in which the onlooker — the kibitzer — can participate mentally, while not indulging in physical action. There is, however, a subtle difference which makes football more interesting than the "sitz" game. Chess pieces never fail to make their allotted movements, while the twenty-two pieces on the chalk-marked field are subject to the unpredictability of the human equation.

Really and truly to enjoy a football game, the spectator must have a deep-dyed, special rooting interest. Looking at a game from an objective viewpoint is as exciting as seeing a horse race without placing a bet. Pick your team, and then mentally try to quarterback it, and you'll get a double kick out of the few hours you spend looking on.

Let's start our grandstand quarterbacking with the theory of attack. To tackle this we need first a clear picture of the playing field itself.

The conventional football field is 100 yards long, with an extra ten yards (collegiate) at each end of the field designated as the *end zone*. The width of the field is 160 feet, and at the termini of the chalk-marked gridiron, exactly 70 feet 9 inches from the side lines, a pair of goals are erected 18 feet 6 inches in width, with a crossbar intersecting ten feet from the ground. This field itself is marked with stripes, the center of which is the fifty-yard stripe. It is from this focal point that most coaches, quarterbacks and armchair strategists figure their plans.

Between the thirty-yard stripes (twenty yards on each side of the fifty-yard line) is a zone of play which is known as the *solid offense zone*. Here running plays and feints are common. Going toward the opponent's goal, from the thirty- to the fifteen-yard line, is the *free zone*. This is a pass zone. From the fifteen- to the ten-yard line is the scoring zone. At the opposite side of the thirty-yard line (in the direction of your own goal), the thirty- to fifteen-yard line becomes the *caution zone*. From the fifteen-yard line to the goal line is the *danger zone*.

There are three basic weapons of attack. These are, respectively, the kick (punt, when manpower and wind conditions are favorable, and place-kick or dropkick for point after touchdown and scoring field-goals), the forward pass and laterally running plays, which often combine with the former in an interminable series of variations and patterns.

Once you digest the theory, you can forget all the fancy nomenclature that goes on over the airways. Modern collegiate and pro football teams operate from five basic types of offensive formation. These are known as the Single Wing, the Double Wing, the T, the Winged T and the Short Punt formations.

The line-up for the Single Wing operates from an unbalanced line and looks like this:

SINGLE WING

The Single Wing is one of the simplest and soundest of all formations because it stresses power. All that it needs for success is a heavy line and powerful backs to operate on fundamental plays. It is not particularly well adapted to hipper-dipper stuff, but it more than compensates for this by massing power at weak points and developing end and tackle offense. However, the Single Wing lends itself to a fast moving air attack, because a fast backfield and end combination can be shaken free, releasing at least three men downfield. The pattern of Single Wing play is set by the Tailback. In fact, only the Tailback and the Fullback are in position to receive a ball from the center, so that by watching these two intently you can see

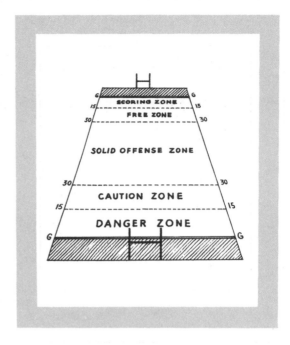

the set-up of the pattern of the play.

The usual types of plays developed include the Spinner — a deceptive play in which the receiving back adds deception to the attack by faking to one of his backfield men and carrying himself. A complete spin sometimes ends in a hand-off. This is true when the opposition starts crashing in and breaking up the spin pattern. Half spins operate from the same formation, except that the ball carrier makes only a half turn before starting toward the scrimmage line, either carrying or handing off. The beautiful part of the hand-off from a spectator's viewpoint is the timing. The swap is made at the exact split second when the spinning back's left shoulder and the receiver's right shoulder are in fleeting contact.

One of the ways to alert yourself to the play's pattern . . . that is, to predetermine whether it's a running play, a pass or a spin play . . . is to watch the pass from center.

When the pass leads the tailback . . . that is thrown to the right or left of him . . . you may be reasonably sure it's a running or pass play. If the pass is directed at the hip or knee of the receiving back, the chances are it will be a spin play.

The line-up for the Double Wing, which also operates from an unbalanced line, looks like this:

DOUBLE WING

The pivot back in the Double Wing is the fullback. He is a veritable magician who must be able to fake, pass, spin and buck. The two wingbacks double in brass as pass receivers, blockers (particularly putting blocks on opposing tackles), but the fullback almost invariably is the first man to handle the ball and to start single and double reverses, spins, bucks and trap plays. In pass plays, the two ends and the two wingbacks are deployed down field, allowing four potential receivers.

The line-up for the T formation which operates from a balanced line (three linemen on either side of the center) looks like this:

CONVENTIONAL T

The T formation quarterback is the important man to watch. He receives ninety percent of the passes from center and must be an adroit ball handler. He does the hand-offs or tosses them to one of the other backs on running plays. The straight T formation is a tough pattern from which to pass. This gave rise to the use of men-in-motion and flankers from the conventional T set-up. Even when you know the pattern of play it is difficult to follow the ball when a good T quarterback starts the works moving. Play becomes wide open and really slick. Don't try to follow all the intricacies. Guess at a hand-off man and watch the runners as they reach the line of scrimmage. It is fairly easy to see the unfolding of the play from this point.

The center plays an important part of the T strategy. He usually makes only one type of pass direct to the quarterback. Sometimes this isn't a pass at all, but a snatch of the ball from the center's hands by the quarterback. On kick formations, the center will pass to the kicking back directly, instead of to the quarterback.

One of the prettiest plays developing from the T formation is the *Double Hand-off*. This often completely baffles the opposition because two potential carriers are hitting the line at the same time. The way the play unfolds is like this: The quarterback takes the pass from center and starts his pivot as both the fullback and left halfback start in motion. The ball handler is in a faking spot to slip the ball to either runner. While spinning, the quarter puts on an act of misdirection. He'll fake an empty hand, drop a shoulder, raise his arm as if to pass and pull a whole bag of similar tricks. If you're sharp, you'll watch the cutting backs and see which one gets the ball in his pocket. But don't be disappointed if you miss it. Pros and coaches who expect this play have been fooled by it.

The T sets up a series of fakes on almost every play. One of the cutest wrinkles for gaffing opponents is the *Criss-Cross*. In this play the fullback is the man in motion who starts to his left. The ball is snapped and the quarter pivots and fakes to the left half who catapults into the right side of the line. The quarter pulls a very tricky stunt here.

He *rides* the ball . . . that is, he holds it against the charging halfback's stomach for a few inches pretending to slap it in the pocket, and then withdraws it with the rhythm of his spin. While this is going on, the right half fakes to his right and then changes direction. The fullback turns up field to block the right end while the quarter slaps the ball to the right half who is charging into the left side.

You've probably heard the bards of the airways talk about the *Mousetrap*. This play has nothing to do with rodents. The mousetrap is somewhat akin to judo in that it uses the violence of the defensive player as a weapon against himself. A tricky ball handler will let the ball be clearly seen for an instant so that the defensive tackle or guard will definitely commit himself, thinking that the play is going in a certain direction. Once he sets in motion, he is blocked out (mousetrapped) from the inside by an offensive man and is *dead* as far as that play is concerned.

Another good play to watch from a T formation is the *Lateral Pass*. It is this play that often gets a break-away back into an open field. It may also blossom out into a lateral-forward pass combination. Generally the lateral starts out with a fake by the ball handler who points the ball toward the fullback, then twists back to a halfback in what appears to be a mousetrap play. The quarterback and halfback fake an exchange, while the fullback has slowed his pace and swung deep. It is to the fullback that the pitchout is made.

The bootleg play is another bit of razzle-dazzle that is a joy to the eyes when well executed. This bold bit of trickery starts out with the ball handler having his back to the line of scrimmage similar to a criss-cross play. After faking to the crossing backs, the quarter holds the ball concealed against his right hip and swings deep around the defensive left end. He works slowly to deceive the defenders and if he's wily enough can break out into the clear on an end run. A variation of this play is the *Statue of Liberty,* wherein an obvious pass play is developing from a bootleg formation. But an end coming around snatches the ball from the carrier's passing hand and continues in an end run.

The Winged T formation looks like this:

WINGED T

The quarterback is the boss-man in this formation. He handles the pigskin on practically every play. Fullback and left half can run wide or take hand-offs. Reverses with the wingback are a constant threat. This formation has added strength on the attacking flank and permits at least three pass receivers to break quickly into the open. There is apt to be more passing from the Winged T than

from the conventional T.

The tailback is the key man in this formation. He kicks, passes and is a pivot in the natural series of reverses and bucks. The fullback does the ball handling and should be a tricky spinner. The halfbacks must be good blockers and trappers, able to take two or more men out of play to allow the attack to get moving.

Now, as a grandstand coach, you must have at least an elementary knowledge of classic strategy and a nodding acquaintanceship with tactics. Strategy involves such determinants as wind direction, position of the ball, score, time left, distance to go, etc. Tactics involve the choice of players as to their greatest talents and plays of the team as a whole to reach certain pre-conceived positions.

Elementary strategy consists of the following basics: Before the whistle starts the game, captains check wind direction and condition of the field. A muddy field generally calls for power plays with the pass as a surprise element. A fast dry field calls for razzle-dazzle and pony backs with plenty of speed and deception.

The opening gambit is a series of repeat plays which aim at the defense's weak side. Thrusts inside and outside of guards and tackles determine the opposition's manpower. Usually it is wise to repeat plays which are gaining for the attacker, especially on a try for first down or touchdown.

If the defense shows an outstanding player who is constantly breaking up the attack, a series of plays should be used that will work against him.

The fast tricky stuff is saved until players are inside an opponent's thirty-yard line, and then they cut loose. The opponents won't dare tighten up for fear of a surprise.

In closing minutes of each half, if attack is close enough, a third down field goal is tried for (if it will put attacker ahead) instead of trying a pass. A pass interception will ruin scoring chances.

In danger zone, the kick is on third down unless there is less than two yards to go for a first down.

If the ball is wet and slippery, the best plan is to kick on first or second down in danger zones and pray for an opponent's fumble. Player kicks on first down under these conditions if the wind favors.

All the rules are out if a team is behind in the closing two minutes. The thing to do then is play all out and gamble to win.

If a running game is working smoothly, a player doesn't pass, unless the defense is drawn up into such a tight position that a pass will score.

In goal line stands, it is wise to use the best ground gainer and plays that work successfully without the element of gamble. A place kick on the fourth down might be tried, if the defense holds firm. A player can look over the defense in goal line stands and if it's tight, he unleashes speed and goes wide. If loose, he hits them inside.

When the safety man is playing up close and spoiling an attack, a quick kick is used on second or third down to boot the ball over his head.

Defense is as much a specialized series of patterns as the offense in modern football. Good defense means that every man has a specific job to do and a plotted territory to defend. Centers or key backs often call defensive signals, anticipating various types of plays which immediately shifts the defensive patterns into pre-planned formations. These will vary from a seven-man line to protect against power plays to a four-man line for spread and pass attacks. The defense moves are not solos. The entire line acts as a unit in breaking up certain plays; otherwise holes develop through which it is possible to gain vast distances. Thus we find angling movements . . . that is, movements where the defensive charge is lateral and backed up by line backers who move in the same direction to plug the vacancy left.

The looping line movement means all linemen shift to destroy attacking blockers and prevents them from shifting into the secondary for double blocks, thus throwing the attack off stride.

One of the most thrilling things to watch on the defense is the work of the ends. Like skirmishers in a battle line, these forwards are called upon to do many things. They must strip the runner of his interference, slow up the play to give the backers-up a chance to make the tackle, fend against passes, charge in to break up kicks and make a majority of tackles. They are also called upon to rush the passer or fade back into the secondary to intercept or break up pass plays. Ends like Don Hutson or Mac Speedie make you forget the attack, when you watch their defensive play.

As far as defensive tactics are concerned, these are the basic elements.

Linemen believe that every play is a running play (except where a fourth down kick is a must) until it is proved otherwise. The backers-up consider every play a pass until the play develops otherwise.

Power plays must be broken up with low, submarine power charges. If a quick opening attack is gaining, defense should use a slide with the play defense.

Defense should try shooting a linebacker in a quick charge on pass and kick plays . . . BUT ONLY ONE AT A

TIME. The ends should rush the passer from the sides.

Two safety men are used when time is running out and opponents are trying to score.

Halfbacks must prevent ends from faking a block and then slipping into the secondary to snag a pass.

There are several legitimate tricks that an alert defense can use and these call for your admiration. For example, suppose the defense is leading in the closing minutes of the game: If the attack in desperation gets a runner behind the defender on a pass play, the smart defense will tackle the potential receiver and take the penalty rather than permit a potential score.

If a spread or other unorthodox formation throws the defense into confusion and there is no chance of calling for a time out, a smart defensive center will fall on the ball and stop the play.

With this information under your belt, you should be able better to enjoy a football game despite some florid announcer's jargon. To render him even less bewildering we append a brief glossary of the common argot.

ANGLING LINE: The defensive linesmen move in a charge at an angle.

BACKFIELD IN MOTION: An illegal play in which one or more backfield men move forward *before* the ball is snapped.

BLOCKING BACK: A backfield man whose main function is to clear the path for runners rather than ball carrying.

BOX DEFENSE: When two deepest defense backs are parallel.

BUTTON-HOOK: When a pass receiver starts in a certain direction away from the scrimmage line and then makes a U turn back toward the line to catch a pass thrown at a pre-designated spot.

CLIPPING: Illegal body contact of the defense player from the waist down.

COUNTER: A fake play in which a thrust is ostensibly aimed at one side of a line but which actually develops at the other.

CRASHING: Headlong diving at blockers, particularly to end-play.

DOUBLE TEAM: A two-man block on an opposing key figure.

END AROUND: The end acts as ball carrier, taking the pigskin around the opposite side of his regular position.

FIVE MAN LINE: Six players in secondary, five men on front line of defense.

FLANKER: Offensive back who is positioned outside his own end.

FLAT PASS: Ball thrown toward the side-lines outside of the ends.

GOPHER PLAY: Going all out for a score on a single play. Generally a last minute effort.

INTERFERENCE: Illegal when applied to grabbing a pass receiver to prevent him from catching the ball. Legal when referred to a mass of runners proceeding and protecting the ball carrier.

JUMP PASS: A forward thrown while the passer leaps into the air to throw over the heads of defense.

LATERAL: A pass thrown parallel to the line of scrimmage.

LINE BACKER: Defense men who are directly behind line ready to plug gaps.

LINE BUCK: Runner carries ball directly inside tackles on direct play.

LONG SIDE: The side of an unbalanced line where there are more men to the right or left of center.

LOOPING LINE: When first line of defense moves in a lateral and forward motion.

MAN-TO-MAN DEFENSE: Forward pass defense in which each eligible receiver is covered by a man as in basketball.

OFFSIDE: Crossing line of scrimmage before ball is snapped. Five-yard penalty.

OPTIONAL PASS: In which the passer may throw or run as he elects. Used frequently in the pro game.

REVERSE: Starting play wide in one direction and returning to reverse side.

SCREEN PASS: Forward pass to a receiver who is guarded by blockers. When it works it's a Gopher Play.

SHIFT: To change formation alignment before the ball is snapped.

SHOOTING THE GAP: When a backer dives into offensive backfield before the play is well under way.

SHORT SIDE: The side of the unbalanced line which has the least men parallel to the center.

SINGLE WING: An offensive formation where one halfback (flanker) is outside the end.

SPLIT LINE: A line-up where the linesmen are widely spaced.

SPOT PASS: A forward thrown to a designated place instead of a receiver. The receiver attempts to fool his guardians and make a last minute catch at the spot predetermined.

STRONG SIDE: That portion having the most players.

TAILBACK: Deep offensive threat . . . usually a triple-threat man.

TRAP (MOUSETRAP): Sucking a defensive player past the line of scrimmage, then blocking him down and out from the side.

TRIPLE-THREAT: A back or end who can run, pass or kick.

UNBALANCED LINE: One that has more players on one side of the center than the other.

WEDGE: A V-shaped formation of blockers ahead of the carrier. Prevalent in returning kick-offs and punts.

WINGBACK: A back positioned outside of the offensive end.

ZONE: Defensively, territory assigned for positive protection. See chart of strategy.

For the height of luxury as a spectator — 100% pure cashmere woven by Einiger in a sports jacket hand-tailored by Carey.

Babe Ruth as he hit his 60th homer breaking his own record.

Sultan of Swat Slams Number Sixty

BABE RUTH PROVES HE'S MISTER BASEBALL

New York, October 1, 1927 . . . The happiest man in the world today, even happier than the great Bambino himself, is Joe Forner, 40-year-old Yankee fan of 1937 First Avenue, Manhattan, who caught the sixtieth and record breaking home run ball that the mighty Babe bashed into the stands. If you value your eardrums keep away from that First Avenue address for the next week, for Mister Forner is no shrinking violet, as even the Babe can attest.

The mighty blow came off a southpaw throw of Tom Zachary, Senator pitcher, as he saw his low, hard one belted into Babe's favorite parking place, the right field bleachers. This hit not only set a record, but won the game since the score was deadlocked at two-two in the eighth, when the Pasha of Bash stepped to the rubber with one out and Koenig on third.

Zach and the crowd alike were tense for here was raw drama in the making.

Pre-season writers had speculated that the Babe was washed up and about ready for the shelf. If so, they forgot to mention that whoever did the washing put in an overdose of starch, for the Bambino's stickwork got crisper and more devastating as the season progressed. Here was a chance to perform a home run feat that was almost impossible. 59 homers had been laid to the Babe's credit. This was the moment. Zachary sneaked the first throw over for a called strike and the crowd moaned. The next one was high and outside for a ball. On the next pitch, the Sultan of Swat crashed his willow against the horsehide which went sailing like a bat out of the nether regions. The gang in Ruthsville stood up and outlined the path of its flight. It dropped half way to the top of the bleachers and was a fitting hit to break his 1921 record of 59 homers.

While his teammates went as crazy as the crowd, the king of belters jogged slowly around the sacks making sure to touch each bag firmly and carefully. As he reached home a truly presidential rain of torn paper confetti deluged him while the ball game to all intents and purposes ended then and there. The Babe grinned sheepishly as he ambled out to the field where the citizens of Ruthsville rose to a man and gave him a handkerchief salute. The happy hero entered into the spirit of clowning and did a series of comic salutes to the adoring crowd.

The disconsolate Zachary, unwilling conspirator in the record setting feat, said in an interview that the pitch he threw had *everything* on it. It was low, fast and on the inside. The Babe pulled away from the plate, then stepped up and golfed the pitch on a line into the stands. Catcher Muddy Ruel and Umpire Bill Dinneen both claim the ball was more than ten feet fair as it sailed over the bleacher barrier.

Note: George Herman (Babe) Ruth is unquestionably the greatest figure ever associated with our national pastime. He was born in Baltimore, February 6, 1895. Most of his childhood was spent at an orphanage, St. Mary's Industrial School, in that city. He left the institution in 1914 to become an outfielder and pitcher for the Baltimore Orioles. That same year he was sold "upstairs" to the Boston Red Sox where he became a great left-handed pitcher. He played with the Yankees from 1920 to 1934 and such was his skill and his hold on the fans that the Stadium became known as the House That Ruth Built. His last public appearance was at a premiere of the "Babe Ruth Story," a moving picture made in his honor. He died a few months after this (August 16, 1948) after a two-year war against cancer, at Memorial Hospital, New York City. The records he set would fill volumes. On the page opposite we list a few of Ruth's records.

Perhaps the greatest Ruthian moment came during the world series game played against the Cubs at Wrigley Field on October 1, 1932. The Babe came to bat in the 5th with the score locked at four to four. He had already hit a homer in the first inning to give the Yankees a 3-0 lead and as he stepped to the plate to face Cub pitcher Charlie Root, the crowd razzed him mercilessly. As Root whisked a strike past him the Babe turned and, in an eloquent gesture, raised one finger to the crowd. A second strike, and Babe turned again raising two fingers. Then like an actor who, having played a part so often, knows it by heart, Ruth majestically waved toward the right center field wall. A moment later the Babe's pantomimed prediction was a reality. As the crowd, sensing the finale of the drama, rose to its feet, Ruth slammed a homer almost exactly where he had pointed.

Old Pete to the Rescue

New York, October 11, 1926 . . .

Sports writers, fans and other second guessers all swore that young Rogers Hornsby's mind had jumped the track when, without a warm-up, he signaled the bull-pen for Grover Cleveland Alexander to relieve blister-fingered Jess Haines in the crucial seventh inning of the 6th game of the 1926 World Series between the Yankees and the Cardinals.

Alex rose from his catnap in the bull-pen, shaking off weariness with a nod of his head as if he were shaking off a catcher's signal, and shuffled down the baseline to face this set-up: He had pitched and won a full 9-inning game the day before. Now it was two out, a world's series at stake, and the Cards one paper-thin run ahead. Combs, Meusel and Gehrig each occupied a sack. Hit-hungry Tony Lazzeri was at bat. The short conversation that took place between worried manager and veteran pitcher shuffling out to the mound is worthy of its place in baseball history.

Hornsby: "Jeez, Pete, we're in a tough spot. You see how things are."

Alex (spitting a brown stream into the dust): "Yeah, Boss! There don't just seem to be no place to put Lazzeri. Guess I'll have to get him out!"

A funereal hush blanketed the ball park as Old Pete calmly threw his five warm-up pitches to Bob O'Farrell. Lazzeri fidgeted, the tense fans edged forward on their seats, Umpire Hildebrand poured buckets of sweat before he nervously shouted, "Play Ball!"

This was it! The clutch was on and every one of the 40,000 in the park knew it! But Old Pete was as unconcerned as if he were pitching a Florida exhibition. He'd been through this before. His first pitch to Tony was low and the crowd groaned as it went for a ball. The next was a hook that bent over the outside corner and broke Lazzeri's back. Another outside fast ball . . . a crack of wood . . . but the blast went foul! Pete was the only soul in the park grinning; he was ahead of the batter.

His next pitch was a hook so low that a worm couldn't hit it. Neither did Lazzeri! That was the pennant!

The eighth and ninth innings were nticlimactic. Pete breezed through them as the Baseball Gods were busy inscribing the name of Grover Cleveland Alexander on the ivory tablets of the immortals.— I.M.M.

BUILD

YOUR OWN

GOLF COURSE

You own eight acres. You're a golf addict. Want to

combine your holdings and your hobby and make an old wild dream come true?

Gentry, in association with Edward P. Brady, shows you how

EDWARD P. BRADY is Director of Golf and Special Projects for the Department of Parks of the City of New York. For 25 years he has been connected with the building and the maintenance of the city's 10 publicly owned courses. These courses are known for their beauty and their toughness. Mr. Brady, then, is the man to tell you how to build your own. Here's his expert advice:

With a recent development in golf-course design it is now practical to construct a nine-hole, par-32 golf course on a tract of land as small as eight acres. It can boast such features as "water holes" and green and fairway traps. The cost of such an undertaking can vary from a minimum of $5000 on a "do-it-yourself" program, to possibly $25,000 if constructed professionally. Of course, the nature and topography of the land will be reflected in the cost.

The secret of this new design is in the utilization of only four putting greens, each used for two holes and one for three holes of play.

The ideal tract of land to develop would be approximately 420 feet wide and 840 feet long, of rolling meadowland, free of trees, stumps and rubble, with a brook running across or parallel to the tract. The initial construction work would involve the removal of all trees and growth on the fairway, green and tee areas. The area should then be thoroughly cultivated by disking with a tractor-drawn disk and graded with a tractor-drawn rake.

The greens should be of at least 2500 square feet minimum area and be elevated above the fairways at least an average of three feet, thus requiring about 300 cubic yards of material each, one third of which is sand. Thus, 200 cubic yards

each—800 cubic yards in all—of good topsoil would be necessary to construct the four greens. The tees could be relatively small, with an area of 500 square feet.

Subsoil, excavated from the pond or from trap locations, will furnish excellent "fill" for forming tees and the base of greens to elevate them. At least one foot or more of topsoil is necessary for growing and sustaining the proper quality of turf grass on the greens and tees.

Sodding of the green is the preferable method of establishing playable turf in a short time. Bentgrass sod is available for the various climatic areas across our nation and costs only about 25 cents per square foot. Seeding the greens to bentgrass is possible but perhaps not too practical except for the professional agronomist.

The same operation as above applies to tees except that the front of the tee should be slightly higher than the rear of the tee, actually only about ½ inch for every 100 feet of length. Tees may be sodded to bentgrass or other good strains of permanent grasses.

The fairways should be sterilized before seeding with one of the many products now available for this purpose, such as Allyl alcohol, Crag #1, Vapam, Dowfume or Aero-Cyanamid. Such sterilization will eliminate the germination of weed seeds ever present in soils. Fairways should then be fertilized with an 8-6-4 fertilizer at the rate of 1000 pounds to the acre. Seeding of fairways should not exceed 150 pounds per acre and the seed can be applied by various methods, perhaps the best being the use of a wheelbarrow seeder covering a swath of eight feet in width. Each climatic

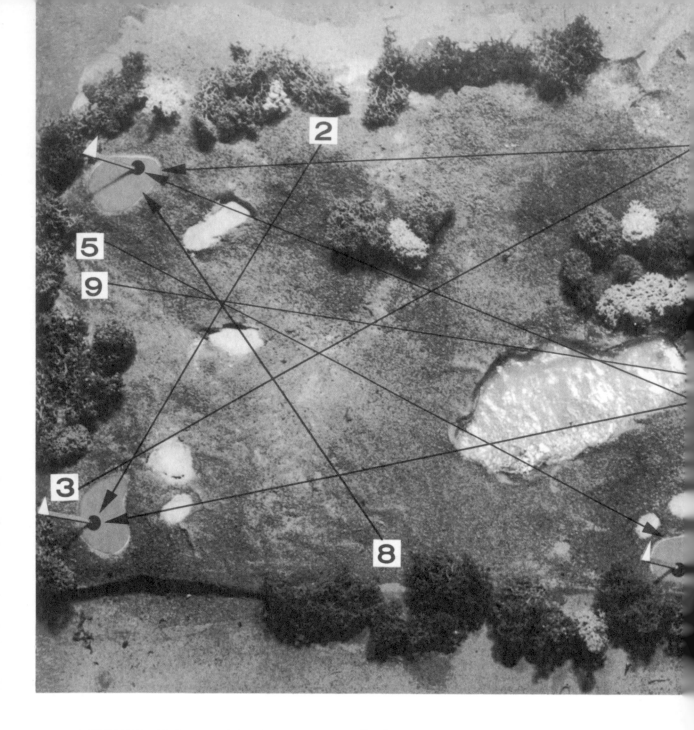

GENTRY'S PLAN FOR YOUR PERSONAL GOLF COURSE

NINE HOLES

FOUR GREENS

EIGHT ACRES

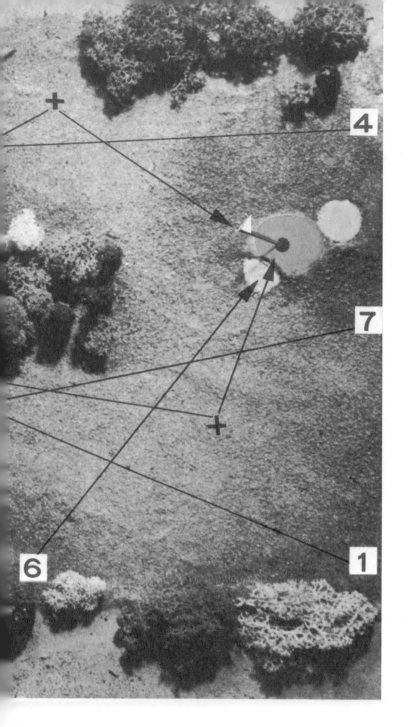

HOLE	YARDS	PAR
1	275	4
2	120	3
3	300	4
4	245	4
5	175	3
6	110	3
7	270	4
8	125	3
9	265	4
	1,185	32

area favors a different type of grass seed; however, a mixture containing about 35 per cent of Creeping Red Fescue, 35 per cent Chewings Fescue and 30 per cent of Kentucky Bluegrass generally proves reasonably good. Uganda grass, a fine, new leaf-textured strain, similar in growing habits to the Bermuda grasses, makes excellent putting greens and tees.

Prior to the construction or seeding of fairways the pipelines for irrigation should be installed. It is imperative that there be a water outlet for each green, and preferably at each tee. Fairway irrigation is desirable; a necessity if bentgrass is used.

Initial equipment for this golf course would include:

1 power greens mower	$400.00
1 Gravely Tractor or equiv.	325.00
3 Gravely Mowers or equiv.	300.00
1 Gravely Rotary mower or equiv.	120.00
1 Gravely Spray attachment or equiv.	150.00
1 Gravely Cast attachment or equiv.	100.00
1 Gravely riding sulky or equiv.	75.00
1 Land lawnmower	35.00
¼ bundle bamboo poles	15.00
Misc. rakes, shovels, etc.	50.00
1 Gandy 5′ fertilizer spreader with Gravely attachment	150.00
Hole cups, hole cutter, flagpoles flags, ball washers, tee markers, tee benches	150.00
400′ water hose	200.00
6-8 sprinklers (automatic)	200.00
Repairs to equipment, parts, gas, oil, etc.	250.00
	Say...$2750.00

Materials for maintenance would include annually:

4 tons fertilizer	$250.00
4 tons limestone	40.00
25 cubic yards topsoil	100.00
100 pounds seed	100.00
25 cubic yards silica sand	100.00
50 pounds fungicide (Tersan)	75.00
50 pounds insecticide (Chlordane)	30.00
Misc., 2, 4D weed-killer	100.00
	Say...$1000.00

It would be well for any individual planning such a development on his property to enlist the assistance of his County Agricultural Agent and the golf-course superintendent of his country club. These people are trained to understand the soil and the production and maintenance of turf grasses. No fees are charged by County Agents, and golf superintendents are generally willing to help anyone to enjoy golf more. They can also recommend where to purchase the necessary specialized equipment and appurtenances.

Gentry will be happy to supply additional information concerning topsoil problems, drainage, seeding, equipment, maintenance costs, etc. to readers, free of charge. Write Gentry, 551 Fifth Ave., NYC NY

ART

AND

CULTURE

6

On the surface, *Gentry* was as aspirational as a Chrysler Imperial Sedan: wildly attractive, smoothly packaged, and silver-spoon stately. Yet for its time, the magazine was a thoroughly subversive manifesto.

This was a decade steeped in glorifying a postwar ethic that urged American men—whether they were returning from the Korean War, entering the workforce, or moving to the wilds of suburbia—to work together to build a community, to be good company and dutiful family men, and always to see themselves as part of a team. *Gentry* dared to ignore all entreaties. Instead, the majority of its pages were deftly infused with hearty doses of unrepentant narcissism. Luckily, narcissism's usual sidekicks of arrogance and foppishness were deflected by the magazine's relentless enthusiasm and an editorial position that unwaveringly promoted individuality through affluence and nerve. But there is no denying that the quarterly was conceived as a testament to "It's all about me!" thirty years before our culture gave birth to a contrary version of the *Gentry* man—the yuppie.

Perhaps the most significant way *Gentry* resisted devolving into a parade of self-absorption was that in between all the "how-tos" directed toward self-improvement, self-confidence, and self-celebration, there regularly appeared text-heavy, well-researched features about extraordinary men who had already achieved singular greatness. In presenting such formidable ideas and achievements, the magazine subtly directed its potentially cultured audience to shift gears. Now was the time to shut up, listen, and learn.

Gentry curated the lengthy feature "Looking at Pictures" not simply to slow down a man's pace while he was in a museum, but to change his point of view. The editors sought an understanding that the James Whistler masterpiece commonly referred to as *Whistler's Mother* is, in fact, an abstraction entitled *An Arrangement in Gray and Black: The Artist's Mother*, which might make it easier to see that a painting generally regarded as a classical portrait is actually a noteworthy precursor to modern art due to its minimal distillation of color and graphic composition. In addition, modern art becomes more exciting, relevant, and diverse when you are suddenly made aware of the deliberate mathematical precision that went into making Fernand Léger's angular *Three Women*, and that the energy circling through Paul Klee's *No. 23* was the result of "planned accidents."

Nothing Oscar Wilde ever declaimed or wrote was an accident either. In recognition of this dazzlingly brilliant linguist who never sent forth a knowing epigram without adding a dash of venom, *Gentry* presented "An Alphabet of Uncommon Sense," a compilation of bon mots derived from Wilde's work, with entries such as "Lying, the telling of untrue things, is the proper aim of art" and "The old believe everything; the middle aged suspect everything; the Young know everything." Probably the densest and most edifying biographies commissioned in the magazine's tenure are gathered in "Ten Men Who Changed the World." Today, tabloids flaunt such an accolade to spotlight Wall Street Ponzi schemers, jihadists, and producers of reality television, but *Gentry* was steadfast in urging the reader to dive into these complex, bullet-point-free histories of such daunting nonconformists as Copernicus, Galileo, Darwin, and Einstein, not to make him feel less of a man, but to remind him that life is filled with so much yet to discover.

Finally, there is the weirdly compelling, head-scratchingly hypnotic, and slightly eerie elevation of "The Obstinate Number 9." True, once you've absorbed its uncanny properties—and the strange truth that you can multiply any number by nine and the resultant figures add up to nine—can you really do anything with it? Well, it does give you something to talk about at parties—and a dinner guest who sits at a table prepared with something stimulating to talk about is one of the key signs of a cultured man. And that's what *Gentry* was all about.

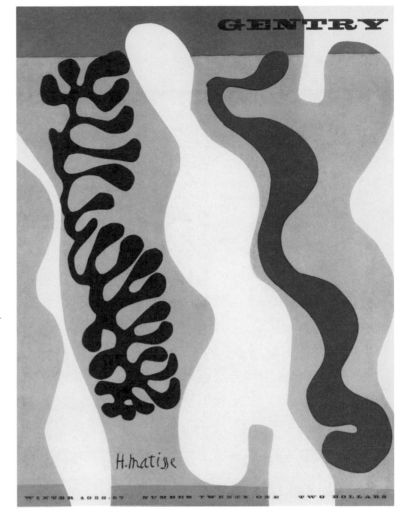

**CLOCKWISE,
FROM TOP RIGHT:**

Gentry, Number Twenty-
one, Winter 1956–57;
Number Seven, Summer
1953; Number Six,
Spring 1953.

ELVIS

by FELIKS TOPOLSKI

The artist-editor-author-publisher-printer
of Topolski's Chronicle, *the London*
fortnightly, recently visited America. These are
his drawings and comments on an
American-Greek-god-sex-hero phenomenon

Presley with his manager and agent

RECENTLY AT A TV variety audition, the wise girl who conducted it held forth for me expertly on the merits and demerits of Elvis Presley. I was just preparing my *Chronicle* on him and I suggested that she write for that issue a professional piece of assessment as if, job-seeking and unknown, he had come for an audition. She was agreeable then, but later must have lost heart. She became unobtainable on the telephone.

Indeed, the Presley case escapes the purely expert measure. I, as an irresponsible amateur, can only attempt a few random shots—hoping that, however wide, they will encompass the mark:

The public's behavior is tremendously conditioned nowadays by the ever-present TV, film and press cameras. The speakers at the Presidential Conventions, when mounting the rostrum, would go through an extraordinary ritual of ham-acting: big gestures, toothy smiles, embracings, kissing their State's pennant—all out of character as revealed in the meek speech-delivery which would follow, all utterly for the benefit of the cameras. Any crowd conscious of being "recorded" will also ham-act to the limit its expected part. *Life* showed some time ago a series of photographs taken during a Presley act: groups of young females "beside themselves" as if on the edge of an epileptic trance. How far did these catch the truth, or merely camera-conscious amateurs eager to act the elation which was expected of them?

These films, these photographs, are pushed out to the millions and engender "mass snobbery"—the inescapable order of behavior. And joy at be-

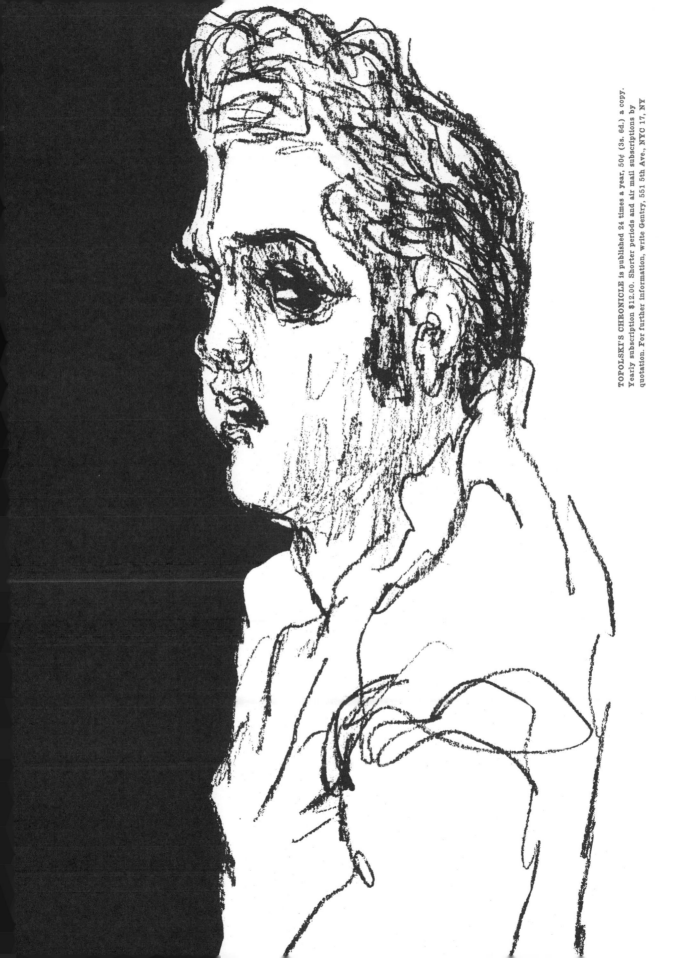

TOPOLSKI'S CHRONICLE is published 24 times a year, 50¢ (3s. 6d.) a copy. Yearly subscription $12.00. Shorter periods and air mail subscriptions by quotation. For further information, write Gentry, 551 5th Ave, NYC 17, NY

No photographers near . . .

The cameras appear

longing to the mass-order of behavior is probably the core of the matter. Not Mr. Presley . . .

After a full day made up of Presley's rehearsals, his TV show and his teen-agers, I was inclined to see the whole as a piece of skilled *management*-cum-crowd-snobbery. The teen-agers demonstrating at the stage-door, with mounted policemen and barriers to restrain them, seemed gathered, as any crowd, by curiosity—and, as any crowd out for a spree, eager to be amused and to show off. Their noisiest outbursts were good-humoured, either caused by the appearance of Mr. Presley (having been chanted to the window of his dressing-room) or by press photographers staging a momentary pandemonium for a "take."

When, before the Presley appearance, the announcer prepares the public (that is, the girls) and tries out the loudness of their unison-scream (*"Is that all you can do? Try again!"*), he is working not on their libido, but on their "esprit de corps." Indeed, Presley's face shows, again and again, a childish and rather touching surprise mingled with contentment when a single swing of his hip causes unfailingly the SCREAM.

But this cannot be all. Some people talk learnedly of his possessing the secret of the youngsters' emotional mime-cum-sound, which apparently withers with maturity. (Some talk of his great acting gifts, some of his Greek god features.) I watched him closely at a press conference and rather liked his good, posed-into-toughness shape, but was worried by his facial diversions from Greek exemplars, such as the upturned tip-of-nose, sloppy half-open mouth and also sloppy but half-closed eyes.

Yet the "god" aspect must not be dismissed.

My generation's puberty was rather private. We would steal our parents' books, thus learning the theory long before they thought it the right time to give us their progressive enlightenment. Nowadays, as in antiquity, Sex seems to be becoming an open and foremost preoccupation of the adolescent—in fact, it is developing its public rituals. The chosen god-symbol, supplied periodically from amongst the "Stars," serves as the approved fixation-object for awakening desires. And, since his sanctification is performed by the supremely august Business of Entertainment, the young virgins are free, even encouraged, to sublimate their urges in the public rites of adoration.

But, however mystically chosen, why Elvis Presley? Because, I think, he possesses very happily the godlike value of all-embracing popularity: he is vulgar, yet stylish in the "zoot" manner—hence he appeals both to the sophisticated and the simple. And his manhood is above suspicion . . .

Feliks Topolski

P.S. Yet here is still another assessment. Back in London, my daughter Teresa, age 9, gave this verdict: "Better than Roy Rogers."

THE OBSTINATE NUMBER

9

by

WILLIAM S. WALSH

If it be true that figures won't lie, that they won't even equivocate, that two and two exhibit an unbending determination to make four and nothing but four, at least figures do often play strange pranks. They abound in paradoxes, and though a paradox is rightly defined as a truth that only appears to be a lie, yet the stern moralist, who hates even the appearance of evil, looks with scant favor upon a paradox. Luckily, we are not all so stern in our morality. Most of us welcome a little ingenious trifling, an amiable coquetting with the truth; we are willing that Mr. Gradgrind shall have the monopoly of hard facts; we like to find romance even in our arithmetic. And we don't have far to look.

There is the number nine. It is a most romantic number, and a most persistent, self-willed and obstinate one. You cannot multiply it away or get rid of it. Whatever you do, it is sure to turn up again, as did the body of Eugene Aram's victim.

Mr. W. Green, who died in 1794, is said to have first called attention to the fact that all through the multiplication table the product of nine comes to nine. Multiply by any figure you like, and the sum of the resultant digits will invariably add up to nine. Thus, twice 9 is 18; add the digits together, and 1 and 8 makes 9. Three times 9 is 27; and 2 and 7 is 9. So it goes on up to 11 times 9, which gives 99. Very good. Add the digits together, 9 and 9 is 18, and 8 and 1 is 9. Go on to any extent, and you will find it impossible to get away from the figure 9. Take an example at random. Nine times 339 is 3051; add the digits together, and they make 9. Or again, 9 times 2127 is 19,143; add the digits together, they make 18, and 8 and 1 is 9. Or still again, 9 times 5071 is 45,639; the sum of these digits is 27, and 2 and 7 is 9.

This seems startling enough. Yet there are other queer examples of the same form of persistence. It was M. de Maivan who discovered that if you take any row of figures and, reversing their order, make a subtraction sum of obverse and reverse, the final result of adding up the digits of the answer will always be 9. Example:

$$2941$$
$$\text{Reverse, } 1492$$
$$\overline{1449}$$

Now, $1 + 4 + 4 + 9 = 18$; and $1 + 8 = 9$.

The same result is obtained if you raise the numbers so changed to their squares or cubes. Start anew, for example, with 62; reversing it, you get 26. Now, $62 - 26 = 36$, and $3 + 6 = 9$. The squares of 26 and 62 are, respectively, 676 and 3844. Subtract one from the other, and you get 3168 $= 18$ and $1 + 8 = 9$. So with the cubes of 26 and 62, which are 17,576 and 238,328. Subtracting, the result is $220,752 = 18$, and $1 + 8 = 9$.

Again, you are confronted with the same puzzling peculiarity in another form. Write down any number, as, for example, 7,549,132, subtract therefrom the sum of its digits, and, no matter what figures you start with, the digits of the products will always come to 9.

$$7549132, \text{ sum of digits} = 31$$
$$\underline{31}$$
$$7549101, \text{ sum of digits} = 27,$$
$$\text{and } 2 + 7 = 9.$$

Again, set the figure 9 down in multiplication, thus:

$$1 \times 9 = 9$$
$$2 \times 9 = 18$$
$$3 \times 9 = 27$$
$$4 \times 9 = 36$$
$$5 \times 9 = 45$$
$$6 \times 9 = 54$$
$$7 \times 9 = 63$$
$$8 \times 9 = 72$$
$$9 \times 9 = 81$$
$$10 \times 9 = 90$$

Now, you will see that the tens column reads down 1, 2, 3, 4, 5, 6, 7, 8, 9, and the units column up 1, 2, 3, 4, 5, 6, 7, 8, 9.

Here is a different property of the same number. If you arrange in a row the cardinal numbers from 1 to 9, with the single omission of 8, and multiply the sum so represented by any one of the figures multiplied by 9, the result will present a succession of figures identical with that which was multiplied by 9. Thus, if you wish a series of 5's, you take $5 \times 9 = 45$ for a multiplier, with this result:

$$12345679$$
$$45$$
$$\overline{61728395}$$
$$49382716$$
$$\overline{555555555}$$

A very curious number is 142,857. When 142,857 is multiplied by 1, 2, 3, 4, 5 or 6, the answer always gives the same figures in the same order, beginning at a different point, but if multiplied by 7 gives all 9's. Multiplied by 1, it equals 142,857; multiplied by 2, equals 285,714; multiplied by 3, equals 428,571; multiplied by 4, equals 571,428; multiplied by 5, equals 714,285; multiplied by 6, equals 857,142; multiplied by 7, equals 999,999. Multiply 142,857 by 8, and you have 1,142,856. Then add the first figure to the last, and you have 142,857, the original number, the figures the same as at the start.

Now note this about the number 142,857: The digits $1 + 4 + 2 + 8 + 5 + 7 = 27$, and $2 + 7 = 9$.

From A Handy-Book of Literary Curiosities, by William S. Walsh
Reprinted by permission of J. B. Lippincott Company

GORDON B. WASHBURN, *Director of the Department of Fine Arts at the Carnegie Institute, composed and narrated a series of films for TV. Gentry's editors saw the first rough cuts of these films. Because Gentry agrees so vigorously with their purpose—to help Americans understand the art of our time—we have created this special section to present the first of Mr. Washburn's lectures in this unique endeavor. Financed by the Ford Foundation's Educational Television and Radio Center and created in Pittsburgh, the series was produced and directed by Robert Snyder, designed by Norbert Nathanson.*

LOOKING AT PICTURES

Washburn speaking:

Before looking together at some paintings in the field of modern art, let's examine a few points in the history of the movement—a movement which, as we all know, can not be dated exactly. It begins somewhere in the 19th century, and so far as we are concerned is largely a 20th-century affair, but we must go back to the 19th century to understand what the big rebellion was all about, what the artists who have changed the whole face of art meant by their revolt.

I suppose there's no other point equal to their attack on the illusionistic copying of nature; that is to say, the copying of nature which allows nature itself to dictate the subject matter of art. The modern artist was against the idea that a pretty girl makes a pretty painting. He was against the idea that you must go to the seashore to get a handsome view of boats for your newest picture for the salon. He hated being told by the model what was beautiful and what made a picture.

In the idea of the modern artist the picture is made by the painter.

After all, nature has never undertaken to make human clothing, architecture, furniture. Why should it make our pictures for us? These lie in the province of man, and in his artistry. And so the 20th-century painter, before all else, has dispensed with the model as his dictator.

Let us look at a few pictures—for instance, a portrait by Bonnat of Puvis de Chavannes. I trust the old gentleman wasn't as pretentious as he looks here. He was a very fine artist, de Chavannes, but here he looks as though he were trying to imitate Bismarck.

We can compare his picture with one by a revolutionary painter, a deeply beloved painter named Whistler—and to a revolutionary picture known today as ''Whistler's Mother.'' The point we would like to make about it now is that it was not called ''Portrait of My Mother'' by Whistler himself, but rather, ''An Arrangement in Gray and Black.'' By this title he pointed strongly to the notion that a picture, before being a portrait of his mother or anything else, must be a construction, a composition, an organization of material. He said, ''I am making an *arrangement*,'' and by so doing he leads us through a long route to abstraction. Artists who follow him have decided it might not be necessary to include mother at all, or indeed any subject matter. If you are making an arrangement of gray and black, then all you need is gray and black . . .

As opposed to Whistler, let us examine another artist well known to all of us—Van Gogh. His portrait of Roulin the postman shows us the other great tendency that art was to take—the tendency toward emotional expression, toward painting not what you saw in the outer world but what your inner eye expressed, what your inner heart felt. It's the painter's reaction to the world, rather than its physical appearance to his eye. This whole somewhat tortured outline, the whole character of the postman, has been interpreted by a painter who felt thus torturously, thus forcibly, about life.

Let us look at two other objects in this same connection. First, a 19th-century painting of Christ's head. The idea here is pure sentimentality. If one looks carefully one even sees a small bird chirping in the branches of Christ's crown.

Courtesy, Museum of Fine Arts, Boston

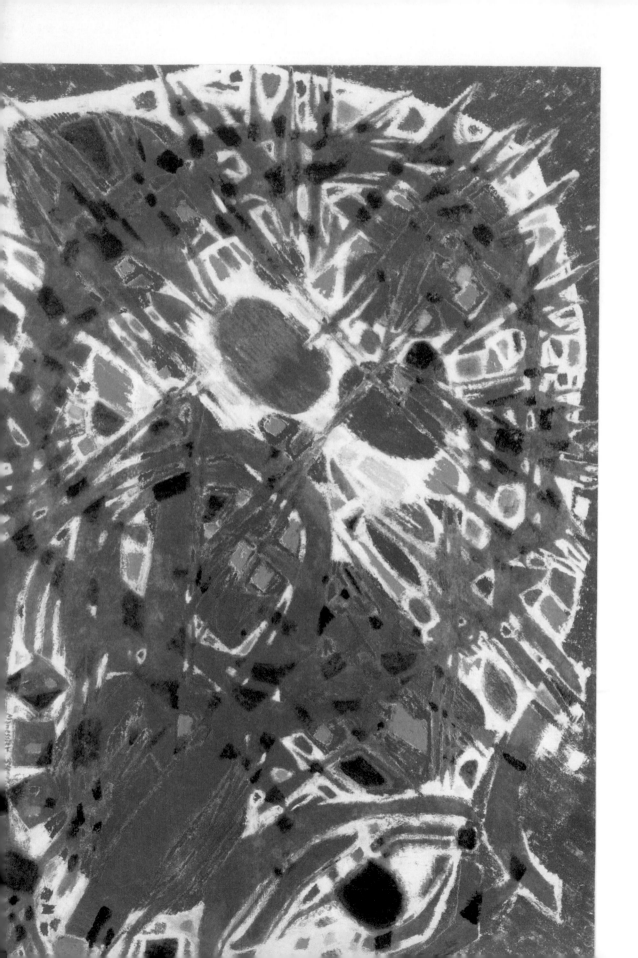

Now let us compare the 19th-century head with a 20th-century image of the same subject. This is abstraction, to a very considerable degree. In this picture by the great French painter Alfred Manessier, Christ is represented by light. This is a metaphor; this is a plastic painting, the painting of an *idea* rather than the painting of an object. Here the idea of Christ as the light of the world is expressed by light pouring in from behind, as through a stained-glass window . . .

I'd like to show you some other aspects of the rebellion which the 20th-century artist expressed toward the imitation of models. In this figure (above) by the 19th-century painter Bouguereau, a figure copied in a studio, an extremely seductive girl, is offered to us in place of a picture. This is not a work of art, it is a tour de force—but this girl has noble ancestors. Here (right) you see the famous Medici Venus of the 4th century B.C., which more or less established for Western art the form that illusionistic painting would follow—illusionistic sculpture, of course, as well. The next turn occurs when this art is rediscovered in the Renaissance, as in this other view of a Venus (left) by Botticelli. It was against this tradition, as it developed over the centuries, to the 19th, that the modern artist has reacted.

(Cast), Courtesy, Metropolitan Museum of Art

We'd be more correct if we said that this is not a nude, but, in the excellent distinction made by an English critic, a naked woman. In this painting by Fichel, of the same period as Bouguereau, we see, again, a piece of seduction rather than a picture. It represents the ultimate decay of the classical and Renaissance tradition.

ART AND CULTURE 235

This wonderful picture by Miro is called "With Hair Unbound in the Train of the Constellation." Dreamlike fantasy is another aspect of the subjective primitivism of modern painting. In the 20th century, as we have seen, painting has tended to go in two directions. There is the Whistlerian one of calculated arrangement, which ends up in abstraction—and this, which Miro shows us, of subjectivity, deriving from the Van Gogh point of view. That artist paints not any aspect of the external world that is known to us, but rather his own feelings, his own thoughts, his own fantasies . . .

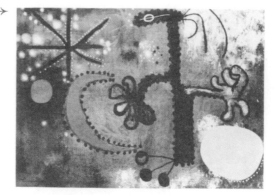

. . . as in the instance of this Leger, where we see the artist using what might be called the inartistic material of our time—machinery, the 20th-century appearance of things as we know them mechanically. The picture is organized with a totality that is machine-like in its unity, its precision, its repetition of forms.

Courtesy Museum of Modern Art, "Three Women" by Leger

←

There are two forms of distortion in modern art. They were identified at the beginning of this century by Maurice Denis—I refer to his "subjective" and "objective" distortion. Subjective distortion refers to an art which is distorted through emotion, through psychological expression, as in this painting by Soutine, "The Woman in Red" (left, above). Soutine is dealing with an ugly woman, but the picture itself is organized in terms that make it beautiful: its color, its color relationships, its forms and lines . . . The same thing is true of this famous picture (left, below) by Matisse, "Pink Nude," but the distortion here is "objective" distortion. By this we mean that the painter actually distorts the anatomy of the human body. He does not use it in accordance with its true visual appearance, but only to make his picture balance. We see here not a naked woman at all, but a nude. She is not a human being, she is simply part of a picture. Leger has said, "I have no more interest in the human beings in my canvases than I have in key rings or in bicycles." Neither has Matisse. You are not invited into this room, as you were invited into Bouguereau's room where his model stood. I have some photographs of this picture, taken as it was being painted. They show us that Matisse started with naturalistic images—a model, a chair, a bunch of flowers. But he transformed these to make his picture, a transformation of the most extraordinary complexity. In the finished picture the chair has become absolutely unidentifiable. You would never guess that those two curls on top were once a chair. Neither could you guess that there are flowers here, a bunch of flowers. That is not necessary. The beauty of this picture lies in the proportion of the parts, in the equilibrium of the colors, the vitality of which produces a sense of life movement, of life excitation.

←We can see a similar activity in the art of another great modern painter, Paul Klee. Look carefully at the drawing, which is called "Play on the Water." Now, how did Klee start making this drawing? In my opinion, he first drew a few parallel lines—this is the plastic motif, a little thing, a very simple, little thing. From that, he begins to wonder—if he curves a line, what will happen? So he goes on drawing, with the line curving, and making little modulations, and he begins to see that this is water, and perhaps he begins to see that in the ripples of the water are faces, or a face. And so a face forms in the water, which wasn't water at all when he started.

In comparison with Klee, let us look at an American painter's abstraction, which is formed in an entirely different way. It is, I suppose, a series of planned accidents. Inevitably, if you paint a picture like this, as Jackson Pollack did, by putting the canvas on the floor and dripping paint on it with a series of rapid motions, accidents will occur which must be taken advantage of in the development of the picture. What we have here is a form of handwriting, propelled by the temperament of the artist, which produces a canvas all parts of which are equally lively, equally expressive from corner to corner.

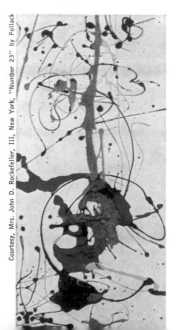

Another abstraction, one of the most famous of all time, is that produced by Piet
Mondrian, the Dutch painter. Such a picture (right) gives us the extreme of abstraction which has been produced in the 20th century. Mondrian does here what we saw Matisse doing, except that he starts with no naturalistic material at all. He turns his back entirely on both the visible world and the subjective world. He seeks to do something I think no other painter has more consciously, or more successfully, tried to do—to give us the final, the pure reality lying behind all appearances in the natural world, in terms we might call symbolic. The lines represent form in the universe; the spaces represent space. This is, as it were, the essence of reality; this is Plato's concept of the pure reality lying behind truth. In a wonderful way, Mondrian has exemplified in this painting, and in others he did, one whole aspect of the modern revolution which we have been observing—that is, the attempt of the 20th-century painter not only to purify painting, but to purify himself as a human being.

Courtesy Museum of Modern Art, "Broadway Boogie Woogie," by Mondrian

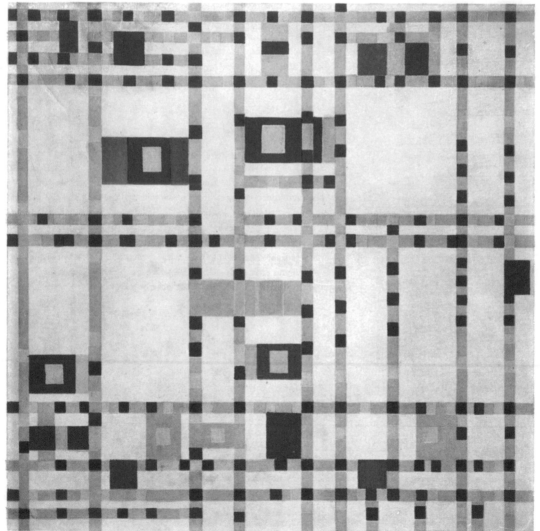

THALES

PYTHAGORAS

ARCHIMEDES

COPERNICUS

KEPLER

GALILEO

NEWTON

DARWIN

PLANCK

EINSTEIN

TEN MEN WHO CHANGED THE WORLD

Ideas, said Plato, are the only reality. Thought brings order out of chaos and patterns the world as we know it. Reality for us is what we know, as we know it, when we know it; the world otherwise becomes meaningless. In the Western world a small group of men have been responsible for the pivotal ideas. Some of these men were ignored or persecuted in their own time, some have been forgotten in ours. Nevertheless, their ideas, like those of their better-known confrères, changed the thinking of and about the world as they found it, and formed some of the essential structures and patterns of our Western civilization.

THALES

FOUNDER OF GREEK PHILOSOPHY; ORIGINATOR OF THE IDEA OF PROOF.
Born in Miletus, in Asia Minor, about 640 B.C. His exact dates are not known, although he is believed to have lived until 546 B.C.

Thales is the first of the forerunners of what is now called scientific method. He departed from the loose and irregular thinking of the Egyptian and Babylonian thinkers by maintaining that no mathematical proposition can be accepted as true unless it can lend itself to proof. He anticipated modern atomic theory by asserting that everything in the universe is composed of a primary world-stuff, a single substance, which he called *arché*.

Not a great deal is known of Thales' life. None of his writings survive, and his biographical data are available to us only on the retelling of the later Greek philosophers and historians. Herodotus believed him to have been of Phoenician parentage, others have him a Milesian noble. Some say that he acquired his early training from a Babylonian priest who set up a school of mathematics on the island of Cos; others maintain he was self-taught.

His place in Greek history was formally established by an incident which occurred in the year 585 B.C. Equipped perhaps with knowledge of what the Chaldeans had called the *Saros,* the cyclic configuration of bodies which results in a total eclipse of the sun every 223 lunar months (18 years, 11-1/3 days), Thales announced the day on which an eclipse would be expected. It happened that the Medes and Persians were in battle at the announced time; the eclipse blackened the sky and the combatting armies, interpreting the darkness as a bitter omen, retired from the field. Subsequently, the citizens of Miletus acknowledged Thales' prediction as a sign of cosmic wisdom. He was referred to as *sophos,*, the wise one, and is established as the first of the Seven Wise Men of Greece.

But what is significant of Thales is not his singular personal achievements, which were many, but the revolutionary quality of his approach to thinking. He is the first historical man to deal systematically with abstract, universal truths — general principles not rooted in time or confined to transient utility. His materials were ideas; and these were pronounced freely for their own sake as the supreme expression of human adventure.

Yet more than this, Thales was the founder of the geometry of lines — what we now call plane geometry. His object was the introduction, for the first time, of a system of demonstration by which precise relations of the different parts of a figure could be established, and by means of which known facts could make possible the discovery of measurements or relationships previously unknown. This is the core of what today is scientific method.

Such a method was new to the world which preceded Thales; it generated the abstract spirit, the cool objectivity and sense of the importance of integrated form which together have come to us from the Greeks.

PYTHAGORAS

ORIGINATOR OF NUMBER THEORY AND THE ASSUMPTION THAT THE EARTH IS SPHERICAL AND IN MOTION. *Born in Samos, about 530 B.C.; taught at Croton in Southern Italy. Time and place of his death are not known.*

Pythagoras represents the first effort to explain the nature of the universe in relationships expressed by numbers. The relationships of the tones in a musical scale, the parts of geometric figures, the heavenly bodies, and probably everything else in nature, he felt, are established in terms of an ordered harmony; and this harmony is based on simple numbers. In a somewhat different form, and without the arbitrary requirement of simple numbers, this is an idea which has made the structure of modern physics possible; modern science interprets the phenomena of nature almost entirely on the basis of number relationships and constants, although these are necessarily more complex than those envisioned by the Pythagoreans.

The conception of the earth as a sphere and as a member of a family of bodies which revolve around a central fire is another signal achievement of the Pythagoreans. It was not until the time of Copernicus, two thousand years later, that this idea was incorporated into Western culture.

Pythagoras is a half-legendary figure. Little is known of his personal life. Although born at Samos, he lived most of his life within the folds of a secret society or brotherhood which he founded at Croton, a Greek colony in southern Italy. Because of the secrecy which surrounded the research and studies of the brotherhood, later writers found it impossible to disentangle the work of Pythagoras from that of his followers.

Among the many geometric propositions ascribed to the Pythagoreans is the famous theorem which still bears the founder's name: that the square on the hypotenuse of a right triangle is equal to the sum of the squares on the other two sides. A discovery in physics, said to have been made by Pythagoras while hearing the musical tones given off by the hammers which struck anvils in a smithy, was the foundation of the Western theory of musical structure. Reproducing the sounds with lengths of strings, Pythagoras found that the musical tones which are harmonious are those sounded by strings whose lengths were proportionate to one another in terms of simple numbers. This observation became the basis of Western musical harmony.

Pythagoras and his followers attempted to apply the idea of number harmony in its simplest form to all the phenomena of nature; but applying it too crudely and in an over-simplified form, they encountered difficulties. Nature proved to be not so simply organized as harmonically related strings. This embarrassing fact was brought home to the brotherhood by the problem of finding the length of that side of a triangle whose square was two. The length, obviously, is the square root of two. But the square root of two is not a simple whole number. It is a number which never terminates — 1.4142 . . . and so on, to infinity. It is said that Archytas, the Pythagorean who first disclosed this fact, was drowned by the gods in punishment.

All extensive projections of thinking tend to develop initial contradictions and difficulties; these are the costs of genius. With the growth and development of the new ideas, the difficulties are sloughed off . . . the genius remains. And nowhere is this process more clearly demonstrated than in Pythagoras, the first of the great Western innovators of thought. His ultimate greatness lies in his passionate search for universal ideas. He sought not only the generality underlying every group of particulars, but the generalities of generalities, the all-embracing, unifying principles of nature and the universe. In this he displays a kinship with Einstein.

His inner eye seems to have been trained on the universal and constant element in all things and all happenings. He distinguished between what is temporary and accidental and what is constant and cosmic. We may have our moods, illnesses, moments of elation or depression. These are but passing aspects of our nature; but do what we will, or feel as we may, the eternal relationships are in no way altered; all the angles of a triangle still add up to 180 degrees and the area of a circle remains *pi* times the radius squared.

This is an attitude Santayana has expressed with great charm:

> *It fortifies my soul to know*
> *That though I wander, Truth is so.*

ARCHIMEDES

GREATEST PHYSICIST AND MATHEMATICIAN OF ANCIENT TIMES; DISCOVERER OF BASIC PRINCIPLES OF MECHANICS. *Born in Syracuse, c. 287 B.C.; killed during the capture of Syracuse by Marcellus, 212 B.C.*

Many of the geometric propositions contained in the books of Euclid were the developments of Archimedes. Among these are the theorems covering the calculation of the area and circumference of the circle, the surface and volume of the sphere and the cylinder, and the basic propositions relating to cones and conic sections — all of which are fundamental in modern science and mechanics. Archimedes also calculated the decimal value of *pi* to four places, declaring it 3.14129 (correct value is 3.1416).

Many of his mechanical achievements, which he despised as matters beneath the level of philosophical concern, became founding elements in Western engineering science. Among these are the discovery of the principle of the lever, the screw, the pulley, and of means for determining specific gravity. The last was supposedly a consequence of an attempt to find out whether or not the gold in a crown had been adulterated. Archimedes' discovery, now a classic story, was arrived at in the bath, and consists merely of weighing the amount of water displaced by an object and comparing it with the weight of the original object. This was the accomplishment which evoked the historical exclamation *Eureka!*

His discovery of the principle of the lever is associated with another much-quoted remark, *dos moi pou sto kai kino ten gen,* "Give me a place to stand and I will move the earth."

Archimedes was criticized by the Syracusans for his lack of concern in the siege of the city by the Romans. His reported reply, whether or not correct, was at least characteristic. The siege of Syracuse, he maintained, was an unimportant detail in the childish sport of history; the consideration of mathematical truths, which monopolized his attention, was of moment to all people, in all times, in all places.

Nevertheless, Archimedes developed many war inventions, among which were burning glasses which were said to have set fire at a distance to the attacking Roman fleet. When Syracuse finally fell and its inhabitants massacred, Archimedes remained calmly at work on diagrams drawn in sand. He is said not to have bothered to glance up at the Roman soldier who plunged a spear through his back.

COPERNICUS

FATHER OF MODERN ASTRONOMY: FIRST SCIENTIFIC FORMULATOR OF THE HELIOCENTRIC THEORY. *Born in Torun (Thorn), in Polish Pomerania, 1473; died at Frauenberg, 1543.*

Mikola Koppernigk, Latinized to *Nicolas Copernicus,* a Polish ecclesiastic of supposedly unimpeachable orthodoxy, dealt a death blow to medieval orthodoxy by establishing as scientific hypothesis the Greek notion that the earth moves around the sun. This idea, which is suggested in Pythagorean doctrine, was first clearly and formally announced by Aristarchus of Samos, who lived in Alexandria around the middle of the Fourth Century B.C. Like many other Greek insights it hibernated during the dark ages, covered by scholastic dust.

Copernicus was a cautious man. Convinced early in life that the earth has a two-fold motion, a daily rotation and an annual revolution around the sun, he delayed publication of his affirmations until the year of his death. Even then his disclosures were wrapped in tact; his magnum opus, *De Revolutionibus Orbium Coelestium,* was dedicated to the Pope and prefaced by a note, written by his friend Osiander, asserting discreetly that the heliocentric theory was only put forward as a hypothesis. In some miraculous way this work for many years escaped censure, although Giordano Bruno who, a generation later, espoused the theory — and extended it to show the relation of the solar system to the fixed stars — was imprisoned for seven years by the Inquisition and then burned.

Like many of the great men of the Renaissance, Copernicus took all knowledge to be his province; he was a cultivated classicist, a physician, poet and painter, as well as a mathematician and astronomer. He tended the sick, manufactured his own scientific instruments, and advised the Polish government on matters relating to currency and economic policy.

That Copernicus' assertions came to be rejected by the authorities of his period can be attributed in part to the gulf which separated his astonishing culture from the intellectual poverty of his critics. Copernicus knew virtually all that could be known, with the instruments then available, of the apparent motions of the celestial bodies, and it naturally occurred to him that, among other things, the earth, rather than vast configurations of galaxies which compose the universe, was the entity revolving; this assumption was simpler, more economic than its opposite. If it was opposed by tradition, tradition must yield to reasonableness.

Yet the critics, in reformation as well as orthodox countries, were denied both Copernicus' observed facts and the objectivity which derived from his culture. When word of his pronouncements came to Martin Luther, the reformer was profoundly shocked. "People give ear," he said, "to an upstart astrologer who strove to show that the earth revolves, not the heavens or the firmament, the sun and the moon. Whoever wishes to appear clever must devise some new system, which of all systems is of course the best. This fool wishes to reverse the entire science of astronomy; but sacred Scripture tells us that Joshua commanded the sun to stand still, and not the earth."

JOHANNES KEPLER

DISCOVERER OF THE ELLIPTIC ORBITS OF PLANETS AND FORMULATOR OF THE LAWS OF PLANETARY MOTION. *Born in Weil, in the Duchy of Württemberg, 1571; died 1630.*

Throughout the middle ages the belief was held that the circle is the symbol of perfection, and that the perfect circle is the fundamental form in the structure of the universe. The Pythagorean notion persisted that eventually all cosmic motion could be explained by simple geometric forms.

Kepler exploded this assumption by making a startling observation: the earth and other planets travel in ellipses, not circles.

Kepler established three laws which cover all aspects of planetary motion. The first specified the path along which a planet moves. The second indicated how it moved along this path — the way its speed varied. The third determined the time required for a planet to complete its revolution around the sun.

In his famous book, *Astronomia Nova* (1609) and *Epitome Astronomiae Copernicae* (1618), Kepler stated his laws as follows:

1. The planet moves in an ellipse which has the sun as one of its foci.
2. The line joining the sun to the planet sweeps out equal areas in equal times.
3. The square of the time which any planet takes to complete its orbit is proportional to the cube of its distance from the sun.

GALILEO

FATHER OF MODERN SCIENCE; FORMULATOR OF THE PRINCIPLE OF ACCELERATION AND FIRST SCIENTIST TO MAKE ASTRONOMICAL OBSERVATIONS WITH THE TELESCOPE. *Born in Pisa, 1564; died 1642.*

Galileo Galilei was distinguished in many branches of scientific observation, but his most distinctive achievement was his establishment in a practicable way of the principle of formal experiment, thus sounding the changes against the purely intellectualistic or schoolman's approach to science. Prior to Galileo, the world of nature was considered fixed and immutable, and its principles were believed almost entirely embodied in the writings of Aristotle.

Galileo's maxim was to test and observe. Typical of this approach was his experimental approach to Aristotle's dictum that heavier bodies fall faster than light objects; a test incorrectly said to consist of the dropping simultaneously of a cannon ball and musket shot from the Leaning Tower of Pisa disclosed the observable fact that all objects fall through space with the same velocity. The consequence was Galileo's formulating of the principle of acceleration.

Although Galileo is commonly accredited with the invention of the telescope, the pioneer development in this field was the work of two Dutchmen, Hans Lippershey and James Metius; working independently of one another, Lipper-

shey and Metius coincidentally announced their invention in the same year, 1608. Galileo, however, was the first to use the telescope for systematic astronomical observation; he discovered the four satellites of Jupiter and upset the prevailing theological notion that there could be no more than seven heavenly bodies.

Although Galileo's social position was secure, and despite the added fact that he enjoyed cordial relations with many scientifically-oriented high dignitaries of the Church, his published writings caused his arrest and trial by the Inquisition. In 1638 he was formally condemned by the Inquisitional tribunal for advocating two heretical doctrines: (1) that the sun is the center of our universe, and stationary, and (2) that the earth revolves annually around the sun and daily about its own axis.

Under duress, as is well known, he recanted. According to a discredited legend, his withdrawal of his theses was accompanied by the whispered comment, *Eppur si muove* — the earth moves nonetheless.

An explanation now generally accepted for Galileo's readiness to withdraw his claims is that the new astronomical observations made the movements of the earth and planets so patent and incontrovertible that the progress of science could in no way be affected.

ISAAC NEWTON

FORMULATOR OF THE LAWS OF GRAVITATION AND MOTION; FOUNDER OF MODERN MECHANICS; CO-INVENTOR OF DIFFERENTIAL AND INTEGRAL CALCULUS. *Born in Lincolnshire, England, 1642; died 1727.*

Isaac Newton was perhaps the greatest scientific genius of all time; nothing in the realm of natural science seemed outside his grasp and unifying capacity. Building on the groundwork established by Galileo, Newton established the general principles of gravitation and established the laws which accounted for such seemingly diverse phenomena as the motion of the tides and the elliptic orbits of the planets. Independent of the German mathematician Leibniz, Newton developed the principles of the calculus, thus laying the mathematical foundation — with Leibniz — for computations relating to bodies in motion. Since modern research has established the fact that all objects and forces in the universe are in motion relative to one another, the calculus has played an indispensable role in the interpretation of the nature of the universe.

Newton developed a body of doctrine which put an end to the sterile speculations of the Scholastics and indirectly fathered the optimism of the Eighteenth Century Rationalists — men who believed that the exact methods of science could eventually solve all problems of society. The Rationalist belief was founded on the Socratic notion that no man does evil knowingly; that all social evil is a consequence of ignorance of ends. The assumption followed that science, which could furnish exact knowledge, would sooner or later banish ignorance and thus develop an age of reason and virtue.

The core of Newton's theory of universal gravitation is the demonstration that all motion in the field of our universe takes place in accord with the following laws:

1. Every body maintains its state of rest or of uniform motion in a straight line, unless it is compelled to change that state by impressed forces.

2. Rate of change in motion is proportional to the motive force impressed, and takes place in the direction in which the force is impressed.

3. To every action there is always opposed an equal reaction.

The first law accounts for the motion of the earth and the planets. The second tells us how to measure force. The third explains the flight of birds, the movement of projectiles, today's jet engines and guided missiles, and tomorrow's possible inter-planetary rockets.

The Law of Gravitation: Every body attracts every other with a force directly proportional to the product of their masses and inversely proportional to the square of the distance between them.

From this formula Newton was able to deduce all the events which were the subject of planetary theory: the motions of the planets and their satellites, orbits of comets, the ebb and flow of tides.

Newton's laws stood unchallenged for two hundred years, until Ernst Mach, a Viennese professor, pointed out that they were not actually universal laws but merely assumptions. And as such, they postulated the existence of a certain kind of mechanical system — that which characterized the behavior of objects of a certain mass in a certain kind of field. They did not hold for the events of sub-atomic space.

CHARLES DARWIN

ORIGINATOR OF THE THEORY OF EVOLUTION THROUGH NATURAL SELECTION AND THE SURVIVAL OF THE FITTEST. *Born in Shrewsbury, England, 1809; died at Down, 1882.*

There have been many theories of evolution, beginning with the Ionian, Anaximander, and extending, in pre-Darwinian times, to Jean Baptiste Lamarck, who maintained that new needs in animals developed new organs. All of these theories were in the main speculative; they expressed what their propounders thought reasonable or likely, not what was necessarily in accord with the facts of nature.

Darwin's extraordinary contribution to Western thought was a combination of fact and procedure. The first, which was the result of his method, established beyond scientific question four conclusions which underlie modern social thought:

1. Different forms of animal life are descendants from common ancestors.

2. Evolution is not the consequence of the inheritance of acquired characteristics; it is the chance outcome of variations in species in a competitive struggle for existence.

3. Every group of living forms exhibits a variation in physical characteristics; among these only the fittest survive. Changing environments establish changing criteria of fitness.

4. The controlling factor in evolution is natural selection; the individuals surviving longest breed most. Natural selection breeds to survival qualities.

What is most significant about Darwin, however, is not his conclusions but his methods. "I have steadily endeavored to keep my mind free,"

he wrote, "so as to give up any hypothesis, however much beloved (and I cannot resist forming one on every subject), as soon as the facts are shown to be opposed to it."

The theory of natural selection has been much misunderstood. Many still believe that it implies conscious choice in animals themselves; others, that it is the effect of some active power.

A generation ago it was common practice to distort Darwinism to imply that humans are descendants of apes — an attitude which overlooked both the evidence and the extensive time intervals required for biological change. It was held by Darwin that the anthropoid apes and man are developments from a common ancestral type. There is no evidence that modern man is in any way physically or mentally superior to any types of historical man, or even to some, such as the Cro-Magnons, who are known to us only through the survival of skull and bone segments.

Evolution, in the Darwinian sense, is not synonymous with progress; it does not imply value in terms either of development or regression. It means merely structural change as a consequence of the combinations and recombinations of the factors determining selection and heredity.

MAX PLANCK

ORIGINATOR OF THE LAWS OF QUANTUM MECHANICS WHICH ACCOUNT FOR THE AVAILABILITY AND DISTRIBUTION OF ENERGY. *Born in Kiel, Germany, 1858; died in Göttingen, 1947.*

Perhaps the central notion in modern physics is the concept of quanta, the capsule units in which energy is available. Classical physics assumed energy to be emitted in a continuous stream, infinitely divisible. In a signal paper published in 1900, Max Planck, then a professor at the University of Berlin, suggested that all matter consisted of vibrators, each emitting energy at some fixed frequency. The radiated energy, however, was only available in individual gushes. No vibrator was capable of emitting a fraction of a gush; the energy unit had to be taken as a whole or not at all.

This basic unit of energy, which can be compared to a gush, a capsule, or a BB shot, Planck called a *quantum*.

Planck was able to define the force of a quantum in mathematical terms, and this fundamental achievement has made it possible to determine the energy available in atoms and to calculate many of the force relationships which are fundamental in nuclear physics.

It led to the possibility of dealing in a concrete way with the calculation of atomic energy. It was

the cardinal link in the chain of events which led to explosion of the atomic bomb. It became the bedrock of the study of atomic fission which, in its constructive applications, may prove to be the catalyst of a global civilization of abundance.

Planck's constant, the mathematical expression in erg-seconds of the energy contained in a quantum, is designated by the letter h. In sufficient amounts, this can be translated into horsepower.

With Planck's discovery the questions asked by Thales and the Ionian Greeks, and by Pythagoras and his followers, are to some extent both answered and made meaningless. Thales sought a universal world-stuff, the *arché* of everything that exists. *What is it?* was his question; the answer is energy which comes in quanta. Pythagoras sought universal numbers which could explain nature; What are they? The answer is Planck's constant and its multiples. The number of the world-stuff is h.

Yet with these answers reality again eludes definition. For despite the resemblance in behavior of quanta to capsules, particles, or BB shot, they are qualitatively quite different. They are not solid. They cannot be seen, heard, or felt. They have no material existence. Modern physics speaks of them merely as *events;* and events in the life of a non-corporeal substance can convey little concrete meaning to anybody.

Matter thus turns out to be not a tangible, perceptible substance, but merely a convenient way of collecting events into bundles. The ultimate inference of quantum theory is that we, as individuals, are literally tissues of dreamstuff; and if it were not for the peculiar *events* which comprise our bodies we would haphazardly walk through one another!

ALBERT EINSTEIN

FORMULATOR OF THE THEORY OF RELATIVITY AND OF THE PRINCIPLES OF THE INTER-RELATIONSHIPS OF ENERGY, MASS, AND ELECTRO-MAGNETISM. *Born in Germany, 1879; now living in Princeton, N. J.*

Einstein . . . when his Relativity Theory was first announced

Einstein is probably the greatest mathematical genius since Newton; but his greatness does not lie in this singular fact alone. His greatness is a consequence of his universal mind, of his ability to embody in the fullest human as well as scientific spirit the ideal expressed by Matthew Arnold — to see the world whole and see it constantly.

His several published theories are part of a single philosophical approach: an attempt to interpret the complex interrelationships of all the energy phenomena of the universe in such a way that their structures become meaningful both in themselves and in their manifold entwinements with other structures. Einstein thus carries to a scientific framework of conclusions the speculations about a primal world-stuff or *arché* which was naively undertaken by Thales and the Greek philosophers of the Fifth Century B.C.

Einstein's Relativity Theory, broadly conceived, has changed our concepts of space, time, weight, energy, gravitation, and the geometry of the world. Departing from the simplified, or, more properly, over-simplified world of classical physics, it has demonstrated that none of these concepts correspond to any fixed or certain entity. The terms become meaningful only under two conditions: when related to one another, and when all collectively are related to some special frame of reference.

A few examples may clarify this thesis. Space is only meaningful when thought of as a distance which can be traversed in time. Time, on the other hand, is defined in terms of distance traversed — as when the hands of a clock move around the circumference of the dial, or when the earth completes a revolution around its axis. Weight is only a way of speaking of the gravitational pull against a body; a given body will have different weights in different gravitational fields.

When these facts were established it became clear that the laws of Newton and classical physics were by no means universal laws. They were statements of relationships which held only for one gravitational field — that which governed the behavior of relatively large objects in the everyday world of experience.

Newtonian physics did not account satisfactorily for the behavior of so-called particles within an atom; neither did it provide a frame of reference for the phenomena of intra-galactic space. It gave us no clue to the meaning of a concept such as time when it relates simultaneously to events on the earth and within a galaxy a million light years away.

Einstein's Special Theory of Relativity established a generalized form in which these events or entities could be given meaning for all conditions and places.

Einstein was later able to show that matter and energy are interchangeable, that the property called mass is simply concentrated energy, and that energy is relaxed mass.

With Einstein, the search for a universal substance — arché, initiated by Thales — and the search for a universal explanation of nature in number relationships, initiated by Pythagoras, come to a high point of scientific development. It would not be correct to say that they have been concluded; it is probable that the refinement of such investigations and formularizations is capable of indefinite extension. But it is noteworthy that a cyclic process has taken place.

The scientists of relativity physics have extended the boundaries of the knowable world. They have penetrated both sub-atomic and intragalactic space. And in so doing they have introduced concepts outside the realm of human experience, and, because of this fact, incapable of representation in terms of meaningful models. The new reality is one which yields only to mathematical description . END

Games of Talk and Touch

How to Play Conversational Monopoly

Two are chosen from the group and asked to leave the room. The group decides on a statement or question for each. When they return, each learns his query or remark in private and they begin a friendly conversation, talking as two strangers who have just met at a cocktail party. The one who is first able to inject his sentence naturally into the conversation is the winner. Under no circumstances can the statement be thrown in haphazardly; it must be led up to by clever guiding of the conversation. The choice of statements is the clue to a successful and amusing game. These should make reference to the other player, be slightly outrageous and not usual in conversation between strangers. A couple who are good talkers will provide great fun as they jockey the conversation.

How to Play Touch and Guess

SAMPLE TEXTURES

1. VELVET
2. SILK
3. WOOL
4. FUR
5. TERRY CLOTH
6. CORK
7. SPONGE
8. FOAM RUBBER
9. SANDPAPER
10. BLOTTING PAPER
11. TISSUE PAPER
12. FEATHER
13. WOOD
14. CELLOPHANE
15. ALUMINUM
16. COTTON
17. LACE
18. LINOLEUM
19. CHAMOIS
20. BAMBOO
21. HORSEHAIR
22. SOAP
23. NYLON SPONGE
24. RAFFIA
25. PITH
26. CORRUGATED PAPER
27. LEATHER
28. FELT
29. BURLAP
30. LEAD

Any number of players, children or adults, are first provided with a pencil and a piece of paper numbered from 1 to 30. The first player removes an envelope from the box and while holding it behind his back removes the contents, determining the nature of the object by feeling it, and returns it to the envelope. After writing down what he thinks he felt, he passes it to his neighbor, who feels and guesses in turn. Care should be taken that no player sees the contents of any envelope, and it is important that the envelopes be circulated in the same sequence throughout the game and returned to the box in their original order.

When all 30 materials have been touched and guessed, one player may open the envelopes in the order that they were circulated and announce their contents so that players may tally their scores. A score of 15 the first time around is good and 25 or better indicates someone who really knows what's at his fingertips.

In one team variation — along the lines of the game — two teams race against time, each player taking turns to make his team-mates guess the material he is holding behind his back. He can only describe how it feels, without giving any clues as to use, color, etc. The other team will, of course, enjoy knowing what feeling he is trying to put into words.

Touch and Guess is by Design Group, Inc., Gage Hill, Brewster, N. Y.

THE CULLINAN
WORLD'S LARGEST CUT DIAMOND

This replica is the exact size and shape of the famous Cullinan diamond, which weighs 530 carats. It is also the principal stone cut from the largest rough diamond ever found, weighing 3,106 carats. The gem was named for Sir Thomas Cullinan who opened up the historic Premier mine where the big diamond was discovered. The Transvaal government bought the gem and presented it to Edward VII on the occasion of his sixty-sixth birthday. Pear-shaped, it is in the British scepter.

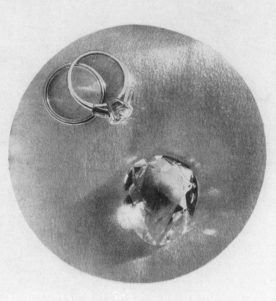

THE STAR
STARTED THE DIAMOND RUSH

The historic Star of South Africa is credited with starting the diamond rush on the South African veld in 1869. The rough stone, which was nearly twice the size of the replica shown, was picked up by a shepherd on a farm near the Orange River. He traded it for 500 sheep, ten oxen, and a horse. The new owner sold the stone for $56,000. As the story spread, prospectors poured into the district. The replica shows the 47-carat gem compared with a one-carat diamond in an engagement ring.

THE ROMANCE OF DIAMONDS

The curious lure of diamonds has long been a puzzle to psychologists. The value of the stone, which for centuries was not even considered beautiful, depends solely on its combined exotic appeal and rarity. Many objects, psychologists have observed, are exceedingly rare without acquiring undue value on this account alone. Many museum items are in this category: Tanagra figurines, Greek intaglios, Minian jewelry. What then gives diamonds their peculiar fascination and worth? The answer seems to be simply that in times past they were believed to have magic properties. Since they could win kingdoms, they were worth kingdoms. Today, we no longer credit them with supernatural virtues; but tradition has decided their worth, and scarcity has maintained it. Thus diamonds, by continued demand, have become established as an international symbol of luxury.

The original home of diamonds was India. Nowhere else in the ancient world was this unique stone — the hardest of all substances and the purest of all gems — found, polished, and prized. Europeans who visited India in the Sixteenth Century returned with tales of a mysterious land called *Golconda* — the source of all diamonds. Golconda was actually a small native village which was the center of India's medieval diamond trade. It has been estimated that by the year 1720 Europeans, fascinated by the spell of this costly gem, had exported from India some 12,000,000 carats of diamonds. The worth of these,

THE KOH-I-NOR

THE SANCY

THE REGENT

at current prices, would be roughly equivalent to one-fifth of all the gold in Fort Knox.

Although the Hindus were the first to discover the curious fact that only a diamond will cut a diamond, the Indian lapidaries did not make use of this knowledge to make decorative or light-reflecting cuts. The diamonds were left largely in their original shape.

Perhaps it was the very naturalness of the early shapes which caused such critics as the astute Isidore, Bishop of Seville, to remark that the diamond is "a dull stone, lacking in beauty." For here, more than anywhere else in the realm of craftsmanship, nature takes its quality from art. It is only the imaginative use of faceting that has enabled lapidaries to capitalize on the purity and clarity of the diamond's structure.

Diamonds, which were once believed to endow their owners with supernatural power, have played a strange role in the history of the world. They have been held as the insignia of empire, the ransom of kings, and the price of love. They have provided an international currency for men and women whose destiny was intertwined with revolution and political upsurge. They have created sudden wealth and prosperity.

Many of the great diamonds today represent value commensurate only with royal treasuries. The Koh-i-nor, for example, the largest and most valuable diamond in the world, and now one of the British Crown Jewels, was once appraised at $10,000,000. The Cullinan, which was presented to Edward VII on his birthday in 1907, was insured at that time for $2,500,000. A deep blue, heart-shaped diamond weighing 31 carats — the only diamond in the world of this combined color, shape, and weight — was recently acquired by Van Cleef and Arpels and valued at $300,-000. The famous Hope diamond, which legend has associated with a mysterious curse, was last worn by the late Mrs. Edward McLean, and was appraised at $176,920. It was purchased from her estate in 1949 by Harry Winston.

Some of the great diamonds of the world have been involved in affairs of love and state equally tempestuous. Among these are such well-known gems as the Hope diamond, the Cullinan, the Jonker, the Great Mogul, the Regent, the Pigott, and the Sancy.

Of no less dramatic significance is the Koh-i-nor, which is believed to have been discovered many centuries ago in India's Gadavary River. According to legend, it was worn in battle by one of the heroes of the great Hindu epic, the Mahabharata, and to have preserved his life. In the days of the Mogul Empire, the Koh-i-nor was said to have been one of the eyes of the peacock which comprised the *Peacock Throne.*

Catherine the Great was perhaps history's most avid collector of diamonds. She is said to have had 2,536 in her crown alone, and to have given diamonds freely to her courtiers and favorites. The famous Orloff diamond figured in her royal romances, however in reverse order: it was a gift she received for favors hoped for **and** ultimately withheld. Today, the Orloff diamond

PHOTOGRAPHS ON OPPOSITE PAGE . . .

Elizabeth II wearing the diamond-and-pearl circlet of Queen Victoria. The design incorporates the Tudor rose, Scotch thistle, and Irish shamrock. The diamond necklace was a wedding gift from the Nizam of Hyderabad.

The famous Koh-i-nor diamond was presented to Queen Victoria, in 1850, by the East India Company. Since Victoria's time, the Koh-i-nor has, by tradition, been worn only by queens. It is now in Queen Elizabeth's crown.

The historic Sancy diamond is believed to be one of the first cut with symmetrical facets. Bought in Turkey by the French Ambassador, Nicolas de Harlay Sancy, for Henry III, it was later owned by Queen Elizabeth, Louis XIV, and Marie Antoinette. It is now in a diadem owned by Lady Astor.

The Regent diamond, which originally weighed 410 carats, was discovered by a slave in an Indian mine. It was later owned by Thomas Pitt, who had it cut as shown in the photograph opposite. The stone was sold to the Duke of Orleans for $500,000. A state treasure of France, it is on exhibition in the Louvre.

A classic diamond necklace by Van Cleef and Arpels, lower left. A row of pear-shaped diamonds is surmounted by a line of round, marquise diamonds, these, in turn, topped by baguettes. Model at lower right, at a recent fashion show, wears a three-million-dollar array of diamonds from the collection of Harry Winston.

Shown in necklace, blue heart-shaped diamond of 31 carats, valued at $300,000. It is the only known diamond in the world of this size and color. From Van Cleef and Arpels' collection.

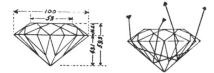

A diamond cut with proportions indicated at left, above, will return the majority of rays falling upon its upper facets, as indicated at right.

A diamond cut too deep or too shallow below girdle allows unnecessary amount of light to escape through its pavilion facets.

Diamonds cut with too little weight above the girdle. Both stones exhibit less "fire" than correctly proportioned diamonds and have less value.

lies in the Soviet Diamond Treasury, a reminder that unrequited and consummated love can be equally costly.

Another of Catherine's diamonds was later named the Eugenie, after the Empress of France. It was worn for some time as a hair ornament by Catherine, then presented, for gallant services, to favorite Grigori Potemkin, who simultaneously became Prince of Tauris.

After Potemkin's death, the gem was sold to Napoleon III. The Emperor, at that time, was courting Eugenie Montijo, a young Spanish beauty. Eugenie demanded two wedding gifts: a wild Barbary horse and a diamond necklace. Napoleon bought the horse, then negotiated for Potemkin's diamond. When Eugenie saw the gem, she forgot the horse — and perhaps Napoleon. Nevertheless, she became Empress and acquired the diamond, which still bears her name.

Eugenie left France after Napoleon III was deposed. Her jewels were smuggled from the Tuileries wrapped in newspapers. They were shipped across the Channel in shoe boxes and eventually were auctioned at Christie's. Eugenie's diamond was sold to the Gaekwar of Baroda for $75,000, and was thus lovingly returned to the land of its origin.

No one believes any more that diamonds have magical virtues, or that they can convey secret powers and cast the destiny of empires. Yet their spell endures. And today they still stud the annals of love, intrigue, and mystery. Whether accompanied by love, respect, veneration, or venality, they still symbolize the eternal lure of possession, prestige, and power.   **END**

HOW TO JUDGE A DIAMOND

Diamond quality is determined by the four *Cs:* carat weight, color, clarity, and cut. Each has its own set of standards and its proper virtues. To buy diamonds discriminatingly, it is helpful to know what to look for.

CARAT WEIGHT. The weight of a diamond is measured in carats, a word derived from the carob tree of the Orient whose seeds were used to balance the scales in the bazaars. It would take a diamond of about 142 carats to weigh an ounce on ordinary scales. The unit smaller than a carat is a *point;* there are 100 points to the carat. Small stones are usually referred to as weighing 10 points, 12 points, etc., and even one-point diamonds are used in jewelry.

As the size of the stone increases, the value increases by more than normal scale because the larger stones are rarer. For this reason, a two-carat diamond is worth more than double a one-carat stone of the same quality.

COLOR. Diamonds are not always white. They come in many shades — pale yellow, coffee brown, red, pink, green, blue, even black. The famous Hope diamond is as blue as a sapphire. The Dresden, one of the Saxon crown jewels, is apple green. The standard for the engagement ring is a clear, frosty, sparkling white — the white of the drops in a waterfall. There are many shades of white. All can be beautiful in a well-cut diamond. Because the purest white is the rarest, it commands a higher price.

The term *blue-white* is sometimes used commercially to describe diamonds that are actually white. This usage is not accurate. Diamonds with any tinge of blue are very rare — one in five hundred among high-grade diamonds examined in one test. The finest diamonds regularly sold in engagement rings have the clarity of a drop of pure water, colorless except for the rainbow fire produced by the diamond's power to break up light and give back a flash of each hue in the spectrum. But diamonds reflect color around them. To judge the color of the diamond itself, you need to look at it on a white paper or handkerchief in north light on a clear day.

CLARITY. Under the Federal Trade Commission rules, a diamond may be sold as perfect or flawless if it shows no flaws to a trained eye when magnified ten times. Other diamonds are valued according to the number, kind, and location of the inclusions. In many cases, the inclusions do not affect the beauty of the stone as seen by the naked eye, but they affect the price.

CUT. Whatever the color and clarity of a diamond, only fine cutting can reveal its full beauty. It must be properly proportioned to a minute accuracy. Each tiny facet must be symmetrical, polished into the world's hardest substance at an angle that may not vary by more than half a degree. Diamond cutters are among the most skilled and best paid of all craftsmen. It is their work which turns a whitish pebble into the most brilliant of all gems. The quality of the cutting has much to do with the final value.

From the work of two almost forgotten geniuses who worked in the latter part of the nineteenth century in France and Germany arose almost all the essential features of the comic strip and the cartoon film, which exert so vast an influence in this country today.

Wilhelm Busch, born in 1832 in the province of Hanover in Germany, was a caricaturist on the staff of *Flying Leaves* (Fliegende Blätte), the leading German humorous paper; Caran D'Ache, as Emmanuel Poiré called himself—the name is Russian for lead pencil—was born of French parentage in Moscow in 1859, and lived and worked in Paris, beginning his contributions to *Caricature* while still doing military service in the French Army.

The originality and force of these two remarkable men can best be appreciated against the background of the tendencies prevailing in art in

their time. Draftsmen were trained to make elaborate studies, with cross hatching and stippling, mostly from plaster casts of the classical sculpture then in vogue. Extreme realism was the fashion and linear freedom and simplification were frowned upon in the academies.

Working in the field of children's stories and humorous illustration, where full conformity with these standards was not demanded, Busch developed a style which even today remains remarkable for its extreme simplicity and expressiveness. With a few pen and ink strokes he recorded the spirit and movement of a figure.

In series such as those of the adventures of Max and Moritz, forebears of the Katzenjammer Kids, he introduced the idea of telling a whole story in a few sequential pictures which, though accompanied by a text, could be followed by a child who was not yet able to read.

In one of these stories can clearly be seen the first treatment of animal life, with the same penetrating observation of them and their movements, which Walt Disney afterward developed.

A flock of chickens performs in the cartoon like a well-trained ballet and there is, in their greed, confusion and untimely end, all the tragedy and pathos which can be felt for domestic favorites. From the moment of their demise begins the new excitement of bent-pin fishing down the chimney, of the scene between the farmer's wife and the dog, whom she suspects of the theft and, finally, of the surreptitious feast and happy

II

I

III

IV

V

VI

VII

VIII

replete slumber under the hedge. Throughout, the economy of means is extraordinary and the drawings' strength, which stems directly from the German woodcut, has not been surpassed.

Caran D'Ache, who admitted that he owed much to Busch, learned from him a sure formula for romantic fun-making by the discovery of hidden humor in everyday affairs. This method was a novelty in France in his day, and the army, in which Poiré served, was a happy field for his observations which abound in love scenes, duels and so forth in which uniformed men appear.

The scene in which a butterfly hunter gets mixed up in a duel is full of his sublime sense

of fun, which we recognise again and again in French humorous films today. The butterfly's nonchalance as it settles on the upturned pants seat of the fallen duelist and the professor's enraptured expression as he sees his specimen impaled on the point of the rapier are inimitable.

Caran D'Ache brought the comic strip out of the realm of the children's book into the sophisticated world of every day, and brought its simplification and subtleties of characterization to its highest point ●

An AlphaBet of UnCommon

Always! that is a dreadful word. Women are so fond of using it. They spoil every romance by trying to make it last forever

The Soul is born old, but it grows young; that is the comedy of life. The Body is born young and grows old; that is Life's tragedy.

Conscience and cowardice are really the same things. Conscience is the trade-name of the firm.

One can survive everything except Death, and live down everything except a good reputation.

Nature hates Mind. Thinking is the most unhealthy thing in the world, and people die of it just as they die of any other disease. Fortunately, in England at any rate, thought is not catching. Our splendid physique is entirely due to our national stupidity.

Young men want to be Faithful and are not, old men want to be faithless and cannot.

The public is wonderfully tolerant. It forgives everything except Genius.

Health—the silliest word in our language, and one knows the popular idea of health. The English country gentleman galloping after a fox—the unspeakable in full pursuit of the uneatable.

There is only one thing worse than Injustice, and that is Justice without her sword in her hand. When Right is not Might, it is Evil.

Every great man nowadays has his disciples, and it is always Judas who writes the biography.

In modern life nothing produces such an effect as a good platitude. It makes the whole world Kin.

Lying, the telling of beautiful untrue things, is the proper aim of Art.

All women become like their Mothers— that is their tragedy. No man does. That's his.

Spies are of no use nowadays. Their profession is over. The Newspapers do their work instead.